The 'Golf Stream'

MORTONHALL
GOLF CLUB
1892–1992

MORTONHALL
GOLF CLUB
1892–1992

SCOTTISH ACADEMIC PRESS

56 Hanover Street
Edinburgh EH2 2DX

ISBN 0 7073 0712 0

Printed in Edinburgh, Scotland by
Pillans & Wilson Ltd.

Bound by
Hunter & Foulis Ltd.

Mortonhall Golf Club
acknowledges with much gratitude
and appreciation the financial
contribution which

Marks and Spencer plc

have made towards the production costs
of this book

ACKNOWLEDGMENTS

Many have encouraged and many have helped me in the production of this book. To all, I am most grateful but to those who follow I am particularly indebted:

To Ian Isles and Eain Robertson, who unfailingly supported and exhorted me when my spirits flagged, painstakingly read my drafts and researched many an obscure area.

To Leslie Mitchell, who kindly lent me some early golf records and expertly created the layout of the first four courses.

To Fred Hawtree, who generously provided me with information I would not otherwise have found.

To Bill Barton, who discovered that priceless hoard of his father's 'Odes' and freely made them over to me.

To the late Fred Gray, who supplied me with the 121 verses of the 'Mortonhall Mafia' and allowed me to make my own selection.

To Dr Kenneth Robertson who beautifully re-created Tom Scott's 'Golf Stream' for the frontispiece.

To George Burnie, who, simply and sincerely, wished to do something for Mortonhall and produced the Index.

To Christine Morrison, who curbed my chauvinism, deciphered my writing and cheerfully laboured to present the whole production to the publisher.

To Dr Douglas Grant, who, with his anonymous editor, guided me with tact, courtesy and patience and made the final offering so much better than the original.

To John Gaffney who, as a new member of the Club, became caught in its spell and ensured with Martin Clarkson the excellence of the printing arrangements.

And finally to my wife, who, over the long years, brought me coffee, tea and sympathy, made some frank and novel suggestions and never envied my love for Mortonhall.

W. G. P. COLLEDGE
October 1991

CONTENTS

ILLUSTRATIONS

APPENDICES

PROLOGUE

Till down the eastern cliffs afar
Hyperion's march they spy and glitt'ring shafts of war

(Gray)

It was after the lambing in the Spring of 1892 that they
restored nine holes of golf on the Meadowhead Hill
Grazing and on 7th May, Andrew Usher who, a few
years earlier, had gifted to the City of Edinburgh the
Usher Hall, struck the first ball on the new Course . . .

This is not the story of a golf club but rather of successive
generations of men who, by their diverse skills and
talents, made, sustained and developed Mortonhall Golf
Club. For these were the Mortonhall Men, united and
motivated by a mystic affection, peculiar to the whins,
trees and grasses of that part of the Braid Hills known as
Mortonhall.

1

THE MORNINGSIDE GOLF CLUB
1891–1892

> And lo! already on the hills
> The flags of dawn appear
>
> (Hosmer)

There is a painting by the well-known Border artist, Tom Scott (1854–1927) of that part of the Braid Road as it dips past the Hermitage and sweeps up to the Braid Hills Hotel (Frontispiece). Painted in 1895, and entitled 'The Golf Stream' after the caption to a cartoon in 'Punch' of that period, it portrays, in the roadway, a throng of golfers mounting the rise with eager and expectant steps. Their destination is the Braid Hills where, in 1889, the City of Edinburgh had laid out the Braids Golf Course. The 'Golf Stream' followed the route used in its time by the Kings of Scotland to hunt or make war and flowed upwards to those 'furzy hills of Braid' where, particularly until the turn of the century, lay the golfing Mecca of Edinburgh. The ancient Bruntsfield Links on the Burgh Muir had been so encroached upon by housing that it could no longer afford room for a golf course; Leith Links, also of much antiquity, had long since flourished and died; and it was outside the city, at Musselburgh and beyond, where the famous clubs – the Honourable Company of Edinburgh Golfers, the Edinburgh Burgess Golfing Society and the Bruntsfield Links Golfing Society, – all played.

The creation of the Braids Golf Course acted as a catalyst among a growing band of golf enthusiasts in Edinburgh and led to the founding of a number of non-course owning clubs of which, for the purpose of this story, the most significant was the Morningside Golf Club. On the evening of Tuesday, 27th January 1891, a 'Meeting of Gentlemen who had intimated their intention to become members of a local Golf Club proposed to be formed in the Morningside District' took place at 41 Comiston Road, Edinburgh, the home of W. K. Murray, Builder. Duncan MacLaren S.S.C. was called to the Chair and, having explained the object of the meeting, requested Mr Murray to read the names of the 28 gentlemen who had agreed to become Members of the proposed Club. It is unfortunate that these names have not been recorded.

The business of this historic occasion comprised the following items:

Name of Club
Two names were proposed for the new club – the Morningside Golf Club and the Pentlands Golf Club – and, after a vote, the former prevailed by a large majority.

Election of Office Bearers
The name of Duncan MacLaren was proposed and seconded as Captain and this was carried unanimously.

W. C. Sturrock was elected Secretary, A. Ker, Treasurer, and a Committee or Council of Messrs. Murray, Grey, Brodie and Watson appointed.

Competitions
It was considered that there should be twelve ordinary monthly competitions and, in addition, four quarterly ones. The former were to be played on the Braids, not on Saturdays but on the first Monday in each month, and two ballots or drawings for partners were to take place – one in the early morning and the other during the forenoon or 'after part of the day'. The venue of the quarterly competitions was remitted to the Committee for consideration.

Entry Money and Subscriptions
It was resolved that, for the first 50 Members joining the Club, there should be no distinction between Entry Money and Subscription which was then determined in the composite sum of 7/6d. When the Membership exceeded 50, further consideration would be given to the matter.

Admission of New Members
Power was given to the Committee to admit any new Members, desirous of joining the Club, on condition that all

such Members would be 'balloted for' at the next General Meeting on the basis that those so admitted would be held as duly elected unless 'the black balls were found to be in a larger proportion than 1 in 4'.

The question of a Patron or President was also raised although a decision on the matter was deferred. It was, however, reported, at a subsequent meeting – held a week later – that Andrew Usher who, apart from his other distinctions, was regarded as 'one of the neatest and steadiest players in East Lothian' had been approached with a view to his becoming President. Mr Usher found himself unable to accept but, nonetheless, had intimated that he would be glad to become a Member of the Club and to present a prize to be played for on conditions 'framed by the Committee'. After further discussion of the Office of President, it was agreed that Fleming Johnston W.S. and Councillor Walker should be approached in that order. Mr Johnston also declined the honour whereupon the matter was dropped and never raised again.

Considerable activity took place in February 1891 to establish the fledgling Club – Rules were drafted (unfortunately no copy exists), scoring and fixture cards produced, competitions and handicapping arrangements made and more than a little attention focussed on the question of prizes. Indeed, this, perhaps more than all, was the most recurrent theme in the four General and eight Committee Meetings in the Club's short life of fifteen months. The most significant and impressive prize was undoubtedly the Silver Lamp presented by Andrew Usher. It had been decided that this should be competed for under handicap conditions at the four quarterly competitions and that it become the absolute property of the player having the three lowest scores at these meetings. In due course, John Rose won the much coveted trophy at the last quarterly meeting held on the Braids on 1st January 1892 with a score of 95 less 9, 86, his other two counting scores being 80 and 82.

In the best tradition of the time, the Club purchased a silver medal (cost £2.2/–) to be awarded to the player having the six lowest handicap scores in the monthly medal competitions. The winner, whose name would be inscribed, was to be allowed to retain the medal for one year and, in addition, to be given a 'gold charm', acquired for £1.10/–. In addition, Mr Grey donated the sum of £3.3/– to be used in the purchase of golf balls for the *three* lowest scores at *each* monthly competition. The balls in question would have been 'gutties' which cost approximately 1/– each. The number and range of prizes for the four quarterly competitions was remarkable. At the Spring Meeting, the first prize (unspecified) was donated by the Captain, Duncan MacLaren, while the second and third 3 prizes were an oil painting and a set of golf clubs presented respectively by Mr Anderson and Mr Buchanan. The prizes at the Summer Meeting were supplemented by a grant of £3.15/– from the Club funds and the list in order of precedence was as follows:

1. Silver Biscuit Box
2. Claret Jug
3. Dinner Gong (presented by Messrs Emley, Glasgow)
4. Butter Cooler
5. Jelly Dish
6. Two Mounted Oak Salt Cellars
7. Small Silver Claret Cup (presented by Mr Crouch, Princes Street, Edinburgh)

Donors were not in evidence at the Autumn Meeting when the Club set aside £5 for a Prize Fund, ultimately applied thus:

1. Pair of Bronzed Horses
2. Fruit Dish
3. Field Glasses
4. Barometer
5. Inkstand
6. Two Flower Glasses
7. Golf Ball Muffineer (dish for keeping muffins warm)

At the last quarterly meeting on 1st January 1892, the donors returned in force and the Club had only to provide £2.15/– to produce the following prize list:

1. Silver Teapot
2. Book – Lady Brassy's *Voyage in the Sunbeam* (illustrated edition) – presented by Mr Morrison
3. Barometer
4. Pair of Nut Crackers in Case
5. Book – presented by Mr Morrison
6. Patent Club & Cleek – presented by Mr Brand and Mr Johnston
7. Driver and one ball – presented by Mr Hood
8. Bottle of Brandy – presented by Mr Black
9. Patent Club – presented by Mr Brand, the designer

In all the quarterly competitions, it was stated the winner was to have the option 'of choosing the Prize to which his score entitles him, or any other prize lower on the List – his decision to be declared on the Green' (the golf course). Under such arrangements, it is not inconceivable that the winner of the second prize at the meeting held on New Year's Day might well have opted for the eighth. The initial handicapping arrangements were inevitably fraught with difficulty and a certain amount of dispute. The first handicaps were determined on 18th

February 1891 by the Committee "so far as they were able to settle the matter with the information before them'. Two months later the Handicap List was revised and the limit increased to 27, subject to the approval of the next General Meeting which, in due course, was obtained by a majority of one. In the autumn of the year, the following post card was sent to all Members:

---

63 CRAIGLEA DRIVE,
29th October 1891.

Morningside Golf Club.

THE COUNCIL have resolved that the following principle shall in future regulate the fixing of Handicaps, viz.:—"That **78** shall in the meantime be taken as a Scratch figure, and that an allowance of two-thirds of the difference between **78** and the best recorded score of any Member shall be given, in order to ascertain the Handicap to which he is entitled—fractions to count against the Player, and the limit of **27** to remain as at present."

This Rule to come into operation immediately.

W. C. S.

The 'Scratch figure of 78, assigned to the Braids Golf Course, was probably a fair assessment at the time. This post card provoked criticism, as six Members exercised a right, apparently under the Rules, to convene a Special General Meeting. There was 'considerable discussion' and ultimately it was agreed to amend the 'principle' by substituting the words 'the average of the three lowest or lesser number of scores' for 'the best recorded score'.

While all the monthly meetings were held over the Braids Golf Course as well as the quarterly ones in the Autumn of 1891 and on New Year's Day 1892, the Club was more adventurous in fixing the venues for the Spring and Summer Meetings.

On Monday, 20th April 1891, 26 Members of the Club travelled to Carnoustie to play the first quarterly competition. Certain railway facilities had been afforded and other arrangements made for the comfort of the Members. Prior to play, a General Meeting was held in the Panmure Arms Hotel. After some formal business, 'balloting for Partners was then proceeded with and the Members then adjourned to the Green. On completion of the round, they sat down for dinner together and the

Secretary, having examined the cards, intimated that the following were the Prizewinners viz (1) Hew Morrison (2) A.J. Hodge (3) William Murray (4) Duncan MacLaren and (5) the Rev. Wm. Stevenson. After engaging in a friendly round in the afternoon, the bulk of the Members returned to Edinburgh by the special carriage in which the necessary accommodation had been reserved.

The Summer Meeting took place on Saturday, 18th July 1891 at Gullane and the following detailed travelling instructions were issued by the Secretary, W. C. Sturrock:

> For the convenience of Members, there will be two draws – the first portion travelling by the train leaving Edinburgh at 9.27 a.m.; and the second portion at 1.45 p.m. Arrangements will be made for having Conveyances in waiting at Drem on the arrival of the respective trains, and in order to carry out this and other details, I shall be obliged if you will let me know by the 11th inst. at latest, if you intend to be present and whether you will play in the forenoon or afternoon draw.

As far as other tournaments were concerned, there is reference to the 'Tournament got up by the *Glasgow Evening Times* to be played at Prestwick on the 23rd and 24th October 1891'. James Paul and A.J. Hodge were selected to represent the Club and, in a field of 27 clubs, mostly from the West, reached the semi-final to lose to Edinburgh Thistle. In April 1892, the team, selected for the Dispatch Trophy, fell to the Watsonians in the first round.

In February 1892, the Club decided 'to terminate the first year's proceedings' with a dinner on 11th March of that year in the Imperial Hotel, then situated at 19 Market Street and now occupied by Lothian Regional Council. Forty-one Members of the Club sat down to dinner at a cost of 4/6d each which, considering the extent and range of the menu (shown opposite), appeared to be very good value. It is perhaps inevitable that there would be a toast to the Prize Donors whose generosity had certainly enhanced the Prize Lists at the quarterly Meetings, and intriguing that there should be one to the Ladies who were not present and to whom no other reference is made in the history of the Club.

The last Committee Meeting of the Club took place on Tuesday 29th March 1892 when, apart from discussing arrangements for the ensuing season, the Minutes close with the following paragraph stating,

MENU.

Soups.

Cocky Leeky.   Hare.

Fish.

Cod and Oyster Sauce.   Filleted Whiting.

Entrees.

Haggis and Nips.   Kromiskies.

Sweetbreads and Mushrooms.

Poultry and Joints.

Roast Beef.   Saddle of Mutton.

Chickens and Turkeys and York Ham.

Entremets.

Apple Tart.   Madeira Pudding.

Liqueur Jelly, etc.   Meringues.   Stewed Fruits.

Cheese and Salad.

Dessert.

Grapes, Pines, Apples, Nuts, Pears, etc.

for the first and only time, the proposal which marked the end of the Morningside Golf Club and the birth of that in the name of Mortonhall:

> The Meeting at considerable length then discussed the proposal to acquire by lease a private course on the Mortonhall Estate and the Captain explained what had passed with Colonel Trotter's Factor on the subject.

> Arrangements were made for the Committee visiting the ground. It was resolved that a Special Meeting of the Club be convened for Friday 8th proximo further to discuss the scheme and authorise the Committee to conclude the negotiations.

As will later be observed, the Morningside Golf Club formed the nucleus of the new Club and many of its Members were then called to play an important and conspicuous role. The following names are particularly to be remembered as the first 'Mortonhall Men':

J. Michael Brown	Duncan MacLaren
J. S. Gowans	Rev. W. Stevenson
James M. Johnston	W. C. Sturrock
A. Ker	D. W. Walker

For record purposes, the prize winners of the Club were:

Usher Silver Lamp	J. Rose
Monthly Medal	Winner not recorded

Spring Meeting (Carnoustie)
(1) H. Morrison
(2) A. J. Hodge
(3) W. K. Murray
(4) D. MacLaren
(5) Rev. W. Stevenson

Summer Meeting (Gullane)
(1) D. W. Walker
(2) H. Morrison
(3) W. C. Sturrock
(4) J. Rose
(5) J. Johnston
(6) Rev. W. Stevenson
(7) A. J. Hodge

Autumn Meeting (Braids)
(1) W. C. Sturrock
(2) J. Rose
(3) J. K. Lees
(4) H. Morrison & J T. Morrison – *equal*
(5) A. M. Runciman
(6) T. L. Walker & A. J. Hodge – *equal*

Winter Meeting (Braids)
(1) J. Johnston
(2) J. Rose & J. H. Forrester – *equal*
(3) Rev. W. Stevenson
(4) D. Anderson & F. J. Walden – *equal*
(5) J. M. Brown, G. S. Ranken
  & W. C. Sturrock – *equal*

2

THE MAKING OF MORTONHALL
– THE VICTORIANS
1892–1901

> And when old age shall this generation waste,
> Thou shalt remain . . .
>
> (Keats)

The First Year

There is no doubt that, from 1890 onwards, the focal point of the golfing scene in the City of Edinburgh lay in the Braid Hills and the rapid growth in the popularity of the game during the decade to 1900 created considerable congestion there as evidenced by the following extract from *GOLF – a Weekly Record of Ye Royal and Auncient Game* in 1892:

> The Braids are all very well in their way, but it requires a philosophic mind to climb several hundred feet, burdened with a stack of clubs, and on arriving panting but expectant on the first tee to find a hundred others, ticket in hand, who have precedence of you, and to know that you must possess your soul in patience for more than an hour before being able to make a start!

No doubt a similar situation pertained at Musselburgh when, in 1891, the Honourable Company of Edinburgh Golfers departed for Muirfield. In Edinburgh the congestion at the Braids led to rapid development of a network of courses, particularly on the South side of the City and, by 1900, such clubs as Baberton (1893), Lothianburn (1893), Torphin Hill (1895), Craigmillar Park (1896), Murrayfield (1896) and the Insurance & Banking Golf Club (now Duddingston) (1897), had all been founded. As already noted, it was early in 1892 that certain officials of the Morningside Golf Club were casting a furtive eye on 'fresh woods and pastures new'. The strange and ominous silence which seemed to pervade the Minute Book of the Morningside Golf Club in the months of February and March 1892 was dramatically broken when, at the meeting on 8th April 1892, the Captain, Mr Duncan MacLaren, announced that James M. Johnston, a Member of the Club, and he had acquired *in their own names* a 15 year lease 'of that portion of the Braid Hills (the Meadowhead Hill Grazing) belonging to Colonel Trotter and now commonly known as Mortonhall for the purpose of playing the game of golf thereon'. It is significant that the Minute Book of the Morningside Golf Club refers to the acquisition by lease of 'a private course on the Mortonhall Estate' and further that the Golfing Annual of 1891/1892 states that 'the ground (Mortonhall) has been used as a golf course for a considerable time by the proprietor (Colonel Trotter) and his friends'. These statements clearly establish that the Course is the oldest on which golf is still played in the City of Edinburgh.

The map *circa* 1870 shown opposite shows the whole area of the Braid Hills at that time while the plan of the first nine holes on Page 16 shows the extent (54.959 acres) of the lease acquired by Mr MacLaren and Mr Johnston. In the 1870 map, particular attention is drawn to the line of the various boundary walls, the track from Meadowhead Farm to the Braid Road, the numerous quarries and the absence of the Pheasant Wood and the Plantation i.e. the woods to the right of the present 6th hole and behind the present 10th green.

Although it was the intention of the lessees to give the Morningside Golf Club the opportunity of acquiring their lease, provided Colonel Trotter approved 'of the personnel of the Members thereof' (a list of Members was actually submitted to the Colonel for this purpose), it was discovered that the Constitution of the Club did not allow such a transaction to be concluded. While the Rules permitted the Constitution to be changed, this could only be achieved at an *Annual* General Meeting, which event had occurred some two months earlier. In order to extricate itself from the technical impasse in which it had been placed, Council proceeded to draft a Constitution for a new Club to be called the Mortonhall Golf Club and convened a Meeting in Dowell's Rooms (now Phillips, 65 George Street, Edinburgh). This Meeting took place on Friday, 29th April 1892 and, the Constitution of the new Club being approved, the Mortonhall Golf Club was born. Duncan MacLaren and

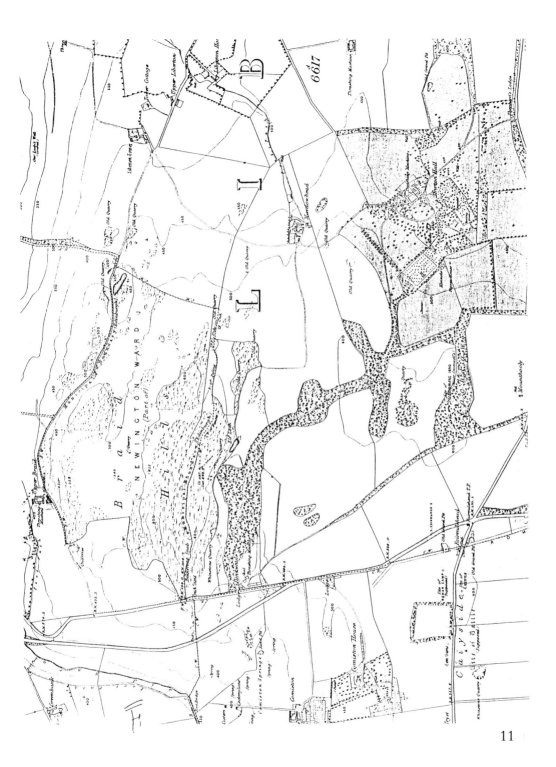

11

James Johnston were thus able to assign their lease to the new Club for which the appropriate legal formalities were concluded on 21st December 1892. Unfortunately, the precise terms and annual rent of this lease cannot be traced.

The Constitution or 'Rules for the Government' of the Mortonhall Golf Club is shown in Appendix K. Particular attention is drawn to Rule 8 – where only *two* days written notice of an Annual or Special General Meeting was required – to Rules 9 & 13 – where a distinction is drawn between Members of the former Morningside Golf Club and other Members – to Rule 14 – where no Member can be admitted unless Council was unanimous in his election (cf. the Morningside Club where election was possible provided the black balls were not 'in a larger proportion of 1 in 4') – and to Rule 15 – where the whole Office Bearers and Members of Council were to be regarded as 'Trustees for the Club'. The Meeting on 29th April 1892 was not solely confined to the Constitution. The following Office Bearers and Council were appointed:

Captain	Duncan MacLaren★
Secretary	W. C. Sturrock★
Treasurer	Andrew Ker★
Auditor	J. Stuart Gowans★
Members of Council:	John T. Watson★
	T. L. Walker★
	J. Michael Brown★
	John Johnston★
	James M. Johnston★
	George Lorimer
	John Macrae
	John Anderson
	C. J. Munro★
	James Ayton

(★former Member of Morningside Golf Club)

Plans for a Clubhouse, which the Meeting of the Morningside Club on 8th April had authorised Sydney Mitchell, Architect and a Member of the Club, to prepare, were also surprisingly submitted for inspection and Council instructed to incur an expenditure 'of not more than £700 in the erection of the building, the introduction of water and the supply of furnishings and boxes' (lockers). Those called to the Meeting numbered 200 consisting of 97 Members of the Morningside Golf Club and a further 103 individuals to whom the Morningside Club had extended Membership on the strength of the lease of Mortonhall. Their names and addresses are listed in Appendix B, the first 97 being the 'Morningside

Men'. Honorary Membership of the Club was unanimously conferred on Colonel Trotter of Mortonhall and his Factor, D. F. Mackenzie. Colonel Henry Trotter, 11th of Mortonhall and Colonel commanding the Grenadier Guards, represented an ancient Scottish family, famed in its time for its loyalty to the Stuart Cause and possessed of a long and distinguished record of military service. (See Appendix A). The then family seat at Mortonhall House, rebuilt in the Georgian style in 1769, lay to the South East of the golf course.

The first Meeting of the Council of the new Club took place on 3rd May 1892 when consideration was given to proposals for the Bye-Laws. These were divided into two sections – Special and Ordinary – and were ultimately agreed in terms set out in Appendix L. Particular attention is drawn to the following:

1. every Member of the Club shall wear the Club Uniform or Cap (Special Bye-Law 2)
2. no caddies shall be brought upon the ground (Special Bye-Law 3)
3. the use of the term 'strangers' for guests (Ordinary Bye-Law 10)
4. the regulations for the commencement of a second round of 9 holes (Ordinary Bye-Law 12)
5. a ball 'driven outside the limits of the Course' shall be treated as a Lost Ball (Ordinary Bye-Law 14)

The choice of the Club's colours was remitted to a small committee of whom Michael Brown was a prominent member. Mr Brown was later to achieve considerable distinction through his paintings of scenes at the Amateur and Open Championships for the annual calendars of the Life Association of Scotland. He lived latterly at 43 Pentland Terrace, Edinburgh, where he died in 1947, aged 94. The Special Committee ultimately decided that the colours of the Club be red and dark blue with the consequence that the 'Club Uniform and Cap' should consist of a 'dark blue velvet Golfing Cap, as furnished by James Barclay, Hatter, Lothian Road' and a Coat 'of a red colour with dark blue velvet collar'. As far as the latter was concerned, it was decided to employ Messrs Macdonald, Middlemass & Wood, Hanover Street, as the Club's Tailors and to provide a 'Coat of three different qualities at £1.1/–, £1.10/– and £2.2/–. The Cap, on the other hand, was to cost 2/6d with 'Monogram included'. On the subject of coat buttons, Colonel Trotter kindly gave his approval to a design bearing his Crest as a consequence of which the Club became liable to the Inland Revenue for an annual licence fee for Armorial Bearings. The initial cost of supplying the   13 buttons, together with the die, was £4.4/– and a charge of 1/– per button was levied on every Member whose coat was made other than by the Club's official tailors.

The Course was officially opened on 7th May 1892 when a Match was played between teams chosen by the Captain and Secretary and the event was duly reported by *The Scotsman*:

> The public opening of the new golf course on the Mortonhall Estate, at the back of the Braids leased from Colonel Trotter of Mortonhall by the Mortonhall (late Morningside) Golf Club, took place on Saturday when a match was played between teams chosen by Captain Duncan MacLaren and the Secretary, Mr W. C. Sturrock. The Course had received a good deal of attention during the previous 8–10 days and was in remarkably good condition for a new green. In spite of the somewhat threatening appearance of the sky, there was a large gathering of Members and their friends, not a few ladies being amongst the onlookers. Previous to the starting of the match, Mr Andrew Usher, addressing the assembled group, congratulated the Members on the acquisition of the ground. He regretted Colonel Trotter, owing to an engagement in London, was unable to be present. He was satisfied from what he had seen of the green that it would be one of the finest inland courses in the country (hear, hear). The turf was very old and the hazards were numerous and big enough (laughter). He considered the Club was exceedingly fortunate in acquiring such a place. They were much indebted to those Members who had personally carried through the negotiations; to Colonel Trotter and his Factor, Mr Mackenzie, for having made everything as smooth as possible; and to the distinguished architect who had drawn up the plans of the fine Clubhouse they proposed to build. To each of these parties he asked for three cheers. The request having been responded to, the Captain, Mr Duncan MacLaren, thanked the Members for having so cordially acknowledged the small services of himself and the Committee in carrying through the arrangements for acquiring the Mortonhall course. They would, he felt sure, find the green a very fine one and if the ponds were too small (laughter) or the hazards too few (laughter) they must just take time until things were got into thorough working order. Thereafter Mr. Usher drove the first ball amidst cheers and the various foursomes started to make the round of 9 holes.

The Scotsman 9th May 1892

At a Meeting two days later, Council 'resolved that the holes should be named' thus:

1. KHYBER	4. POND	7. ELFIN
2. WARREN	5. GATE	8. BUCKSTANE
3. QUARRY	6. SADDLE	9. HOME

The layout of the original course of nine holes was as shown overleaf. A detailed description of these holes appeared in *Golf – a Weekly Record of Ye Royal and Auncient Game* in September 1892:

The first hole is a very long one, and is well named Khyber, because the pass becomes narrower and narrower until at the end thereof you think to find yourself in a cul de sac; but no, a wider gorge is about to open out, and to give scope to one of the most sporting shots with which we are acquainted, the drive for the second hole; on the right within a few feet there is a wall, and beyond the wall a great wood; on the left, not many yards in front is a large pond gaping for balls; *in medio tutus*. These are the longest holes in the round, requiring two drives and an iron. The third is a short but sporting hole, across a ravine and over a quarry; it is just a nice drive. The course then turns back in a westerly direction towards the pond; the tee shot should easily carry the rough stony ground in front, after which a cleek will take you home. The fifth, or Wall hole, takes two good drives, but there is no obstruction. Now begins hill work up to the Saddle, but the ascent is so gradual that it is not a severe strain on the wind. Of the seventh and eighth holes there is little to be said at present, except that they are in a transition state, but, during the winter, there is little doubt that the same energy which has already done so much for the green, will speedily achieve their reformation. The way to the Home Hole is peculiar, the drive being over a cliff. Woe to the man who tops here, as he may then lose several strokes among stones, and perhaps break a club before reaching the course. With a favourable wind, one might drive far enough to get home in two but, as a rule, one has to play round the corner of the rocks, reaching the green in three.

Amid all the enthusiasm and euphoria in May 1892 for the brave new Club, there was regrettably one sour note. This concerned Rule 13 of the Constitution whereby Council had the power of raising an assessment of £1.1/– on the former 97 Members of the Morningside Golf Club for the purpose of defraying the cost of erecting a Clubhouse

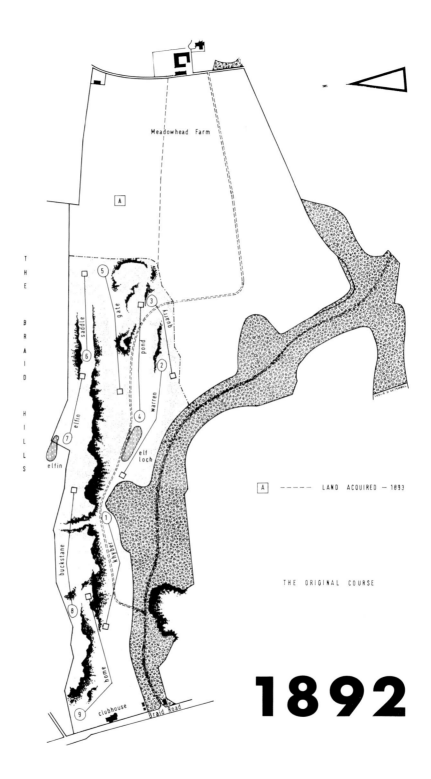

Meadowhead Farm

A

T
H
E

B
R
A
I
D

H
I
L
L
S

5
3
6
2
4
7
1
8
9

saddle
gate
scrub
pond
warren
elfin
elfin
elf
loch
buckstane
khyber
home
clubhouse

Braid Road

A ------ LAND ACQUIRED — 1893

THE ORIGINAL COURSE

1892

16

and other expenses of the Club. All other Members were liable for a total sum of £3.3/– in the first year compared with the basic contribution of £1.1/– from the 'Morningside Men'. On 20th May 1892, Council considered a requisition from 25 Members of the Club, demanding that a Special General Meeting be called to rescind Rule 13 in so far that it imposed an assessment of £1.1/– on certain Members of the Club. After discussion, Council took the view that 'the leading purpose of the requisition was not such as the Council would feel authorised in calling a Special Meeting of the Club'. Simultaneously, however, the Captain, Duncan MacLaren, no doubt regarding the matter as a serious threat to the well-being of the Club, personally sought the Opinion of Counsel on the issues raised by the requisitionists. He was advised that the new Mortonhall Golf Club had acted properly, that the Rules could only be amended at an *Annual General Meeting* and that the remedy for the requisitionists was to resign their Membership. One of those giving the Opinion was G. L. Crole, later Sheriff Crole, who was to become not only a Member of Mortonhall but also its Captain for the three years 1902–05. On the same day on which Counsel's Opinion was received, the Secretary reported that 85 out of the 97 Members concerned were prepared to make a *voluntary contribution* of £1.1/– and that the remaining 12 were prepared to do likewise or resign. Council resolved to give all 97 Members the opportunity to make such a voluntary contribution on the understanding that, at the next AGM, Rule 13 and its offensive 'assessment' would be expunged from the Rules of the Club. This compromise proved to be successful although 8 resignations were received from the 'Morningside Men'.

Sadly, at this time, the Secretary, W. C. Sturrock, who had also been Secretary of the Morningside Club, found it necessary to resign 'in consequence of the work of the Club interfering with his everyday duties'. Council, in accepting his resignation, recorded their appreciation of the 'excellent services' which he had rendered and appointed D. W. Walker as his successor. Tribute must be paid to the outstanding manner and style in which the first Minute Book of the Club was kept – the handwriting, copperplate; the narrative, a model in compromise between detail and economy; the language, at all times clear and unambiguous; the pages, interspersed with a number of blank sheets on which it was obviously the intention to adhere sketches of such items as 'The Opening Day', 'The Club Uniform', 'The Shelter – the Club's First Clubhouse', 'The Club's Crest', 'The First Competition', 'Sketch, characteristic of Willie Park', 'Sampling the Liquors', 'The Examination of the Club's Accounts', 'Sketch of Colonel Trotter's Cup', 'The Wet Clothes line', 'A Club Caddie', 'Editing the Handicap Book', 'The Auditor', 'The New Greenkeeper'. No doubt the artistic talents of

Michael Brown were being invoked but unfortunately no trace of the sketches can be found.

It is inevitably a source of some speculation as to where Members changed or indeed sheltered in the first few months of the Club's existence but, in late June, a temporary shelter was built at a cost of £8.10/–. While it cannot be substantiated, it is considered that the square hut at the East end of the sheds, previously sited on the car park, was, in fact, the Club's 'First Clubhouse'. The first major activity of the Club, after establishing the Rules & Bye-Laws, was the erection of its Clubhouse. Sydney Mitchell, who had prepared the plans, was one of the leading architects in the City of Edinburgh at this time and one of his last works was the design of the Church of Scotland Offices at 121 George Street, Edinburgh in 1909. It would appear from such records as are available that the design of the Mortonhall Clubhouse was a gift from Mr Mitchell as reference is made at the first AGM to 'the obligation under which the Club lies to Sydney Mitchell, Architect, one of its Members, for having generously designed the Clubhouse and furnished the necessary plans for the erection of the building'. Unfortunately, the plan of the Clubhouse is not in existence in the City Archives, but from the plans of a major extension which took place in 1903, it would appear that the basic design of the main floor was as shown opposite.

There was no attic area and, while a Ladies Room was provided on the main floor, quarters for the Greenkeeper/Clubmaster and his wife were situated in the basement. In June 1892, four estimates for the building of the Clubhouse were presented to Council:

William Beattie & Sons	£1250
James Duncan & Son	£ 790
Alexander Calder	£ 750
Alexander Crow	£ 735

As the Club, in General Meeting, had only authorised a sum of £700 to be spent, negotiations took place with Mr Crow, who had submitted the lowest tender, with the result that, subject to certain modifications, a new offer of £650 was received. Enquiries were simultaneously made regarding the source of a water supply and these revealed that the nearest pipe (the 'Swanston Pipe'), belonging to the Water Trust, was a third of a mile distant and that the cost of laying a branch to the Clubhouse might be £100. As it now seemed impossible, both to erect a Clubhouse and to establish a water supply for less than the £700 authorised, Council called a Special General Meeting of the Club on 6th July 1892. This Meeting unanimously empowered Council to accept the estimate of £650 from Alexander Crow or 'other offerer' and 'to procure a water supply from the Swanston Pipe of the Edinburgh Water Trust'. A week later,

18

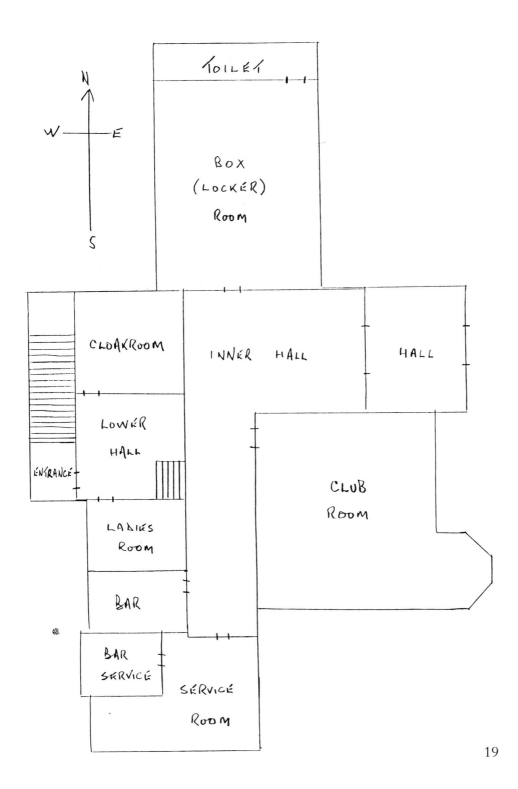

19

however, Council switched allegiance from Mr Crow with whom they had recently been in dispute over the cost (£20.3/8d) of constructing the entrance to the Course from the Braid Road, to Messrs James Duncan & Son who had now offered to construct the Clubhouse for £650 on condition that Ballachulish or Easdale Slate was used for the roof. After consideration, Council decided to award the Contract to this firm at an increase of £5 on their estimate 'provided that they adhered to the strawberry coloured tiles mentioned in the Specification'. Messrs Duncan, on their hand, then indicated their inability to accept the Contract on these terms but were prepared to do so for £670. This new price was accepted by Council and the Secretary instructed to prepare the necessary Contract.

But the saga was not over. In July 1892, Messrs Duncan, for some reason, declined to proceed with the Contract. The Secretary, acting on his own initiative, obtained a further set of estimates, the lowest of which, in the sum of £720, was submitted by Alexander Calder, one of the original offerers. After negotiation, this was reduced to £680 provided that the time for completing the work was extended to 20th October 1892 and that a clause was inserted in the Contract absolving the builder from any further delay due to the difficulty in obtaining the elusive strawberry tiles. In view of the fact that the Contract was only entered into on August 1892 and further that it was decided in early October to contain the W.C. and urinal in a 'small projecting addition' at the North front of the building at a cost of £54, it was remarkable that, in mid–October, Council should have found itself considering proposals for painting and the provision of boxes, while in November accepting estimates for furnishings and napery. In all these ancillary matters, Council wisely left the choice to the Architect, Sydney Mitchell. Satisfactory arrangements were made with Sir William Forrest in regard to the laying of a water pipe 'through the lands of Comiston' and also in connection with the drainage requirements of the Clubhouse.

A Special Committee was set up in November to consider the financing of the whole operation for which it was estimated that a sum of £600 was required to be raised on the security of the Clubhouse. A solution to this problem came very generously in an offer of this sum by C. J. Munro, a Member of Council, at a rate of interest of four and one half percent and for a term equivalent to the remaining period of the Club's lease (approx. 14 years). This offer was gratefully accepted by Council who bound the Club to repay Mr Munro at a rate of £50 per annum, commencing in May 1893.

In keeping with the meticulous style of the Minute Book, a detailed analysis of the total cost of erecting and furnishing the Clubhouse was incorporated therein. Inevitably this is a far cry from the optimistic limits of £700 set by the Club at its first Meeting on 29th April 1892. The facts were as follows:

Building Cost		£767
Furnishing		
Furniture	£93	
Ironmongery	39	
China & Glass	15	
Napery	6	
		£153
Boxes		
(Note: 210 boxes were provided at a cost of 9/1d each – the rent per annum was fixed at 5/–)		£ 96
Water Supply		£ 77
Opening Ceremony		
Silver Key	£ 3	
Sandwiches	2	
Wine	2	
		£ 7
Miscellaneous		
100 tons of sand	£36	
Clubroom Stationery	3	
Gate Bell	2	
Patent Corkscrew	2	
Fee for preparing Bond in Security	8	
		£ 51
Total Cost		£1151

If reference is made to the table appearing in Appendix R, the above cost was approximately £67,700, in 1992 terms.

It was the wish of Council that the Clubhouse be opened by Colonel Trotter and it was suggested that the ceremony take place on 31st December 1892. Unfortunately the Colonel's military duties in London did not allow him to be present on that day and the opening was ultimately fixed for Saturday 11th February at 1 p.m. A Silver Key was purchased for the occasion and a Programme of Proceedings drawn up, providing for the entertainment of the Colonel and 'one or two Members' to cake and wine after the ceremony. The historic opening is perhaps best described by the following excerpt from the Minute Book:

Mortonhall, 11th February 1893.

The Clubhouse was formally opened today at One o'clock by Colonel Trotter of Mortonhall in presence of a company of about 100 Members and their friends, including Lord Stormonth Darling, Colonels McInroy and Stewart, Dep. Surgeon-General Houston, Dep. Inspector-General Messer, the Revds. W. Whyte Smith and Stevenson; Mr. T. Bennet Clark, Comiston House; Mr. Andrew Usher of Blackford Park; Mr. Sydney Mitchell, Architect; &c. &c.

Previous to the commencement of proceedings the Company were photographed in front of the Clubhouse by Mr. Alex: Ayton, Brunsfield Place

The Captain, standing on the Clubhouse steps, then, in name of the Members, expressed to Colonel Trotter their gratitude to him for coming from London specially for the occasion, and presented him with a Silver Key with which to open the Clubhouse. Colonel Trotter then opened the door, and thereafter proceeded with the Company to inspect the interior of the Clubhouse and its appointments, at the completeness and excellence of which he expressed his admiration. The Company having gathered in the Club-room, the Captain, who presided, proposed a vote of thanks to Colonel Trotter for performing the Opening Ceremony. Three hearty cheers were given for the Colonel, who, in the course of his reply, presented the Club with an elegant and valuable Silver Bowl for Competition annually as the Scratch Award of the Club, and he also expressed the pleasure it gave him to accede to a wish of certain older Members of the Club that he would now permit Caddies on the Course under proper regulations. The Captain having thanked the Colonel for his Trophy (and the concession he had intimated, cordial votes of thanks were unanimously awarded to Mr. Sydney Mitchell a Member of the Club, for having generously designed the Clubhouse, and to Mr. Alex: Hay, Surveyor, for services he had rendered in connection with its erection.

The Members thereafter adjourned to the Green where friendly matches were then engaged in. - Colonel Trotter (and the gentlemen who had supported the Chair partook of Cake and Wine in the Clubhouse, and Colonel Trotter afterwards partnered the Captain in a foursome against Lord Stormonth Darling (and) Mr. Andrew Usher, - the match ending in favour of the former. The Course was found to be in excellent order, although

though a stiffish wind somewhat interfered with steady play.

MacLaren

But so much for the government of the Club and the Clubhouse that remains to this day a haven for its golfers – what of the Course concerning which all that has been said is that it opened on 7th May 1892 and that it consisted of 9 holes? To understand and appreciate the first Course, it is necessary to review the early competitions played over it. From the date of the first event on 16th July 1892, competitions took place on alternate Saturdays right up to the first AGM on 29th March 1893. (Two competitions on 3rd December 1892 and 7th January 1893 were admittedly cancelled as snow lay on the Course 'to a depth of 3 inches' and 'at least 6 inches' respectively.) It was however agreed that this practice would not be repeated and for the season 1893–94, the Card of Fixtures was confined to four Quarterly Meetings. In June 1892, the Handicapping Committee, 'having before them the information received from Members as to the handicaps allowed them in other clubs' (presumably at Musselburgh and the Braids), fixed the handicaps to be given to each Member in stroke competitions of 18 holes. It is therefore somewhat peculiar that the first competition on 16th July should have been a bogey competition and that it was 'one of a series to be played monthly, by holes and under handicap and which is to terminate in March next when the player who shall have been first oftenest will be awarded a Gold Charm'. Fifty-two players competed 'in fine weather' when 'the Course showed great improvement after the continuous play of the past 3 months and the excellent state of the Putting Greens did credit to the Greenkeeper'. The eventual winner of 'the series' was the Rev. Wm. Stevenson, who was the only player to be 'first twice'. The first medal took place on 6th August over 2 rounds of the 9 hole Course and while the 'Putting Greens' were found to be in 'capital condition', the length of the grass 'on the lower reaches of the Course, combined with a strong wind on the heights to prevent low scoring'. The winner was C. J. Ray, who, with his handicap of 10, had a net score of 107. John Johnston had the best scratch score of 108 which, in the wind and twice over the ridge, could be regarded as a creditable performance. Reports on the earlier competitions consistently referred to the grass being 'inconveniently long' but on 8th October 1892 when the best scratch score to date of 100 was returned, it was recorded that 'the grass on the Course was now getting less troublesome'. No doubt the more regular traffic round the Course was having some effect.

24

When the plan of the Course is considered against the area of the lease which it occupied, it is astonishing that, at a Meeting of Council on 4th October 1892, the Captain, Duncan MacLaren, should have submitted a plan extending the Course to 18 holes *within the existing boundaries*. Council, in giving its general approval, agreed to go over the ground on 6th October in attendance with either Peter McEwan (1834–1895) the Clubmaker at Bruntsfield, or Willie Park, Junior, (1864–1925) of Musselburgh, who, apart from winning the Open Championship in 1887 and 1889, was, by this time, one of the foremost golf architects in the country. In the event, it was Willie Park who met with Council and who 'expressed a favourable opinion as to the general lines of the proposed Course though also making a number of suggestions for its improvement'. Matters thereafter moved with amazing rapidity – a Special General Meeting was convened on 11th October which not only approved the plan but also agreed to increase the Membership from 200 to 250. The 50 new Members were duly admitted on 14th October – such the popularity of golf – and of Mortonhall. Regrettably a plan of this remarkable lay-out cannot be traced but as subsequent events proved, it must be extremely doubtful if, in fact, it was playable at all. Nonetheless, men were engaged to cut, roll and turf the extra nine greens 'before the arrival of winter' and, in addition, a decision was taken to drain the Marsh in view of the proximity to the first green on the extended Course. The monthly medal on 5th November 1892 was – *mirabile dictu* – played over the new lay-out and 'opinion was generally favourable to the Course as altered, although considerable anxiety was expressed about the amount of crossing at *the three holes* near the pond'! It may well be that the *raison d'etre* of the new Course lay in the comment that it was 'found to be much easier than two rounds on the old one'. The best gross and net scores of 83 and 75 respectively were certainly a considerable improvement on previous returns.

Only two further competitions were played on the new Course before Council was presented with a Requisition, signed by 104 Members, proposing that Colonel Trotter be approached with a view to his letting 'the field lying immediately to the East of the present Gate Hole' for the purpose of 'extending the Green'. Council approved the purpose of the Requisition and authorised the Captain to make the necessary overtures. Within a week, Duncan MacLaren reported that his initial enquiries had revealed that Colonel Trotter was likely to be disposed to lease this additional ground (18.414 acres) whereupon Council agreed to proceed with the proposition, subject to the necessary finance being raised at the next AGM.

In the meantime, it was obvious that the 'three crossing holes' near the pond continued to cause problems and Council resolved to dispense with these holes for the future and reduce the Course to one of 15 holes – play, however, in competitions, was to continue over 18 holes, the first three holes being repeated. Only one competition appears to have been played on this basis as by 3rd March 1893, the Course had mysteriously shortened to 14 holes. Even this seemed unsatisfactory for the four meetings which took place in the 1893/94 seasons, before the new Course on the extended ground opened in May 1894, all consisted of two rounds of the original 9 hole Course. Thus frustrated in its efforts to put a quart into a pint pot, Council turned eagerly to the prospect of the additional ground in what was strangely known as the 'North Field' and, at its Meeting on 3rd February 1893, a plan of an 18 hole course over the existing and new ground was submitted for consideration. Five new greens, each to be 60ft square, were estimated to cost £130. The plan was approved and it was presented, together with terms of a new lease, incorporating the extension as well as the old ground, to a Special General Meeting of the Club on 11th February 1893. Both propositions were unanimously accepted and Council instructed to proceed forthwith. The plan of this course which was ultimately opened in May 1894 was as shown opposite.

Apart from the names of the additional holes, the most noteworthy features were:

1. the introduction of the first tee at the Clubhouse and the consequent use of a common fairway for the 1st and 18th holes
2. the remarkable and sporting fifth hole
3. the use of a common green for the 7th and the 13th holes
4. the introduction of the infamous 8th hole (Perdition)
5. the short 10th and 11th holes
6. the position of the 12th green
7. the introduction of the 16th hole

The ninth hole was remarkable in that, in the early years of the next century, a Scotsman, living in Cordoba in the Argentine, was sent back to his native heath to select 18 holes from various courses throughout Scotland on which a prospective course at Cordoba might be constructed. His choice at Mortonhall was the 9th hole (Cottage) and this was ultimately perfectly rebuilt in the Argentine.

The lease which secured the 'North Field' as well as the original ground was for a period of nineteen years up to 1912 and provided for a rent of £115 for the first four years and £123 for the remaining years. This extended the term of the previous lease by four years. It contained some clauses of which the following are worthy of interest:

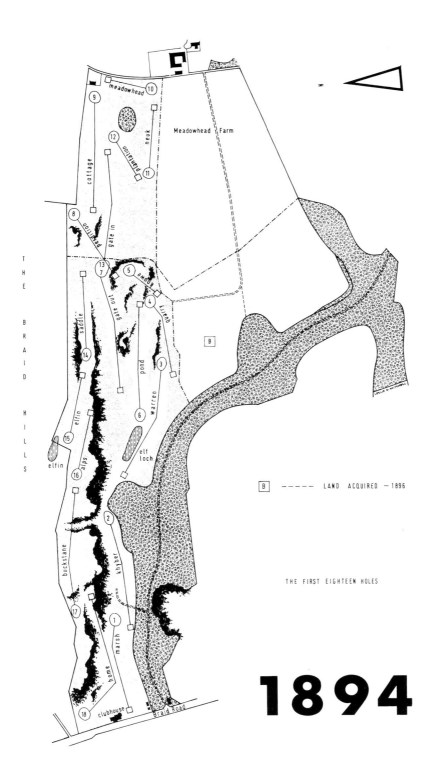

THE FIRST EIGHTEEN HOLES

B ----- LAND ACQUIRED — 1896

1894

27

1. the expression 'which grass they will be entitled to cut, mow or to eat down with sheep'
2. no golf to be played on Sundays
3. the right of Colonel Trotter, namely:
   (i) to work, win and carry away sand, gravel and stones
   (ii) to prune, fell and carry away timber
   (iii) to remove ice from the low pond
   (iv) to reserve to himself the whole game upon the lands
   (v) to hunt – but not with horses or other animals save dogs
   (vi) to reserve the right for himself, the members of his family and visitors at Mortonhall House, to play golf over the said lands
4. each Member of the Club to wear, while on the 'lands' either 'the Club's Uniform Coat or Cap or such other distinguishing badge'
5. the prohibition of crossing boundaries or fences and of entering plantations or coverts
6. the prohibition of interfering with 'ground or winged game'
7. the permission to allow licensed Caddies

The first 'servant' of the Club was a Dirleton man, Peter Lees, who acted as both Greenkeeper and Clubmaster. Evidence of his 'satisfactory services' occurred in October 1892 when he was rewarded by an increase in his weekly wages from £1.1/– to £1.5/–. Mrs Lees was also engaged to wash the Club's linen but apparently her services were regarded as free for, in February 1893, her husband wrote to enquire 'what remuneration Council intended to allow his wife for her services in the Clubhouse'. Not content with this, Mrs Lees, herself, had the temerity to request assistance in the Clubhouse. This proved to be a fatal error of judgment on the part of the Lees. Both matters were remitted to the House Committee together with the somewhat bizarre instruction that they were also to consider the 'best means of disposing of the Clubhouse ashes'! Whether the ashes were satisfactorily disposed of or not is not recorded but certainly the Lees were. The House Committee decided that the time had come for the Club to have a 'proper' Clubmaster and that Peter's duties would be better confined exclusively to those of greenkeeping. In due course, the services of James Sales were secured as Clubmaster together with those of his wife, for an annual sum of £40. But Peter was not altogether forgotten as, through the kindness of a Council Member, the Lodge at Comiston (situated about 100 yards South of the junction between Camus Avenue and Buckstone Terrace) was acquired as a house for him and his wife. A year later, however, Peter Lees left the Club to become Greenkeeper at the Braid Hills.

In retrospect, this was a great loss to Mortonhall – for Peter Lees eventually became the Head Greenkeeper at the Royal Mid-Surrey Golf Club at Richmond where J. H. Taylor was Professional. He is referred to, by Bernard Darwin in his book – *Golf Courses of the British Isles*, in the following passage:

> Much care and money, and a transcendent genius among Greenkeepers, Peter Lees, have combined to make the greens a miracle of trueness and smoothness'.

A leading Greenkeeper of his time, he was frequently consulted later on the techniques of construction and the maintenance of greens and wrote articles which are still of interest to this day.

In its early days, the Club experienced problems over the subject of caddies. In terms of Special Bye-Law 3, no caddies were to be brought upon the ground unless the rule was altered with the sanction of the Proprietor, Colonel Trotter. Some of the Members were, however, ingenious in that there developed in the course of the first season a practice of having 'Gentlemen Caddies' for the 'purpose of carrying Clubs and receiving (NB not giving!) advice'. In October 1892, Council prohibited these arrangements. As will have been noted, however, Colonel Trotter, in opening the Clubhouse in February 1893, graciously granted permission for Caddies to be allowed on the Course 'under proper regulations'.

In due course, Council received applications from persons 'desirous of being licensed as Caddies by the Club' and, after consideration and subject to the approval of Colonel Trotter's Factor, the following persons were granted licences:

> John Stevens, 18 Freer Street, Edinburgh
> William Tait, 34 West Port, Edinburgh
> John Metcalf, 29 High Street, Fisherrow
> Christopher Graham, 6 St. John Street, Edinburgh
> Charles White, 69 Albert Street, Edinburgh
> David Pratt (of no address)
> James Dargo, c/o McEwan, Bruntsfield Links (the famous clubmaker)

A sketch of a Caddies' Badge was approved and a supply of 20 badges was obtained at price of £2.10/–. Each Caddie, on being licensed, was furnished with a print of the *Regulations for Caddies*. These 'Regulations' were in the following terms:

1. No Caddie shall be permitted to enter on the Club's ground unless licensed by the Council, and wearing on his arm the Club's Badge for Caddies. A list of names of the licensed Caddies will be kept in the Club House by the Club Master for the inspection of Members, and no Member shall be entitled to employ any but licensed Caddies.

2. No Caddie shall be admitted to the Course unless under engagement to a Member, who, immediately on completion of the engagement, shall be bound to see him off the Course unless he be again forthwith employed by another Member.

3. Caddies, when disengaged, shall be bound to carry for any Member requiring their services.

4. Caddies are expressly prohibited from, on any pretext whatever —
   (i) Crossing the boundary or other fences of the Course, or entering any of the plantations in or adjoining the Course;
   (ii) Poaching, or in any way interfering with the game or rabbits on the Course or adjoining lands, or doing any act of injury to the property of Colonel Trotter or that of the Club;
   (iii) Entering the Club House, or loitering near the door thereof;
   (iv) Canvassing for employment, quarrelling, or making a noise.

5. Caddies must at once carefully replace any turf cut or displaced by the Members for whom they are carrying, and press it firmly down with the foot, and they must also see that there is no unnecessary waste of sand from the Boxes when teeing balls.

6. The charge to be made by Caddies shall be as follows:— for the first round of 18 holes, 1s.6d.; for each subsequent round or part thereof over nine holes, 1s., and for part thereof not exceeding nine holes, 6d.
   Note:— In paying Caddies, Members are particularly requested to observe this Regulation.

7. Every Caddie infringing any of the foregoing Regulations, or not conducting himself in all respects in a civil and proper manner, shall be liable to the Suspension or Revocation of his Licence, as may be determined by the Council of the Club.

8. The Licence of each Caddie shall also be subject to Suspension or Revocation by Colonel Trotter or his Factor at their discretion and without reason assigned.

9. Caddies on being licensed will be provided with a Club Badge, for which they shall deposit 2s 6d., to be returned to them on re-delivery of the Badge.

10. Without prejudice to the preceding Regulations and in addition thereto, Members shall be responsible for the conduct of the caddies employed by them, and by the Strangers whom they may introduce, while on the Course, and shall be liable for any infringement of the Regulations by the Caddies so employed.

While the establishment of the government of the Club, the building of its Clubhouse and the formation of its Courses undoubtedly dominated the Club's first year of existence, there were also a myriad of other happenings and events which collectively provide a cameo of life in Golf Clubs in the 1890's. As far as open tournaments were concerned, Council nominated the Captain, Duncan MacLaren, and A. J. Hodge to represent the Club at the *Evening Times* Tournament at St Andrews in October 1892 but decided for no apparent reason not to enter the Club for the *Evening Dispatch* Tournament on the Braids in April 1893. On the subject of visiting clubs or matches with other clubs, Council was not accommodating. A request by the Scottish Artists Golf Club to play one of their competitions at Mortonhall in January 1893 was declined on grounds that the Course was in a transition phase. Likewise, offers of matches from the Burntisland Golf Club and ye Monks of ye Braids Golf Club – a non-course owning club which played on Braid Hills – were 'not entertained'.

The quality of the Membership was a subject never far removed from the minds of Council. Even though the Membership was full, Council appeared to indulge in 'observing from the Candidates Book' that, for example, the Hon. Lord Stormonth Darling, Lord Wellwood and Lord Kincairney, all Senators of the College of Justice, together, with Lord Kingsburgh, the Lord Justice Clerk, and Sir Alexander Kinloch Bt., who had the distinction of opening Muirfield on 3rd May 1891 and being 31

Captain of the Royal and Ancient Golf Club in 1892, were all applicants for admission. These distinguished gentlemen were unanimously offered 'the courtesy of the Green and the Clubhouse' and admitted to full Membership of the Club at the earliest opportunity.

As far as the disciplining of Members was concerned, two particular types of infringement stood out above all others – the first, concerning the climbing of boundary walls (Special Bye-Laws 4 and 5) and, to a lesser degree, the second, the introduction of 'strangers' (visitors). (Ordinary Bye-Law 10). As early as June 1892, Colonel Trotter's Factor, D. F. Mackenzie, called the attention of Council to 'the practice on the part of certain Members of crossing the boundary fences' as a consequence of which the Secretary was required to direct this complaint directly to the notice of all Members. Despite this warning, Stirling Paterson was suspended for contravening the Rule and subsequently resigned; J. S. Ferrier was warned as to his future conduct in this matter; J. G. Inglis, whose 'stranger' had crossed the boundary wall, was fined £1 and D. Sime, whose 'stranger' had committed a similar breach, was also relieved of £1. 'Strangers' of Dr Sym committed an indiscretion by leaving the Course via the boundary wall instead of 'going out by the gate' and for this offence, Dr. Sym was requested 'to be more particular in seeing that his friends whilst on the Club's ground did not transgress the Club's regulations in any respect'. Dr J. C. Mercer and J. W. H. Smith., who had been reported for entering the plantation adjoining the Course, adroitly submitted letters of apology which 'after great hesitation' were accepted by Council. On the lesser 'crime', Walter Dickson was reported not only to have introduced two 'strangers' at one time but also to have played some of the holes in reverse order! For the gravity of this combined offence, Council delayed the case 'for further consideration' but ultimately accepted his apology and assurances for the future. Men of the cloth were not averse, apparently, to chancing their arm as the Rev. Dr Charles McGregor was charged with introducing a 'stranger' to play on the Course on the day of the Autumn Holiday. Though Council agreed to take no action in this instance, the learned gentleman was requested to be 'careful to observe the rules in every respect'. In most cases, the 'offenders' were reported by the Greenkeeper who was under an obligation to do so by Special Bye-Law 7.

Following the completion of the Clubhouse, the Secretary displayed admirable enterprise and initiative in arranging a 'Wine Test' for which the sole judge and arbiter was the fortunate Thomas Ainslie. This exercise can hardly be better described than by the Minutes of the Meeting of the House Committee, dated 28th December 1892, which are reproduced opposite.

Edinburgh, 28th December 1892.

At a Meeting of the House Committee held in the Secretary's Office, —

Present :—

The whole Members, the Captain in the Chair.

The Secretary reported that he had some time ago invited those Members of the Club who were retail Wine Merchants to send in Estimates for supplying the Clubhouse with the requisite liquors along with samples of the Wines &c offered, and that these having been received he had, after consultation with the Captain, arranged for the samples being tested by Mr Thomas Ainslie Wholesale Wine Merchant, a Member of the Club, and he now submitted to the Committee the results of Mr Ainslie's test. The Committee having carefully considered these results in connection with the prices quoted for the different articles, and having resolved that the whole of the Club's supplies should be obtained from one merchant, decided to accept the offer of Messrs Douglas & Mason, 96 George Street, as on the whole preferable to the others, and authorised the Secretary to order a sufficient supply of the several kinds to be sent to the clubhouse.

D Maclaren.

It is perhaps not surprising in view of the relatively remote situation of the Club that, in March 1893, Council agreed to submit to the forthcoming AGM that an Agreement be entered into with the National Telephone Co. Ltd. for the use of a telephone at the Clubhouse at an annual rent of £12.10/– for five years. This proposal was unanimously approved but a subsequent suggestion that the telephone be housed in a sound-proof call box was rejected as 'experience had hitherto shown no appreciable inconvenience to arise from the want of it to those using the instrument'. The installation of the telephone is perhaps an indication of the standing of the Membership of the Club at that time for relatively few households then enjoyed such a luxury.

The AGM on 29th March 1893 marked not only what was in effect, the first year of the Club's existence, but the end of a period of intense activity and much achievement. A Club had been formed; a Clubhouse built; a Golf Course restored out of the whins and grasses of predominantly grazing land; and so perhaps, the following somewhat immodest and complacent opening statement in the first Annual Report might be excused:

> The Council, in presenting to the Members its First Annual Report, desires to congratulate them on the success which has attended the Club during the inaugural year of its existence.

The actual Meeting passed without incident. The annual subscription was increased from one guinea to £1.11/6d; the entry money raised from three guineas to five guineas and to finance the cost of the 'North Field' and the extended Course, the Membership was 'enlarged by 25, with power to Council to increase it by another 25, thereby making it 300 in all'. As promised, the offensive Rule 13 was expunged from the Constitution.

The Membership statistics make interesting reading:

Original Members – 29th April 1892		200
Add: Admitted – Special General Meeting – October 1892		50
		250
Less: Death	1	
Resignation	1	
		2
		248
Add: Elected		2
Membership – March 1893		250
Waiting List		138

The financial affairs of the Club for its first accounting period –
29th April 1892 to 17th March 1893 – can be summarised thus:

REVENUE ACCOUNT

Income

Annual Subscriptions	£269	
Entry Money & Voluntary Subscriptions	507	
Donation from Andrew Usher Esq. for Prize Fund	5	
Interest etc.	14	£795

Expenditure

Upkeep of Course, Sand etc.	£ 61	
Greenkeeper's Wages & Assistants	120	
Greenkeeper's Tools	20	
Rent, Taxes, Insurance & Licences	55	
Expenses of Bond	8	
Prizes	11	
Honorarium to Secretary	25	
Printing & Stationery	40	
Miscellaneous Expenses	33	£373
Surplus to Balance Sheet		£422

BALANCE SHEET

Assets

Clubhouse

Building	£650	
Water Supply,. Drainage, Painting, Grates etc.	177	
	827	
Entrance Gate, New Greens & Drainage of Course	139	

Furnishings

Boxes	£96	
Furniture & Fittings	93	
Ironmongery, Napery, Crockery,		
Glass etc.	61	250
		£1216

Less: *Liabilities*

Heritable Bond	£600	
Overdraft at Bank	194	794
Members' Surplus from Revenue Account		£ 422

A historic year in retrospect but what of the future? – perhaps no more
than to wonder if grass would grow in the 'North Field'.

But the grass did not grow on the 'North Field'. In June 1893, Council, along with Colonel Trotter's Factor, D. F. Mackenzie, inspected the state of the new field and found that, over a considerable area 'there was no appearance of the seed springing'. There were nonetheless areas where the grass was well-rooted and, on Mr MacKenzie's advice, remedial action was deferred for a month 'in order that the seed might have an opportunity of germinating after rain'. While some improvement did occur, re-sowing was eventually necessary in certain parts at a cost of £79.15/6d. These steps proved to be most successful as, in the following summer, Council was sorely exercised on the 'inconvenient length of the grass'. In May 1894, the 'North Field' was opened for play and, as a consequence, the Course was extended to 18 holes as depicted in the plan on page 27. Despite the 18 hole Course, which briefly and ingloriously existed on the original ground, this must be regarded as Mortonhall's first 18 hole circuit. Entry to the 'North Field' was by steps crossing the old boundary wall while exit was by means of a wicket in the gate short of the green of the 13th hole (Gate-In). The comments of those who engaged in friendly matches 'to test the capabilities of the ground' were generally favourable although the soil was found to be 'a little harder than on the Old Course' and the grass 'somewhat long for perfect play'. In naming the holes on the new Course, Council instructed that the name and number of each hole be 'painted on the pin'. Stakes with oblong boards had not yet been replaced by flags!

The growth of grass during the playing season posed problems and the most economical and popular method of control was by the grazing of sheep. Originally, the grazings were at the disposal of Colonel Trotter but, in 1894, the Club purchased the lease for an annual rent of £30. The grazings were then put out to tender and out of four offers received, they were given to J. D. Richardson, Butcher, 31 Minto Street, Edinburgh for £25 per annum. While financially this was apparently unsatisfactory, the Club had acquired the important right to cut the grass without restriction. At the end of 1895, however, Mr Richardson requested a reduction in his rent as the Club had 'cut the grass to his detriment'. Council agreed that more had been cut than intended and offered a reduction of £5. Despite all financial considerations, 'sheep did safely graze' at Mortonhall for 60 years until 1954. The other two methods of grass control, employed at this time, were by hand scythe and horse drawn reaper or mower. The former, obviously slow and laborious, tended to be used only in selected areas, leaving the main areas for the reaper. The first reaper was hired from Colonel Trotter's Factor but, following an account for £5.4/– for damage, the Club purchased a Shanks Patent Horse Mower for £21. The cost, however, of hiring a horse and man seemed by comparison expensive, amounting in June 1895 to £7.9/2d. Indeed the horse was by no means cheap as a paling had to be erected at a cost of £10 round the horse paddock (this became known as the 'Horse Park' and lay in the ground between the two copses at the 13th hole), corn and hay for the 1896 season amounted to £9.4/2d while 'boots' for horse were £1.14/–. But 'the horse' remained at Mortonhall till 1926.

As far as the rest of the Course was concerned, special consideration was given in 1893 to defects in the putting green at the 14th hole (Saddle) and a surveyor was appointed to prepare plans to level it. It was agreed to excavate 600 cubic feet at a cost of £30 and secure the sheer face of the embankment at the north end of the green with 100 battens bought for £2.12/9d. In the course of the excavations, there was a strange and exciting find when a series of old graves – considered to date from early Pictish or Dark Age times with their flat side-stones – was laid bare! In reporting this discovery, the magazine 'Golfing' recorded 'The spot is thus one where the imagination of the antiquarian can have free play, for nothing is known of these silent tenants of Mortonhall, and they can be trusted to keep their secret. It is these, other than golfing interests, that lend part of the charm to this Course'. Perhaps these graves marked the first of the 'Mortonhall Men'. There was trouble, too, at the 1st hole (Marsh), which had been drained to allow for the siting of the new first green. Council had, somewhat innocently, become ensnared in a long running feud between Colonel Trotter's Factor, D. F. Mackenzie, and a Member of the Club – the former accusing the latter of not wearing his golfing cap against which it was claimed that the Factor was guilty of introducing more than one stranger to golf with him at the same time. The Factor threatened to cut the pipe draining the Marsh unless it was carried past the Buckstane Farm Steading which, it was alleged, had been occasionally flooded by water from the Marsh. The Club was consequently faced with a bill for £14.19/– for extending the drainage to the Braid Road.

Four shelters were erected on the Course at this time at a cost of £9.7/5d each – much, it must be said, to the annoyance of Colonel Trotter's Factor with whom the vendetta referred to above still rankled. Indeed, this feeling continued to manifest itself in many little ways particularly in an almost obsessional surveillance of the boundary walls. Any Member seen crossing the wall in search of his ball was reported to Council for the appropriate disciplinary measures. Council, in an endeavour to ease the situation, purchased a number of 'ladles' and placed these along the walls to enable Members to scoop their balls out of   37 the forbidden territory. Again, the Factor countered by stating that the use of the ladles was damaging the walls!

In January 1894, almost a year after the Clubhouse had opened, Council were presented with a requisition from 53 Members of the Club which read:

> We, the undersigned Members of the Mortonhall Golf Club, desire to bring under the notice of the Council the insufficient accommodation of the present Clubhouse.
>
> The erection of Boxes (Lockers) in the middle of the box-room has curtailed the space and light to such an extent as to make it impossible to dress there. Members also experience considerable inconvenience on account of the inadequate lavatory accommodation.
>
> We would respectfully suggest for the serious consideration of the Council the necessity for an enlargement of the present House. The opening of the addition to the Course this spring will, we consider, admit of an addition to the Membership, and we would suggest that the funds required for a satisfactory extension of the present Clubhouse should, in whole or part, be raised by the Entry Money on the introduction of new Members.

Council approved this proposal and instructed Sydney Mitchell to prepare two possible 'enlargements' for consideration. Within a fortnight, Mr Mitchell had submitted the two sketches required and it was decided to opt for the larger scheme at an estimated cost of £900. While no plan of this extension can be found, it is considered that it was as indicated on the main floor drawing shown on Page 40.

Fortunately, a photograph of the Clubhouse as extended was taken and this is reproduced facing page 64.

The plans were duly approved at a Special General Meeting in March 1894 and out of 11 tenders received, the work was entrusted to Peter Whyte, Builder, Gilmore Place, Edinburgh at a price of £1052. The Special General Meeting also approved the admission of a further 50 Members at an entry fee of ten guineas, thereby increasing the total Membership to 350. This was even further increased by another 50 Members at a Special General Meeting following the completion of the work. While these entry monies were applied towards the cost of the Clubhouse, it was agreed that the balance be borrowed. Once more, C. J. Munro stepped into the breach, increasing his loan from £500 to £1250.

On the completion of the extension in the autumn of the year, consideration was given to the use to be made of the basement room created under the new Dining Room. This room had a pleasant aspect and the Members of Council no doubt felt that, in the exclusive masculinity of Victorian clubs, they displayed much considerateness and gallantry in allocating it as a Ladies Tea Room. Their apparent chivalry was, however, questionable, as they also decreed that the room was to be used subsidiarily as a Card Room for Members'. Five years later the 'best laid schemes' had 'gone agley' and the room was used for Members' bicycles.

The initial allocation of the room as a Ladies Tea Room was, however, of significance in that it led to the construction of the stairway leading to the main floor. This, Council stipulated, was the only means by which Members could introduce their lady friends to the Dining Room. Lady visitors fell into the category of 'non-playing strangers' and the Club showed a rare delicacy in framing a Bye-Law which stated that while the addresses of all strangers must be entered in the Strangers Book those of ladies were to be omitted. The Dining Room was opened in November 1894 and although this added to the Club's facilities, it also created problems and expense. Catering was initially restricted to Saturdays and Holidays and while there is no record of complaints about the quality of the food – indeed the Clubmistress, Mrs Sales, was reputed 'to make the best tea in Edinburgh' – there were a number relating to service. Previously, the Clubmaster was given £30 per annum towards the cost of keeping a servant to assist him in the Clubhouse and a waiter was also paid for by the Club on Competition Days and Public Holidays. After the Dining Room opened, the Clubmaster was authorised to employ a maid at a cost of 3/6d per afternoon or 5/– per day but this soon proved to be inadequate, and a further waitress was engaged on the same terms. While the food may have been above criticism, the quality of the whisky was not. Following complaints in October 1894, a 'change in that article' was agreed upon and James Gillespie, Wine Merchant was asked to furnish a supply of his whisky at 18/6 per gallon (cost of 1/5th gill = 1 penny). An attempt, however, by George Lunan, to introduce his Aerated Waters in place of those in use was rejected on the 'opinion of experts'. From an early stage, the Club was conscious of the problems of bar stock control and, in 1895, a professional stocktaker was engaged at an annual fee of three guineas.

In the period 1894–1896, with its new 18 hole Course and enlarged Clubhouse, Mortonhall rapidly became a popular golfing centre. Much consideration was accordingly given to improving the comforts and facilities for the Members – hot water was provided by means of a boiler in the basement – the cleaning of Members' clubs and boots was undertaken by the Clubmaster at annual charges of 5/– and 2/6d respectively – ivy and roses were planted round the Clubhouse – an 39

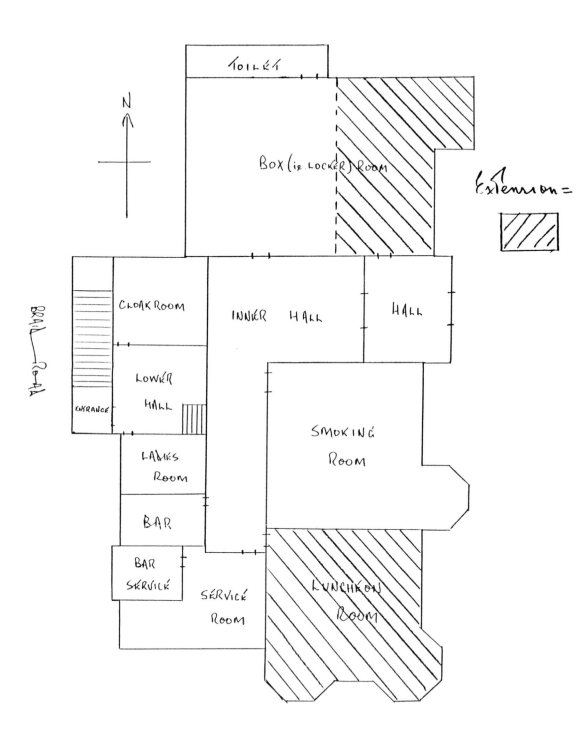

N

BRAIL ROAD

TOILET

BOX (ie LOCKER) ROOM

Extension =

CLOAK ROOM

INNER HALL

HALL

LOWER HALL

ENTRANCE

LADIES ROOM

SMOKING ROOM

BAR

BAR SERVICE

SERVICE ROOM

LUNCHEON ROOM

Artist's proof of Michael Brown's Golfing Picture 'The Open Championship St Andrews 1895' was purchased for four guineas – the introduction of gas was rejected on the grounds of cost (£100) and attempts by Clubmakers, Hutchison of North Berwick and T. P. Waggott of Comiston Road, to advertise their wares in the Clubhouse, were similarly dealt with. From the outset, travel to and from the Club to Morningside Station was by foot or bicycle but, early in 1894, thanks to the enterprise of Mr John Kerr, a brake was run between the Clubhouse and the station. Mr Kerr was given a key to the Members' gate in order that he could announce to Members 'the starting of the Brake on its return journey'.

Despite the excellence of the tea provided by Mrs Sales, complaints alleging incivility by the Clubmaster grew to such an extent that he and his wife parted company with the Club in March 1896 to be succeeded by Mr and Mrs William Cockburn. Sadly, William Cockburn, who had been a steward in the Officers' Mess of the Scots Guards, did not survive a year in the Club's employ. After his death, however, Council was so impressed with the efficiency of his widow that she was retained in sole charge of the Clubhouse. Mrs Cockburn's son, Phillip, was retained also as a Page Boy/Cleaner for which purpose Page Boy livery was bought at a cost of £3.19/6d.

As far as golf was concerned, hole and hole tournaments took place regularly throughout the season during 1893 to 1896 but the medal competitions were restricted to the four major meetings, namely the Spring, Summer, Autumn *and* Winter, the latter being played in November. In 1893, such medal competitions took place over two rounds of the original course (see plan on page 16) and over this telling circuit, the best recorded score of 82 was achieved by the Captain, Duncan MacLaren. The round was made up thus:

$$454 \ 475 \ 444 = 41$$
$$553 \ 545 \ 356 = \underline{41}$$
$$82$$

In 1894 and thereafter, all medal competitions were played over the 18 hole Course and, in the period to 1896 the best recorded scratch score of 76 was obtained by A. Craigie, Gregor McGregor, Michael Brown, the artist, and W. B. Taylor, who, in 1895, 1896 and 1898, had the distinction of having won the Irish Open Amateur Championship whose other winners at that period included John Ball (3 times) and Harold Hilton (4 times). There was a marked increase in the number of visiting clubs and among those savouring the delights of Mortonhall were the Scottish Artists G.C., the Edinburgh Corporation G.C., the Institution G.C. and the Scottish Conservative G.C. At the same time, a number of challenges were thrown down to the Club and the first match to take place at Mortonhall was in May 1895 against the Borders Golf Association which resulted in a win for the home club by 37 holes. Matches were then decided on the total number of holes up in each game rather than on the number of games won. Ten players took part on each side and after the match, all were entertained to dinner in the Clubhouse. This is the first recorded formal dinner at Mortonhall. Offers of matches from the Leith Caledonian G.C. and, as far afield as St Andrews University, were also accepted while, for no apparent reason, a match against the Blackford G.C. was declined.

One of the highlights of the period was undoubtedly the visit to Mortonhall in June 1895 of John Ball, Junr., of Hoylake, the winner of the Open Championship in 1890 and eight times winner of the Amateur Championship and this historic occasion could not be better described than as in the Club's Minute Book:

> Mortonhall, 15th June, 1895
> Mr John Ball, Junr., of Hoylake, again visited the Club's Course today on his way home from the Open Championship Meeting just completed at St Andrws. A foursome was played in the forenoon and also in the afternoon, Mr Ball having for his partner in the first round Mr C. H. Smith of Hoylake, their opponents being Mr George Morris and Mr D. W. Walker, Mortonhall. In his second round Mr Ball partnered Mr Henry Cook, W.S., their opponents being Mr Duncan MacLaren and Mr Gregor Mcgregor, Mortonhall. After a close game in each round, victory rested with Mr Ball and his partner in the first match by one hole, and with Mr MacLaren and his partner in the second match by a like number. A single between Mr Smith and Mr Morris ended in favour of the latter. In this round Mr Morris holed the fifth or Knowe Hole in one stroke.

Photographs were taken and one of these is reproduced facing page 80.

The hole in one by George Morris referred to above, is the first recorded one at Mortonhall and probably the only one achieved at the remarkable Knowe Hole (see Plan of Course on page 27).

An important appointment was made in April 1894 when the Club engaged its first Professional − Jack Simpson of Carnoustie, a former stonemason from Elie. Sadly his tenure of office was of short duration as he died in 1895 aged 35. Simpson, described as a 'mighty driver and dashing player', won the Open Championship at Prestwick in 1884 in a strong gale. At the second hole, he topped his tee shot 10 yards into a whin bush and eventually holed out in 9. Undaunted, he went on to return the best round of 78 and, with an 82 in the second round, secured the Championship Medal.

While the main considerations of the period 1893–1896 were undoubtedly the development of the new Course and the extension of the Clubhouse there were many other interesting incidents and occurrences. A suggestion was made that Commissionaires might be employed to carry clubs on the Course as well as the ordinary caddies and, after negotiation with the Corps of Commissionaires, an arrangement was made whereby Commissionaires could act as Caddies without the necessity of wearing a badge other than their uniform, provided they were remunerated at the rate of 7d per hour from the time they left the Commissionaires Headquarters until the time of their return thereto.

At the AGM of 1895, an addition was made to the Rules of the Club in that 'Officers in HM Service, on the Staff or in the Garrison in Edinburgh and District or on duty on the local Coast, may, during the period of their official residence, be admitted to the use of the Course and Clubhouse by the Council on the written application of two Members upon payment in advance of the Annual Subscription, without any Entry Money'. As a consequence, Lieut. F. G. Tait, of the Black Watch, then stationed at Edinburgh Castle, was, on 4th May 1895, admitted to the Club under this Rule. But of Freddie Tait's exploits at Mortonhall, more will be written later.

Was golf a more dangerous game in the 1890's than of now? Perhaps it was, for in 1893, Dr Sym presented the Club with a box of bandages and lint for use in the case of accidents on the Course. But danger was not apparently only restricted to flying golf balls as, in 1895, there was an incident when a troop of the Inniskilling Dragoons, stationed at Piershill, made an unauthorised entry on the Course and had 'gone galloping over a large part of the Club's ground to the injury of the turf'. The Colonel and the Adjutant of the Dragoons duly apologised.

The period also affected two of Mortonhall's earliest heroes. James M. Johnston, who along with Duncan MacLaren, had entered into the original lease of the Meadowhead Hill grazings, died in October 1893, some eighteen months after the formation of the Club. Duncan MacLaren, who had served the Club with such distinction as its Captain in the first three years of its existence, declined re-election at the Annual General Meeting in 1895 and his place was taken by the Hon. Lord Stormonth Darling. Lord Stormonth Darling, who had been solicitor General for Scotland for two years and Member of Parliament for Edinburgh and St Andrews Universities, was noted, among his many 43 accomplishments, as the author of a number of songs and verses. Indeed, shortly after his election, he gave the Club a copy of his famous ballad 'Keep Your Ee on the Ba''. This poem is recorded in Appendix I – The Barton and Other Odes.

And so Mortonhall entered into the third phase of its making – but what is this? – another Course in the offing?

The Remaining Years

It was almost inevitable that, within 18 months of the opening of the first 18 holes, the novelty and sporting nature of the 4th (Quarry) and the 5th (Knowe) holes (see Plan on page 27) began to pale and to cause considerable congestion on the Course. But the first Mortonhall Men were nothing if not ambitious and early in 1896, there were rumblings of leasing *either* the 30 acres, belonging to Colonel (now General) Trotter on the South side of the 11th (Neuk) hole (the ground purchased by the Club in 1976) *or* a similar acreage, belonging to Captain Gordon Gilmour on the North side of the 9th (Cottage) hole (now part of the Braids). Council, however, exercised caution, claiming that the likely rent of £4 per acre was excessive and would lead to the introduction of more new Members than was in the best interests of the Club. Nonetheless, a more modest extension of 9 acres was proposed in that ground known as the 'triangular' field, lying to the South of the 4th (Quarry) hole. Inevitably, Duncan MacLaren was despatched to General Trotter to negotiate and, within the month, reported that a lease could be arranged at an annual rent of £30 on condition that the Club paid the whole cost of the necessary seed (£29.1/3d). This arrangement was recommended by Council to the AGM of 1896 together with the proposal that the Membership should be increased by a further 25 Members to a total of 425. Both proposals were approved. The acquisition of this additional ground successfully eliminated the short 4th and 5th holes with the result that Mortonhall's second 18 Hole Course was disposed as shown opposite.

The new 4th hole was named the Avenue in view of its proximity to that leading to Mortonhall House while the new 5th hole retained the title of Quarry and the new 7th hole assumed the mantle of Knowe. The extension was opened for play on 8th May 1897. Entry to the triangular field was by a wicket gate near the 4th tee while exit was by similar means in the old boundary wall short of the 5th green. There was certain difficulty in approaching the 5th green from the new angle as any ball dropping short was liable to run back to the base of wall. Council, however, instructed the raising of the ground on the North side of the

44

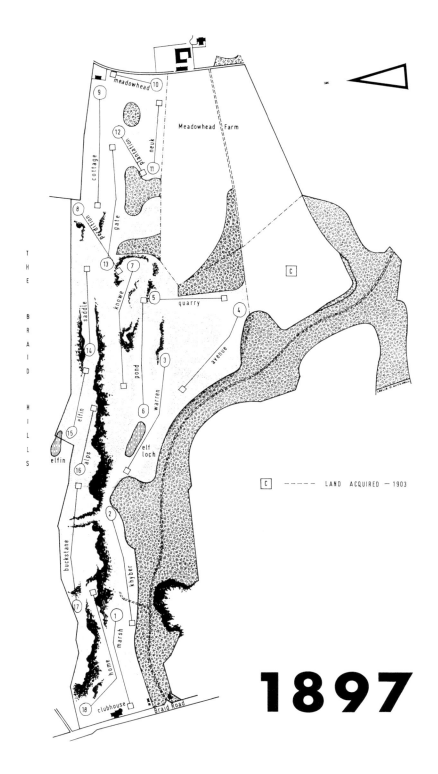

THE BRAID HILLS

meadowhead

Meadowhead Farm

cottage

plantation

neuk

gate

pavilion

knowe

saddle

quarry

avenue

elfin

warren

pond

alps

elfin

elf loch

buckstane

khyber

marsh

home

clubhouse

Braid Road

C ----- LAND ACQUIRED — 1903

1897

45

wall so that balls tended to 'return' to a club's length from the wall. This ridge of raised ground remains in existence to this day. Constant consideration was also given to the general upgrading of the Course and particular concern centred round the Elf Loch or 'the pond' as it was more popularly called. In 1897, no less a Member of the Club than Andrew Usher proposed that it be cleared out and the sludge round the edges used as a top dressing for the greens. Although Mr Usher's proposal was not accepted, the plantation at the East end of the pond was laid down in 1898 while, in 1900, Council, concerned at the decay in the woodwork of the small footbridge which crossed the pond, ordered its removal. This bridge had been useful in the recovery of golf balls as many of the 'gutties' used at the time were 'floaters'. One important piece of work which was carried out in 1899 concerned the 18th (Home) green where 'owing to the configuration of the ground at that place, the putting on that Green as well as the approach shot thereto, are often attended by an amount of luck, good or bad, unmerited by the stroke' instead of presenting 'a test of skill'. A contract which featured the blasting of rock was entered into and eventually, at a total cost of £101.18/6d, Council declared that the levelling work had been done 'in a thoroughly satisfactory manner' and that their expectations had been 'amply justified'.

Around the turn of the century, the Minute Books of the Club were strangely silent concerning golfing activities of the Club but such events as were recorded are of some historical note. First of all, there was the inimitable Freddie Tait – winner in 1896 and 1898 of the Amateur Championship and third in the 1896 Open Championship behind Harry Vardon and J. H. Taylor. Lieut. F. G. Tait, was, as previously stated, admitted to Membership of the Club in 1895 as an 'Officer in HM Services' and from his MATCH BOOK, there are frequent references to matches at Mortonhall, particularly during the Spring of 1896, for example:

> 6th April 1896   versus Colin MacRae – 'one very long drive over pond going to third hole – over 200 yards carry'
>
> 2nd May 1896   playing with Duncan MacLaren in Spring Medal – round in 78, second to W. B. Taylor who had 75. A very hot day and had to carry my own clubs – consequently I did not play my best – greens very bad.
>
> 25th June 1896   playing with Duncan MacLaren in Summer Meeting – round in 72 + 4 = 76 – beat record by 3 strokes – no scratch prize.

And so W. B. Taylor's record in the Spring Medal was shattered.

Tragically, Freddie was killed at Koodoosberg Drift in the Boer War in 1900, aged 30, and Council, in addition to subscribing five guineas (the maximum invited contribution) to the Memorial instituted in his honour by the Royal and Ancient Golf Club, opened a subscription list in order that individual Members of the Club might similarly express their sympathy, appreciation and respect. There was an unusual sequel to the Freddie Tait story in that his brother, J. G. Tait, who had been admitted as a 'Service Member' in 1901, presented the Club with 'his late brother Freddie's favourite mashie'. It is a matter of considerable regret that such a prized possession has been lost but the blame certainly cannot be laid at the door of the Council of 1901 who refused to allow a Member, Henry Bower, to take the club from the Clubhouse in order to have a replica made. Permission was, however, granted to Mr Bower to have an 'impression' taken of the club in the Clubhouse but it is not recorded whether he took advantage of this offer.

Mortonhall featured high in the list of ports of call when the famous came North to play in the 'Championships'. In June 1900, Harold H. Hilton – twice winner of the Open Championship, four times winner of the Amateur Championship, four times winner of the Irish Open Amateur Championship and U.S. Amateur Champion 1911 – played over the Course, to be be followed a year later by the 'great triumvirate' of Braid, Taylor and Vardon plus Alec Herd, Open Champion 1902. They were invited to play an exhibition match at Mortonhall for £20 'seeing they were to be in the vicinity of Edinburgh playing for the Championship'. This was undoubtedly a gala occasion and extensive arrangements were made. It was decided, however, that 'the excisable liquors supplied in the separate Marquee to be erected on the ground should be sold to Members only'. Vardon, incidentally, went round in 68 to beat the Freddie Tait record by 4 strokes. The photograph facing page 81 shows the famous four standing in front of the Clubhouse – seated in front of them the then Captain, Rev. W. Whyte Smith, and Secretary, D. W. Walker.

On a more humble level, there was a challenge to a 100-a-side match from the Edinburgh Burgess Golfing Society – 50 to play at Barnton and 50 to play at Mortonhall. This challenge was eagerly accepted by the Club and the match duly took place on 25th July 1901 and was recorded thus:

> The conditions were that each Club should be represented by no fewer than a hundred players, fifty couples to play at Barnton, and the like number at Mortonhall. The annals of golf contain no record of a match of such gigantic proportions and the event caused considerable stir throughout the golfing world and among Edinburgh golfers in particular. The

47

Members of both clubs entered into the engagement with great zest, and, with very few exceptions, all those chosen to play in the historic event came forward. On 25th July 1901 'this memorable contest was formally opened at Barnton, where Captain Chesser of the Burgess drove off against Captain Whyte Smith of Mortonhall, and intimation having been conveyed by telephone to Mortonhall that play had begun, the match was soon in full swing on both courses'. The Burgess representatives who played at Barnton succeeded in securing a transient victory by seven holes; but Mortonhall Course proved disastrous to the majority of the Burgess players, who were defeated there by ninety-two holes, Mortonhall thus winning the match by eighty-five holes. Reckoned by match play, Mortonhall only won by nine matches.

The match was commemorated in the most chivalrous fashion when the two Captains were elected Honorary Members of their opponents' Clubs.

The general life of the Club, however, continued to be coloured by personalities, incidents and vignettes of Victorian life. The terms of the lease, referred to on page 28 allowed General Trotter the right for himself, the members of his family, and visitors at Mortonhall House, to play golf over the Course. In July 1896, it was, however, represented to Council that some inconvenience was being felt by the General's sons in not being entitled to use the Clubhouse when golfing over the Course. Council extended this privilege and also elected the four to Honorary Membership of the Club.

In 1897, Dr F. W. N. Haultain was appointed Captain in succession to Lord Stormonth Darling. Dr Haultain, who was a fine golfer from East Lothian, was at one time Secretary of the Harum Scarum Golf Club which met once per annum on the Queen's Birthday at Gullane 'to show loyalty to her Majesty by a day's golf'. The winner of each annual meeting was required to entertain the other Members of the Club to dinner thereafter when fines were imposed for all manner of offences. One Member was actually fined for attending the opening of the General Assembly of the Church of Scotland! In 1900, Dr Haultain featured in an unusual incident when, playing an iron shot to the first green, he unearthed a George II farthing which remains to this day as an exhibit in the Club's showcase. In 1898, the Right Hon. Mitchell Thomson, Lord Provost of Edinburgh, was appointed Captain although surprisingly both he and Lord Stormonth Darling resigned from the Club in April 1901.

A bizarre incident occurred in June 1897 when the great Duncan

Duncan MacLaren

Sir Henry Trotter

MacLaren 'Father of Mortonhall' and its first Captain, was reported to Council by Dr Sym for chasing a rabbit on the Course in contravention of the Lease (see page 28). However, after correspondence between Mr MacLaren, Dr Sym and the Secretary the charge was withdrawn.

Council graciously conferred Honorary Membership for one year on A. J. T. Allan of Edinburgh University, in recognition of his winning of the Amateur Championship at Muirfield in 1897.

As the Club grew in stature and so in confidence, it seemed to become increasingly conscious of public and social obligations. The courtesy of the Course was granted in 1898 to Members of the British Medical Association during their Conference that year in Edinburgh as well as to members of the General Assemblies of the Church of Scotland. The 'more deserving boys' attending South Morningside School were permitted after school hours and on Saturdays to act as Caddies on the Course at a charge of 9d per round. This generally reflected the national trend away from the dominance of the professional caddies of the 19th Century. The requirements of the new and rapidly increasing breed of golfers in the 1890's were cheap and simple – bag carriers rather than expert advisers. In 1901, free Temporary Membership was granted for the winter of 1901/02 to the Rev. John Kerr of Dirleton who had, and who has since, in increasing measure, achieved much distinction as the author of '*The Golf Book of East Lothian*. (This is now a collector's item and a copy is presently worth in excess of £1,000.)

While Council rejected a request from General Trotter's Factor to have a bonfire on the highest point of the Club's ground to mark Queen Victoria's 'Diamond Jubilee' in 1897 on the grounds that it might damage the tees and greens nearby, it willingly agreed of its own accord to send a wedding present to the value of £30 on the occasion of the marriage of the General's son, Captain A. R. Trotter, in 1901.

In November 1901, one of the more intimate events in Club life at Mortonhall was instituted – the Captain's Supper. Following a competition among Council Members, a supper was held in the Clubhouse at which the guests were D. F. Mackenzie, the Factor of Mortonhall, and the Captain of the Burgess Golfing Society. The year 1901 also marked, with the death of the old Queen at Osborne, the end of the Victorian era; for golf, it also marked, due to an American invention, the end of the gutty ball; and for Mortonhall, it signalled a 'first nine' of solid achievement – an established Course, a comfortable Clubhouse, a full Membership and an accumulated surplus of £3,276.

Notable among those who contributed so much and are to be added to the first of the 'Mortonhall Men' were undoubtedly:

Sydney Mitchell   C. J. Munro   W. B. Taylor   49

3

THE MAKING OF MORTONHALL
– THE EDWARDIANS
1902–1907

Along the cool sequestered vale of life,
They pursued the noiseless tenor of their way

(Gray)

In 1902, there arose almost concurrently two matters which were to lead directly to securing the future of the Club well into the Twentieth Century and thence indirectly to establishing its position for all time at Mortonhall. Early in the year, there were murmurings about the inadequacies of the Clubhouse. At first, these were thought to be minor but then as the requirements were more accurately assessed, they – and their cost – became more formidable. The second development was the invention in 1898 in the USA of the Haskell core wound rubber ball. This ball – the forerunner of that played today – made golf much easier, flew much further and appeared on the British golf scene around 1900. Although no regulations then existed as to the size, weight and composition of golf balls, the new invention had a distinct advantage over the gutty, particularly in regard to the 'bound' it gave on landing. For a time, it was not considered *de rigueur* to use the Haskell ball against an opponent playing a gutty – indeed, those who did were referred to as 'bounders'! Inevitably, Mortonhall began to look on the short side and once more Council looked longingly at the ground on the South side of the 11th hole (Neuk). (See plan on page 45). While ambition was not a quality lacking in the early Mortonhall Men, it was of a kind tempered   51 with caution. Ambition dictated that both Clubhouse and Course be extended but caution diverted such aspirations to the terms of the Lease. Dare Council embark on their projects when the Lease had but 10 years to run? Good sense indicated otherwise – the Lease must be re-negotiated. The Club was fortunate in having as the newly elected Captain, G. L. Crole, Advocate (later to become Sheriff Crole K.C.) and he, in company with the redoubtable Duncan MacLaren, shortly to be appointed Law Agent to the Club, must have constituted an impressive team to negotiate with Sir Henry Trotter, the General having been knighted in 1901.

Initially a new lease for 99 years was sought but while Sir Henry and his son, Captain A. R. Trotter, the next heir of Entail, were 'anxious to meet the wishes of the Club as far as they could', they could not see their way 'for estate considerations' to extend the Lease for a period of more than 30 years – until 1933. They were, however, in addition, prepared to allow the Club the option to lease the 'coveted land' South of the Neuk at a rent of £66 per annum. Including the additional ground, the rent for the whole lease was to be fixed at £271 per annum to 1912 and £350 per annum thereafter. As the total acreage involved was virtually 99 acres, the respective rents per acre, at £2.14/8d and £3.10/8d were in the opinion of Council, low in comparision to those paid by other Edinburgh Clubs. All other aspects, including the financial implications, were examined and were, in the opinion of Council and its negotiators, considered reasonable. All that remained was to obtain the formal approval of the Members and to acknowledge a further triumph for Duncan MacLaren. But two further obstacles unexpectedly broke the surface.

First, it was discovered that the Estate of Mortonhall was held 'under the fetters of a strict entail' which, notwithstanding the consent of both Sir Henry Trotter and the next heir of entail, precluded the granting of a lease for a longer period of 19 years. It was, however, possible to overcome this hurdle by obtaining the sanction of the Court of Session and this, Sir Henry Trotter was willing to do, on the understanding that the Club met the expense thereof, estimated at £40/£50.

Second, and only some weeks before a Special General Meeting on 13th March 1903, doubts were expressed in Council as to the suitability of the additional ground and as to the extent of the financial burden it would lay on the Club. Nonetheless Council proceeded to submit the following 'package deal' to the Membership:

1. that the offer of a new lease to 1933 be accepted on condition that the necessary approval be obtained from the Court of Session
2. that the option to lease the 16½ acres to the South of the Neuk be taken up on the understanding that 50 new Members be admitted and
3. that the Clubhouse be enlarged at a cost not exceeding £2000 on the understanding that Council be authorised to borrow a sum up to £1500 and that the annual subscription be raised to £2.2/–

After discussion and debate, proposals (1) and (3) were approved unanimously but, after a vote, proposal (2) was defeated by 74 votes to 71. In retrospect, this Meeting was historic in that the annual subscription was increased for the first time in ten years, albeit by only 10/6 to £2.2/– and that the ground which was rejected as unsuitable for golf was the area not only purchased by the Club some 70 years later but also the subject of an interesting observation made, as will be seen shortly, by no less a person than J. H. Taylor, Open Champion & Golf Architect. In due course, Sir Henry Trotter obtained the appropriate sanction from the Court of Session and the Club gratefully acknowledged the consideration and concern shown by Sir Henry and his heir, Captain A. R. Trotter, in the whole matter. As events will show, Mortonhall was to express its appreciation in a most distinctive way. The Special General Meeting over and the lease secure, Council was at last able to address its mind to the enlargement of the Clubhouse.

Sydney Mitchell, the Architect of the original building, had resigned his Membership in 1899 and J. H. Cooper of Messrs Cooper & Taylor, Architects, was appointed to advise on the extension. Mr Cooper's partner was W. B. Taylor, already mentioned for his golfing achievements and now a prominent and active figure in the Council of the Club. Mr Taylor was also the architect responsible for the Clubhouse of the Bruntsfield Links Golfing Society at Davidsons Mains.

Plans were drawn up which featured extensions to the Dining and Smoking Rooms, the improvement of the Kitchen and Lavatory accommodation and the construction of a flat for the Clubmistress in the attic. The contract was awarded to Adam Currie, Builder, South Gray Street, Edinburgh for the sum of £1362.12/–. Certain other 'works', mainly heating and painting, were estimated at £400, thus making the total cost £1762.12/–. Finance was arranged in the form of a Bond for £1500 from the Scottish Accident Life and Fidelity Insurance Co. Ltd. – the previous loan from C. J. Munro amounting to £1250 having been repaid in 1900. Numerous extra works, relating mainly to the Kitchen, were commissioned from time to time and new and additional furnishings bought with the result that the total cost amounted to £2352. Some of the incidental expenses included in this total were as follows:

Cost of special round table to encircle the pillar in the Smoking Room 'for the purpose of holding magazines and newspapers'	£6.18/–
Hand Grenade Fire Extinguishers, hung in baskets	£7.2/6d
Two dozen Black and Gilt Earthenware Spittoons	£1.10/–
Hire of Piano for Opening Ceremony!	£1.1/–

Preliminary arrangements for the opening ceremony were made at a meeting of the House Committee and while these were generally upheld at a subsequent Meeting of Council, 'cake, wine and tea' was over-ruled in favour of 'cake and tea'. On 2nd April 1904, the enlarged Clubhouse was formally opened by Sir Henry Trotter. The occasion was described in the Minute Book thus:

> There was present a gathering of about two hundred Members of the Club and their friends.
>
> Proceedings were opened by Captain Crole giving a brief history of the Club since its institution in 1892, and tracing its prosperity in various stages down to the present time. This prosperity could be attributed to the pioneers of the Club among whom he mentioned Mr Duncan MacLaren, the first Captain, as one to whom its success was largely due. Captain Crole also referred to the interest which Sir Henry Trotter had always shown in the Club and asked him to declare the Clubhouse open. Miss Turnbull in the name of the Club presented Sir Henry with a silver key, and fastened the Club's badge, in gold, on his breast. Sir Henry declared the Clubhouse open and thanked the Club for the honour they had done him in inviting him to perform the ceremony. He congratulated the management upon the prosperity of the Club and commended the conduct of the Members in the sportsmanlike way in which they had observed certain conditions of the Lease of the Course.
>
> Refreshments were afterwards served to the Company.

While the Kitchen was now sited in the basement and connected to the Service Room by means of a hoist, the floor plan of the main Clubhouse area was as shown opposite.

54

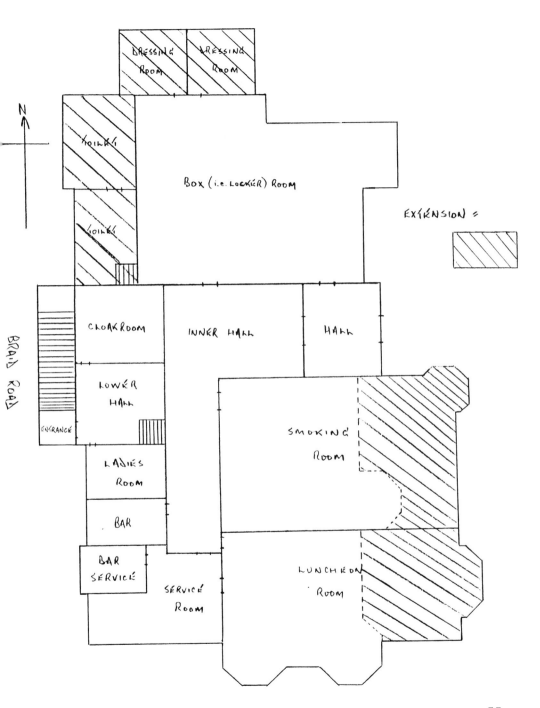

N

DRESSING ROOM

DRESSING ROOM

TOILET

BOX (i.e. LOCKER) ROOM

EXTENSION =

TOILET

BRAID ROAD

CLOAKROOM

INNER HALL

HALL

LOWER HALL

ENTRANCE

SMOKING ROOM

LADIES ROOM

BAR

BAR SERVICE

SERVICE ROOM

LUNCHEON ROOM

55

For most of the period under review, the Clubhouse was in the charge of the Clubmistress, Mrs Cockburn. While maids appeared daily, the only other party who resided in the Clubhouse was the Page Boy for whom suits of livery – and extra trousers – were frequently purchased. After the extension was completed in 1904, new arrangements were made with Mrs Cockburn:

1. that she be paid a salary of £150 per annum
2. that from this salary, she provide and keep *three* servants and provide board for the Page Boy, Philip Traynor (of whom more will be heard) and
3. that, if additional service is required, she provide for their board, the Club paying the necessary wages

In addition, the duties which Mrs Cockburn had previously undertaken in cleaning the Members' boots and clubs for 5/– per annum (provided she was able to collect the money!) were to cease. To carry out these tasks, Thomas Drummond of Musselburgh was appointed at a salary of £1 per week. He was also required to 'repair clubs, sell golf clubs, balls and other requisites of the game and to play with and teach Members who may desire his services, being paid by the Members engaging him 2/– per round for playing 18 holes and 2/– per hour for teaching'. These latter professional activities had previously been performed by the Greenkeeper, William Cunningham, since 1900. Although Mrs Cockburn had tendered her resignation in 1903 and then withdrawn it, her decision to resign in 1906 was final. While Council had decided to appoint a Clubmaster and his wife, Mrs A. Millar was eventually appointed after a considerable number of candidates had been interviewed. As far as the catering was concerned, a review was commissioned in 1902 with the result that the following tariff was agreed:

Cup of Bovril with Bread	3d
Sandwiches (each)	2d
Chicken and Ham Pates (Glass)	10d & 1/5d
Brawn and Boarshead (Glass)	1/2d
Ox Tongues (Glass)	3/5d
(Tin)	2/5d
Lunch Tongues (Tin)	1/4d
Boneless Chicken (Tin)	1/0½d
Sardines in Oil (Tin)	8d & 1/2d
& Tomato (Tin)	8d & 1/5d
& Whitebait (Tin)	8d

56   Potatoes will be charged 2d each person and Bread 1d per person

Cheese with Bread, or Biscuits and Butter

without Luncheon   8d

after Luncheon   3d

Tea Coffee etc.

Cup of Tea   2d

Coffee (Ground)   2d

Cocoa   2d

Tea, Coffee, or cocoa with Bread and Butter   6d

and two eggs   9d

Note: in the event of eggs being scarce the price will be 10d

Lunch

Plate of Meat (Hot) with Potatoes & Bread	1/–
(Cold)	1/–
a further helping of either	6d
Small Plate of Meat (Hot or Cold)	9d
Beef Steak or other Pie with Potatoes & Bread	1/2d
Steak or Chops with Potatoes & Bread	1/–
Basin of Soup (Extract of meat) with Bread	4d
(Specially prepared)	6d

Hot and cold lunches were supplied between the hours of noon and 3 p.m. but no hot meals were to be provided after 8 p.m. and no food at all after 10 p.m.

More particular and frequent attention was directed towards 'the whisky' and, in 1902, Stuart Gowans, the Auditor, to whom many, if not all, financial and administrative problems were referred, submitted a report which was resolved thus:

In accordance with instructions Mr Gowans submitted the following samples of whiskies viz:–

No 1.	Glenlivet	1895	20° u.p.	16/6d
No 2.	Rosebank	1895	20° u.p.	15/–
No 3.	Lagavulin	1897	20° u.p.	14/6d
No 4.	Glengrant	1897		15/6d
No 5.	Ben Nevis	1897		15/9d
No 6.	Talisker	1897		15/6d

and in addition there was submitted a sample from Messrs I. & G. Cockburn of Dalmore 1896.

After the samples had been tested by the Members of Committee the Meeting requested Mr Gowans to order the following:

No 1.	Glenlivet	1895	20° u.p.	16/6d
No 3.	Lagavulin	1897	20° u.p.	14/6d
No 5.	Ben Nevis	1897		15/9d
No 6.	Talisker	1897		15/6d

and to get a quotation as to Dalmore at 20° u.p.

While obviously one of the perquisites of the House Committee was the 'testing' of the whisky, its judgment remains in some doubt as, six months later, it was decided that 'all kinds of whisky at present in the Clubhouse should be mixed in one Cask and sold as the Club's blend'. And it only cost 4d a glass (one–half gill).

Although the life of the Members in the Clubhouse proceeded in a leisurely, relaxing and seemly fashion, it was not entirely devoid of interest and incident. In June 1903, W. B. Taylor reported that he had been 'attacked' in the Clubhouse by a fellow Member and although the assailant apologised for his conduct, Council considered that they could not overlook the offence and suspended him for six months.

In keeping with all the best traditions, the Club purchased a snuff-box in June 1904 but, within six months, the Secretary reported that it had 'disappeared'. In January 1905, however, the Captain, Sheriff Crole 'intimated his desire to present a snuff box to the Club' and handed over a carved Kilmarnock Snuff Box which had belonged to his family for more than one hundred years. This box remains to this day a prized possession of Mortonhall.

As has been said, there were two matters which led to the re-negotiation of the lease, one, the enlargement of the Clubhouse and the other, the extension of the Course. While Council's dream of extending the Course to the South of the Neuk was shattered by the surprising decision at the Special General Meeting in March 1903, Sir Henry Trotter indicated, in the following November, that the Club 'could at any time obtain the land to the South of the Avenue (the 4th) hole'. Inevitably, Duncan MacLaren and Captain Crole re-opened negotiations with Sir Henry on this new possibility. Ultimately, agreement was reached concerning the 13.38 acres involved and the financial terms of the lease amended thus:

Rent of £205 for the first year; £258.10/8d for the next eight years and £337.10/8d for the remaining twenty one years to 1933.

Considerable debate took place as to the merging of the additional ground into the existing Course and eventually, it was agreed that, for a trial period, three holes would be played *anti-clockwise* in the new field, the old 8th and 9th holes would be made into one and astonishingly, a new 13th hole would be played from the old 11th tee to the existing 13th green. (See Course Plan on page 45). This unusual Course was opened for play on 12th June 1905. Within four months, however, criticism of the condition of the new field closed it for play and six months later, this part of the Course still being closed, the extraordinary suggestion was made that the Club should endeavour to effect an exchange for 'the coveted land' South of the Neuk. While this was ruled out of order, a further attempt was made to bring the new field into play but such was the confidence in the plan advanced that the advice of J. H. Taylor, whom failing James Braid, was sought.

On 24th September 1906, J. H. Taylor (1871–1963) five times Open Champion and ultimately partner in Golf Course Design and Management with Frederick George Hawtree, visited Mortonhall and 'for a moderate fee of three guineas', submitted a report to Council. (This report is reproduced in full in Appendix M).

While Mr Taylor's recommendations were accepted in regard to the new field, two features of his report call for special comment. Firstly, his almost envious preference for 'the coveted land' was realised some 70 years later when it was developed by his partner's son and secondly, his construction of the new long 4th hole and assurance that its crossing the line of the 6th hole was not likely to cause difficulty. The latter was probably the greatest hurdle which Frederick Hawtree Jnr. had to face in his development plans of 1976/77. It was, therefore, in 1907, that Mortonhall saw its third amended Course of 18 holes in the form shown overleaf. The holes were renamed and bogey fixed thus:

1.	Marsh	– 300 yards	– 4	10.	Cottage	– 350 yards	– 4
2.	Khyber	– 320 "	– 4	11.	Neuk	– 300 "	– 5
3.	Warren	– 400 "	– 5	12.	Plantation	– 150 "	– 3
4.	Long	– 580 "	– 6	13.	Gate	– 325 "	– 5
5.	Avenue	– 290 "	– 4	14.	Saddle	– 265 "	– 4
6.	Quarry	– 335 "	– 5	15.	Elfin	– 210 "	– 4
7.	Pond	– 340 "	– 4	16.	Alps	– 155 "	– 3
8.	Knowe	– 350 "	– 5	17.	Buckstane	– 340 "	– 5
9.	Perdition	– 170 "	– 4	18.	Home	– 310 "	– 4

TOTAL OUT 3085 " 41   TOTAL IN 2405 " 37

GRAND TOTAL 5490 YARDS 78

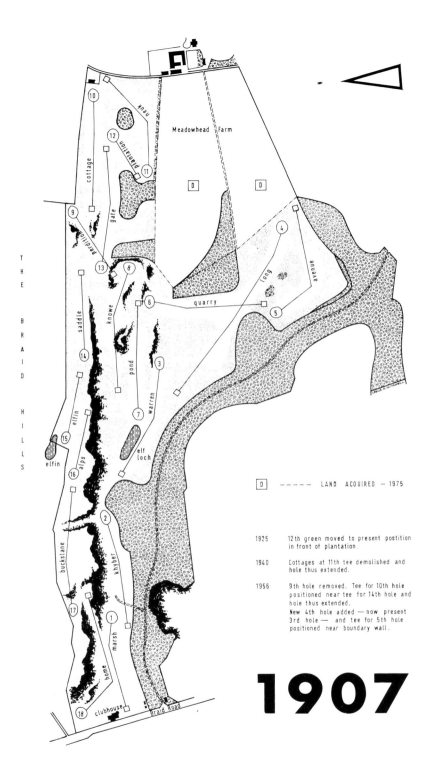

Meadowhead Farm

THE BRAID HILLS

LAND ACQUIRED — 1975

1925   12th green moved to present postition in front of plantation.

1940   Cottages at 11th tee demolished and hole thus extended.

1956   9th hole removed. Tee for 10th hole positioned near tee for 14th hole and hole thus extended.
New 4th hole added — now present 3rd hole — and tee for 5th hole positioned near boundary wall.

1907

The bogey score of the previous Course (see Plan on page 45) was 76, although details of its length are unfortunately not available. Other matters concerning the Course during this period were more of historic interest than importance. In 1904, the flagpole was moved from its original site in front of the Clubhouse to the 'hill South of the last putting green'; the sheep were a continual source of annoyance to the extent that women were frequently employed to pick up their droppings; consideration was given to the purchase of a motor roller and cutter in 1905 but the matter was dropped on financial grounds, it still being cheaper to keep two horses from April till October; a punt measuring 6 feet by 3 feet 6 inches and costing £3.15/–, was placed on the pond for the recovery of balls and poled by a boy on competition days; a stable was erected in 1905 for the horse at a cost of £18.15/–.

As far as golf was concerned, there was much activity as can be evidenced by the growth in the number of visitors, 1903–04 – 1450-; 1904–05 – 2700; 1905–06 – 3300; 1906–07 – 3441, and the plethora of non-course owning clubs who were given the 'courtesy of the green'. These latter included such clubs as George Watson's College, Stewart's College FP, Philosophical Institution, Morningside Parish Church, Heriot, Edinburgh United Free Presbytery, Edinburgh Institution FP, West End Merchants, High School FP, Scottish Artists, Lodge of Journeymen Masons, Distillers Co. Ltd. etc. In 1905, the courtesy of the Course was extended to the Fellows and Guests of the Royal College of Surgeons during their Centenary Week in July.

Well known visitors continued to testify to the popularity and reputation of Mortonhall. Fred Billington and Oscar Asche (1871–1936) who both frequently appeared in Edinburgh with the D'Oyly Carte Opera Company under Sir Herbert Beerbohm Tree and who resided during their stay in the Braid Hills Hotel, were given regular temporary Membership. Oscar Asche is probably best remembered as the author of the lyrics for the musical 'Chu Chin Chow'. One of the members of George Watson's College Boys Golf Club who were given the 'courtesy of the green' in July 1906 was T. A. Torrance who was, in later life, to achieve much distinction as an international golfer at Walker Cup level, appearing in the team on five separate occasions between 1924 and 1934.

Reverting to golf within the Club itself, the highlight of 1902 was the return 100-a-side match with the Edinburgh Burgess Golfing Society. The match took place on 4th July – 50 matches being contested at Barnton and a like number at Mortonhall – and once again Mortonhall ran out the winners by an aggregate of 58 holes. The result of the match was announced in the evening at Messrs Ferguson & Forresters, Princes Street, Edinburgh, where the Secretary of Mortonhall had 'provided sufficient talent for a Smoker'. There seems little doubt that the match was an unqualified success and it is accordingly strange that the Burgess Club was unable to muster a side in 1903, thus ending what might have become a colourful tradition. The loss of this fixture was, however, compensated when, in March 1905, the Murrayfield Golf Club proposed that an Inter Club Competition be held annually among the following Edinburgh Clubs: Edinburgh Burgess Golfing Society, Bruntsfield Links Golfing Society, the Insurance & Banking Golf Club (now Duddingston), Baberton, Lothianburn, Turnhouse, Mortonhall and Murrayfield, each acting in rotation as host and play to be by two foursome teams from each club. The first tournament took place in April at Murrayfield where the Insurance and Banking Golf Club, who defeated Mortonhall in the second round, were the ultimate winners. Mortonhall was represented by W. B. Taylor, W. C. Sturrock, W. H. Hamilton and D. G. MacKenzie.

As far as the Club competitions were concerned, some remarkable scores were achieved in the period. In winning the Walker Silver Club in 1904, D. G. Mackenzie set up an amateur record of 69, while in 1906, W. B. Taylor, in the course of a tie in the Coronation Medal, went round in 67 apart from one putt of 'about a foot on the 8th green where his opponent knocked away his ball'. Not to be outdone, W. C. Sturrock claimed later that year to have gone round in 65 while playing in a private match. Two further manifestations of the increasing popularity of the game and its competitive edge were the introduction in 1905 of time sheets and sweepstakes.

Despite the precise rules and regulations which had been drawn up, the caddie situation at Mortonhall from 1902 to 1907 could only be described as volatile. While in 1902, the Captain was given the privilege of a caddie on medal competition days and a Caddie Master appointed, caddies were in such short supply by 1905 that two boys were engaged at 6/– per week plus tram or train fares to Morningside and a mid-day meal supplied by the Clubmistress who received 1/– per day from the Club for this chore. Early in 1906, the position became more critical when the entire caddie staff consisted of one boy. Whether as part of a publicity drive or for more altruistic considerations, the Club organised a competition for caddies in July 1905 in which a field of eleven participated.

The tapestry of the whole period was enlivened and enriched by incidents both memorable and trivial and by the beginnings of customs and traditions. There were the abortive plans for the celebration of the coronation of Edward VII leading to the purchase of the Coronation Shield (see Appendix H) and the Turnbull incident when, in July 1903, eleven year old Master Turnbull – the son of a Member – was found by Sir Henry Trotter's Factor in a field of oats, searching for balls. The possible recipient of this 'ball' harvest – Mr Turnbull, senior – explained that his son had entered the field without his knowledge or authority during his absence at Gullane. It was a time when the Club Coat and Cap gave way to a silver badge, designed by Messrs Wilson & Sharp, Jewellers and Silversmiths. Happily, in 1902, arrangements were made for photographs to be taken of the past Captains of the Club with the result that to this day Mortonhall has a complete record of all who have enjoyed this distinction. These years saw the appointment of Honorary Members and Trustees and the creation of two types of Membership. In 1902, the Club agreed that the distinction of Honorary Membership could be bestowed on any one in recognition of his being a distinguished golfer, or for services rendered to the Club or to the game of golf. The provisions regarding Trustees were amended in 1903 when four Trustees were appointed by the Club to hold on its behoof, its whole property heritable and moveable, and to remain in office until death, resignation or removal by the Club. The First Trustees were G. L. Crole, Duncan MacLaren, J. Stuart Gowans and D. T. Addis. Their names and those of their successors in office are to be found in Appendix D. In 1905, the Membership was increased to 500 with power being given to Council to appoint within this total 'Morning Players' up to a maximum of 200. Such players were defined as those who would not start to play on Saturdays after 1 p.m. or on other days after 5 p.m. No doubt these players could be regarded as the first 'Five Day Members'.

A proposal in 1905 that 'the wives, daughters and sisters of Members and the sons of Members under 18 years of age' be admitted, under payment of a special subscription, to certain playing rights was abandoned on receipt of a petition from 35 Members. There were several interesting new admissions to the Membership. W. C. White and W. B. Torrance, both of whom were to bring honour and distinction to the Club as golfers, were admitted in 1903 and 1905 respectively while in 1906, W. Willis Mackenzie, perhaps Mortonhall's greatest golfer, enjoyed temporary Membership for the month of August. Lieut. Shackleton R.N., the Antarctic explorer, was admitted a Member in 1904 under the rule for 'Officers serving in H.M Forces'. Some prospective Members were not – initially at least – so successful. Following a black–balling incident in 1906, the efficiency of the ballot box was challenged and, after the device was 'repeatedly tested' in the presence of Council, it was found to be defective and the victims of its recent machinations were, as a consequence, duly elected Members of the Club. Also joining Mortonhall in 1907, was Adam Tait who, in 1934, donated a prize fund to the Club for annual competition (see Appendix H). Adam Tait became Cashier and General Manager of the Royal Bank of Scotland, retiring in 1917. The methodical Tait resided at

22 Braid Avenue, where each day, he would work for an hour in his garden before breakfast, walk the three miles to the Royal Bank in St Andrew Square and then back again in the evening. He died in 1939, aged 90.

In April 1905, Sir Henry Trotter graciously accepted the Captaincy of Mortonhall and it is manifestly evident that the distinction was not given in return for the many favours and courtesies which Sir Henry had shown but rather as a mark of his very genuine concern and regard for the Club which now played golf on his estate. Sir Henry, the 11th holder of the Mortonhall Estate (see Appendix A), resided, at the time of Captaincy, with his wife and family at Mortonhall House and it was, therefore, a matter of very real regret when, only some three months later on 16th July 1905, he died at the age of 61. The following tribute was paid by Sheriff G. L. Crole at a Special Meeting convened on 17th July 1905:

> This meeting has been convened on short notice in consequence of the death of Major General Sir Henry Trotter of Mortonhall, G.C.V.O., the Captain of the Club, who from the formation of the Club thirteen years ago has, as our landlord, shown a deep interest in its welfare and has greatly contributed to its success; and who has since his unanimous election as Captain by the club in April last presided over the Council's Meetings with much acceptance and assisted in the management of the Club's affairs; Sir Henry has been held in the highest esteem by all the Members of the Club and those Members especially who have come into personal contact with him will know the geniality of his disposition and the many benefits which he has bestowed upon the Club. I move that this Council record their sense of the great loss the Club has sustained by the death of Sir Henry and resolve to convey to Lady Trotter and Sir Henry's family their sincere and heartfelt sympathy.

The flag was flown at half mast and both the Course and Clubhouse closed on the day of the funeral.

One direct link with the period was established in 1976 with the late Sir Alexander Brebner who became a Member in 1903 and whose Membership of more than 75 years has never been surpassed. Sir Alexander clearly recalled playing golf at Mortonhall with his father in 1897, the fairways being cut by hand scythe and the Members playing in red jackets and blue velvet caps. He was a spectator at the exhibition match in 1901 with Vardon, Taylor, Braid and Herd, and

The Clubhouse from the East

The Khyber Pass

was, for some reason, drafted in as a participant in the 100-a-side matches against the Edinburgh Burgess Golf Club. He had a high opinion of Duncan MacLaren as a golfer and of Michael Brown as an artist.

At the end of this era, both Clubhouse and Course had been rendered into a state which, essentially, was to remain unchanged for 60 years and 70 years respectively. Mortonhall was now made, and one of the most momentous periods in its history concluded. It is accordingly fitting that further accolades be bestowed on the following 'Mortonhall Men':

Sir Henry Trotter

Sheriff G. L. Crole

Michael Brown

66

4

MORTONHALL – AT PEACE
AND WAR
1908–1918

> In peace, there's nothing so becomes a man
> As modest stillness and humility
> But when the blast of war blows in his ears . . .
>
> (Shakespeare)

Peace

The period between 1908 and 1914 marked, for Mortonhall, years of peace and plenty. The birth pangs of the Club had long since passed and the Members had begun to enjoy to the full the timeless pleasures and delights of the Meadowhead Hill Grazing and the other lands which they had leased.

While there were no structural changes to the course, the sheep remained a perennial problem and there were many references to the 'dirty state of the greens'. In 1908, the let for sheep grazing was withheld but as the grass grew too long, Council had to think again. The tenant was asked to restrict his flock to 250, but this meant that the horse drawn mowers had to be increased to three. The following season, Councillor Laing kindly presented the Club with a horse on condition that when it became unable to work, it would be shot not sold! But the Greens staff were not capable of such ruthless measures and within three months they returned Councillor Laing's horse as 'unsuitable'. In January 1908, the Greenkeeper, William Cunningham died after a reign of 8 years to be succeeded by William White of Burntisland who, in 1913, emigrated to Canada to make way for the 'second man', Alexander Thomson. 'Thomson', as he was always known, started at Mortonhall in 1913 and died in the Club's service in 1957. Between those years, he had threatened resignation many times when at odds with the Council and Greens Convener of the day. He was a legend in his time, commemorated in verse and anecdote, tireless in his devotion to the Club and fierce in his affection for 'his' Course which he oft declared 'naebody wid make a bluidy fool o''. More will be heard of this remarkable character.

Little change took place also in the Clubhouse and apart from an alteration in 1910 in the water supply from the 'Swanston' pipe to that from the Talla reservoir, the main concern was the installation of electricity. In 1911, an estimate of £128 from Messrs Blackie & Sons for 'installing electric light' was accepted and in reporting its decision, Council submitted that:

1. 'by getting rid of the oil lamps, it will be possible to dispense with the page boy' and
2. 'there will also be a saving in the annual expenditure on painting and cleaning'

The page boy was accordingly dismissed and the oil lamps sold. The remaining incidents in and around the Clubhouse were no more than a flickering tableau of the times – Council agreed to give Jemima, the kitchenmaid, a month's 'holiday' so that she could undergo an operation for housemaid's knee; the provision of tooth picks was remitted to the Secretary 'with powers'; a 'small' barrel of beer was purchased on request and the hut at the Clubhouse was converted into a hen-house. In 1912, the Clubmistress, Mrs A. Millar resigned on emigration to Australia and was given a brooch to the 'value of about £6 bearing the Club's crest and a suitable inscription'. From a large number of applicants Miss Barbara Campbell was selected as Mrs Millar's successor.

But what of the early exploits on the Course that was to serve Mortonhall for over 70 years? In 1907, when bogey was fixed at 78, age proved to be of no great handicap to John Johnston who, in his 74th year and in partnership with Peter Taylor, won the Summer Foursomes (Colonel Stewart's Medal). Other golfing achievements were both many and varied – Drummond, the Club's Professional, qualified for the final of the *News of the World* Tournament at Sunningdale and was given £5 from the Club 'towards his expenses'. In 1908 Oscar Asche – the operatic singer – holed out in one stroke at the 18th hole from the tee 'at the top of the steps' and so made the shortest walk recorded at Mortonhall to the inevitable celebrations. Strangely, the only other hole in one recorded during the period occurred at the 12th hole (Plantation) when Miss E. Kyle of Fife Ladies struck the 'perfect' shot but, the bar being an exclusively male preserve, the consequential rejoicings may have been delayed to a point when the actual achievement had faded from the memory. William ('Willie') C. White of the classic swing, so admired for its simplicity and repetition, shattered the bogey of the new Course in 1909 with a score of 71 to be followed three years later with an even better 70; and then D. P. Watt, who had succeeded Drummond as the Club's Professional in 1910, won the Scottish Professional Championship at North Berwick in 1914. This was somewhat of a unique achievement as Watt was a left-hander. As far as Club Matches went, Mortonhall held their unbeaten record until 1910, when they were defeated by the Bruntsfield Links Golfing Society at Bruntsfield by 11 matches to 10. For four years this was regarded as a minor blemish in the team's proud record until, in June 1914, the same Golfing Society again achieved the 'impossible' by winning by twelve matches to nine at Mortonhall. Success, however, came to the Club in 1914, when its team won the Inter-Club Tournament at Duddingston. Mortonhall was represented by J. D. Lownie, D. M. More, W. C. White and A. I. MacLaren (son of Duncan MacLaren). The first Council Match against Murrayfield took place in 1913 on a home and away basis and it was reported with satisfaction that this 'minor' team managed to square the match.

In the wider context of the game, Mortonhall tended to take an independent, almost stuffy line. In 1909, the Club was asked for its opinion on the management of the Amateur Championship but Council agreed 'not to take any notice'. In the same year, however, Council agreed to adopt the Rules of Golf as approved by the Royal and Ancient Golf Club but subject, of course, to the existing local Bye-Laws of 'this Club'. Again, in 1910, the attention of the Club was drawn to an edict of the Royal and Ancient Golf Club that 'mallet shaped clubs did not form proper implements for playing the game'. After consideration, it was decided that 'no action need be taken'. Nonetheless, the Club showed considerable respect for the most famous of all golf professionals – Tom Morris. On the day of the great man's funeral on 27th May 1908, the flag was flown at half mast as a mark of respect, while two months later a donation of three guineas was remitted to his Memorial Fund.

The caddy facilities at the Club continued to be provided by youths aged between ten and fifteen and one of these, James Henderson, recalled that caddies were always in great demand at the beginning of each season. This was due to the rust which had formed on the 'masters'' 69 clubs during the winter and it was one of the caddy's chores to remove it by emery paper, which he was expected to provide. As the season progressed and the clubs began to gleam, the demand for caddies diminished. The caddy fee at the time was 1/1d, of which the odd penny was payable to the Professional in his capacity as Caddymaster. Mr Henderson enjoyed two distinctions – first, Lady Edith Trotter, whose regular caddy he was, allowed him to cross the Mortonhall Estate on his way to the Club from his home at Straiton: second, he was the winner of one of the annual Caddy Competitions in which his clubs were carried by Major Ramsay and for which he received a prize of 7/6d plus a ball and a meal.

A study of the Membership is of interest not so much for those who joined as for an apparent softening in the attitude towards lady golfers. But was this change of heart entirely free of ulterior motive? In 1909, for the first time in the Club's history, there were vacancies in the Membership, probably due to the recent opening of such clubs as Craiglockhart (The Merchants), Kingsknowe and Cammo (later to move to Dalmahoy) and to the lowering of the Entry Fee at Baberton. Other clubs without a waiting list were Burgess, Bruntsfield and Duddingston. As Mortonhall expenditure was generally increasing in response to the Membership's demands for higher standards and better facilities – and with an increase of £79 due for rent in 1912 – the admission of lady members appeared an attractive option to Council. Accordingly, with the approval of the AGM in 1909, the matter was considered in some depth but mindful of the rebuff in 1905 when the attempt to introduce the wives and daughters of Members had been abandoned, Council doubted whether lady members would join in sufficient numbers to generate the necessary revenue, particularly in view of the 'capital expenditure' required for the necessary accommodation. In its 1910 Report, Council made a submission which, on the face of it, seems remarkable for its concept of 'capital expenditure' –

> With regard to the admission of ladies, the Council are of the opinion that there need be no serious objection if the number be limited to 50, and reasonable conditions be made to safeguard the interests of the Members. It is considered that with very slight alterations – viz the removal of the glass screen separating the Committee Room from the passage, so throwing the passage into that room, and closing up the door communicating with the lavatory – the cost of which would not exceed £10 – sufficient accommodation could be provided for such ladies.

In fairness, however, £10 would represent approximately £526 in 1992 terms. After discussion, it was agreed that Council's recommendation on the matter be 'delayed'. The question was raised again in 1912 on the motion of an individual Member only to be firmly rejected on a show of hands. In 1913, however, Council found themselves in a dilemma when Colonel Trotter's tenants at Mortonhall House – Mr and Mrs Findlay – were both admitted as Temporary Members on the grounds that 'Mrs Findlay stood in an exceptional position being the wife of Colonel Trotter's tenant'. It would seem that some embarrassment continued to linger as, in 1914, it was agreed to allow Morningside United Free Church Ladies Golf Club to hold a competition over the Course free of charge.

Among the the new Members joining the Club in 1911, was W. Willis Mackenzie who, in the 1920s, was to gain great distinction by winning two Scottish Amateur Championships and by representing Great Britain in the first two Walker Cup Matches against the USA. The transgression of Members in crossing the boundary walls in search of balls continued unabated as did the imposition of fines by Council. While some sympathy might otherwise have been shown to the Member who admitted crossing in search of his snuff box which had fallen from his pocket while leaning over the wall, this quickly evaporated when it was learned that he appeared in the Clubhouse in a state of intoxication and had borrowed £1 from the Clubmistress to boot. It is however significant that following the death of D. F. Mackenzie, Factor on the Mortonhall Estate, in July 1910, the incidents regarding the boundary walls abruptly ceased.

The news of the death of Edward VII on 7th May 1910 prompted the Captain to order the flag at the Clubhouse to be lowered to half-mast till after the funeral on the 20th, except for the day of the 9th when George V was proclaimed King. On the day of the funeral, both Clubhouse and Course were closed. The subsequent coronation of George V was sedately and simply acknowledged by raising the flag, in sharp contrast to the 'fireworks' which surrounded that of his father. (See Appendix H – Coronation Shield)

The month of June 1912 saw a happy reunion of the original Members of the Club reported in the Press in the following terms:

> To celebrate the twentieth anniversary of the Mortonhall Golf
> Club's existence, and to do honour to Mr Duncan MacLaren,
> the Club's first Captain, a dinner was held in the Clubhouse
> last night, attended by 50 original Members. Sir Thomas S.
> Clouston, MD, LLD, Captain of the Club, presided, and was
> surported by Councillor Inman, Dr Ronaldson, and Mr Henry
> Brown, ex-Captain Mr C. J. Munro, and Mr J. Ogilvie Kemp

KC. After the loyal toasts had been honoured, the Chairman proposed 'the Guest'. It was now twenty years, he said, since the Mortonhall Club had been instituted, and as they all knew they were there to do honour to the man who had had more to do with its institution than any other person. (Applause) Mr MacLaren well deserved the honour they had given him that evening. There was a Club called the Morningside Golf Club, which existed previous to 1892, and of that Club Mr Duncan MacLaren was President. It had no long existence, and no eventful history. Play was conducted over the Braids. It occurred to a man living at that time that this was not quite a satisfactory state of matters. Accordingly negotiations were entered into with the proprietor of Mortonhall entirely on the initiative of two gentlemen Mr Duncan MacLaren and Mr Johnston. The conception of starting a new Club was, he thought, a great one, and deserved a great deal of credit. They must remember that Edinburgh was not then surrounded by scores of golf clubs, and the local public depended entirely on Bruntsfield Links, the Braids, and Musselburgh. Sir Thomas Clouston then outlined the negotiations which preceded the forming of the Club, and remarked that in regard to the history of the Club it had been from the very beginning a most extraordinary success. Not only this, it had been a stimulus to a great number of other clubs. They were undoubtedly the premier private club and the origin of it was his friend Mr MacLaren. Captains of the Club had been Lord Stormonth Darling, Dr Haultain, Professor Lodge, Dr Ronaldson, and many others.

In the following year, the twenty first since the inception of the Club, it was proposed that Colonel A. R. Trotter might see his way to accepting the Captaincy but unfortunately his military duties did not allow him to take up the appointment.

As has been previously stated, there was an incipient financial crisis which, in 1909, had been of sufficient gravity to contemplate the admission of lady members. The following synopsis of the Balance Sheet at 28th February 1909 shows the Club to have been solvent but, with vacancies on the waiting list, a surplus for the year of only £53 and a rent increase in the offing, Council was prudent to view the position with some alarm:

Fixed Assets

Clubhouse and Furnishings		£4851
Course – capital expenditure not written off		291
		£5142

Current Assets

Stock etc.	£ 58	
Cash in Bank	88	
	146	
Less Creditors	99	47
		£5189
Less Loan over Clubhouse		1064
Net Assets		4125

represented by

Members Surplus

At beginning of year	£4072	
Add: surplus for year	53	£4125

In a detailed report, the Finance Committee suggested three courses of action for increasing the annual revenue of the Club – these were:

1. increasing the annual subscription
2. admitting Lady Members
3. charging Visitors introduced by Members

While the fate of the 'Ladies' is known, Council took the view that an increase in subscription costs could well be self-defeating as a large proportion of the Membership played little or no golf. Accordingly the third option was preferred and Council resolved that, from 1st June 1910, the estimated 3,200 visitors, annually introduced by Members without payment, would require to obtain a ticket at a cost of one shilling.

The main interest, however, in the Finance Committee Report is not the conclusion to which the club was ultimately led but rather the information relative to other Clubs in the Edinburgh area at the time:

	Subscription	Rent & Rates	Course	Clubhouse	Management
Mortonhall	£2.2/–	£284	£565	£409	£178
Burgess	£2.2/–	875	583	844	214
Bruntsfield	£2.12/6d	965	503	441	175
Duddingston	£1.6/–	587	459	309	127
Baberton	£1.15/–	268	363	292	159
Murrayfield	£2.2/–	566	565	120	156

War

Events at Sarajevo in June 1914 and the subsequent embarkation of the 'contemptible little army' for France appeared to have had little effect on the tranquillity of life and golf at Mortonhall in the glorious summer of that year. Indeed, it was not until 15th October 1914 that the Minutes of the Club made any reference to the fact that the nation was at war. The Autumn Meeting for the year was cancelled 'on account of the War with Germany now raging'.

Events now began to move with some rapidity – the courtesy of the Course and Clubhouse was extended to all Officers in the Regular and Territorial Armies; donations of £100 were made to the Prince of Wales Relief Fund (£50), the Red Cross (£25) and the Belgian Relief Fund (£25); a list of Members serving 'King and Country' was posted in the Clubhouse and their subscriptions reduced to nil; a member of the Greens Staff (Russell), the Professional (Watt) and his assistant (Inglis) joined the 'Colours'; in November 1914, Colonel Algernon Richard Trotter DSO, the 12th of Mortonhall and Colonel of the 2nd Life Guards, was severely wounded; Michael Brown designed a Christmas Card (the original of which now hangs in the Dining Room) and this was sent to each Member of the Club on active service along with 100 cigarettes – Mortonhall was at War!

Over the next year, the few minuted Meetings of Council seemed almost to reflect the sad and sinister silence which had fallen over Country, Course and Clubhouse alike. There were no competitions – the Club trophies, except for some reason, the Coronation Shield and the Duncan MacLaren Cup, were deposited with Messrs Hamilton and Inches for the duration of the war – although two matches took place in July and August between a Club team and Officers of the Argyll and Sutherland Highlanders who were at that time encamped at Mortonhall. A small yet significant alteration did, however, take place on the Course when the wall in front of the present 6th green was removed and two bunkers put in its place. The base of the wall is still evident to this day and presents a challenge to any player essaying a running rather than a pitch shot to the green. Inflation manifested itself in an increase in the price of a cup of tea in the smoke room to 3d while a cup accompanied with bread and butter rose to 4d. In anticipation of proposals by the Government to increase duties on wine, beer and spirits, Council proceeded to lay in a stock of whisky.

Among the Membership, the first war casualties occurred when Captain Reginald Baird Trotter, an Honorary Member, was killed in action in May 1915, to be followed in September by 2nd Lieut. F. Kinloch Anderson of the Black Watch. There was, too, a touching moment when, in October 1915, a postcard was received from Philip Traynor, who had been a Page Boy in the Club in 1904, stating that he was now a prisoner of war in Germany and enquiring whether the Club might send him – as it did – a food parcel.

The year of the Somme, 1916, with its record of 57,000 British, dead and wounded in one day, dawned bleakly over a desolate Mortonhall. The Clubhouse – the scene of so much fellowship and jollity in past years – had now assumed a sepulchral mien and, like the Course, was simply and quietly tended for the return of those at war. So few Members visited the Club that the Clubmistress was given a bonus of £20 to compensate for the 'great falling off in catering'. New Lighting Regulations, issued by the Scottish Secretary of State, obliged the Club to 'obscure' all the windows at the Clubhouse and, as the war wore on, the shortage of coal forced Council to announce draconian measures:

1. on Mondays to Fridays inclusive (except Public Holidays), no fires are to be lit in the Dining Room and
2. no fires are to be lit in the Committee Room.

While both Club and Council accepted without demur all the restrictions of wartime, they certainly did not appear to regard the problems associated with the wine and spirit trade with equal equanimity. In April, the price of whisky was raised to 7d a glass and, two months later, Council was alarmed by a decree of the Liquor Control Board that all spirits were to be reduced to 'at least 25° under proof strength'.

The Greens Staff was reduced to a 'Head Man' and two men but, in the summer, the redoubtable Thomson was called up for military service. His brother, Joseph, took his place at a wage of £1.10/– per week while his wife was paid a weekly allowance at the pleasure of Council. Similar arrangements were made for the dependents of other Club servants – 10/– a week being paid to the wife of Watt, the Professional, while the mother of Russell, one of the Greens Men, received 5/–. Sadly Russell was reported missing in November and Watt was to die of wounds in April 1917. The services of Joseph Thomson did not appear to be highly valued as strenuous efforts were made to obtain alternative employment for him as a ploughman. Joseph was, however, unwilling to oblige, and proceeded to exploit his position by making frequent demands for wage increases. Although these were as frequently refused, Joseph did manage to boost his earnings to £2.5/– a week before the return of his soldier brother.

While Officers in the Armed forces had been granted the courtesy of the Course from the outset of the War, a similar privilege was extended to all ranks in 1916. In addition, private soldiers were allowed – after a debate, it has to be admitted – to enter the Clubhouse. Furthermore, it was a regular practice for wounded soldiers to be entertained in the Clubhouse and to be taken for picnic teas on the Course.

The desolation of 1916 yielded to an ever-deepening gloom in 1917 and there was much comment in the national press as to whether golf courses should be utilised for the production of food. This issue was taken up by Council and the suggestion that cattle might be grazed as well as sheep drew an unfavourable response from the grazing tenant. In the summer, the District Agricultural Committee of Midlothian made enquiries as to the possibility of sowing corn in the '13 acre field' leased in 1903, but after investigation, the matter was dropped. Nonetheless a small portion of ground near the present 6th green was cultivated to provide vegetables for the Clubhouse. This plot was tended carefully and faithfully long after the war by Thomson and became known as 'Thomson's Garden'. Remnants of this garden, in which rhubarb was an outstanding success, were still evident in the 1970's.

While mention has been made of the two matches which took place in 1915 with the Argyll and Sutherland Highlanders, none was played in 1916 although, in 1917, two more were engaged in with the same regiment, now stationed at Dreghorn Castle. Also in 1917 the Club played against Officers stationed at Craiglockhart War Hospital including Captain Siegfried Sassoon of the Royal Welch Fusiliers. Sassoon's Mortonhall connection reflects much credit on the Club for the peace and recreation it provided for those suffering from shell-shock and other scars of war. To appreciate the Sassoon saga, a foray into his background is necessary. Sassoon was born in 1886 of the extremely wealthy banking family of that name and, as a young man of means, indulged in writing poetry and in pursuing sporting instincts, mainly hunting and golf. He enlisted at the outbreak of war and, by 1917, had earned himself the sobriquet of 'Mad Jack' and the Military Cross. However, in April 1917, badly wounded in the chest and disturbed by the influence of the pacifist, Bertrand Russell, he threw his M.C. into the Mersey and, with the same courage, he had displayed at Mametz Wood and the Somme, made public in July 1917 a statement which he had sent to his Commanding Officer, protesting 'against the political errors and insincerities for which the fighting men are being sacrificed'. In normal circumstances, Sassoon would have been court-martialled but for the intervention of his friend and fellow poet, Lieut. Robert Graves, also of the Royal Welch Fusiliers, who managed to persuade a Medical Board that Sassoon was suffering from shell-shock. As a consequence, Graves, who had been so seriously wounded at the Somme that his 'obituary' had appeared in *The Times*, was detailed to escort Sassoon to the Craiglockhart War Hospital in

Edinburgh where many similar casualties were treated by the distinguished neurologist and psychologist Dr W. H. R. Rivers. In the event, Graves missed the train and Sassoon arrived alone in Edinburgh to be followed by an embarrassed Graves on the next express. Sassoon spent the last six months of 1917 at Craiglockhart during which he golfed regularly at Mortonhall and paid the following tribute in his book *Sherston's Progress*:

> I must admit, though, that I wasn't worrying much about the war when I'd just hit a perfect tee shot up the charming vista which was the fairway to the first green at Mortonhall. How easy it felt! I scarcely seemed to be gripping the club at all. Afternoon sunshine was slanting through the golden brown beeches and at last I knew what it was like to hit the ball properly.

Such was his affection for Mortonhall that it is tempting to conjecture whether the following little-known lines might have been inspired by his view from the ridge at the then 17th hole:

> Then will you look upon your time to be
> Like someone staring over a foreign town
> Who hears Church bells, knows himself set free
> And to the twinkling lights goes gladly down

This verse was written in 1917/1918 and it could perhaps be that the memory of the Braid Hills, the city stretched out beneath and the 'twinkling lights' of the Clubhouse were its stimulation.

Unknown to Sassoon at the time of his arrival at Craiglockhart, there was already in residence Lieut. Wilfred Owen of the Manchester Regiment, also suffering from the malady attributed to Sassoon. But for a common love of poetry, the two were hardly alike. Wilfred Owen was born in 1893 of a modest middle class background and prior to the outbreak of war was strenuously seeking to make his living as a tutor and teacher. He was small in stature, compared with the tall, elegant and stately Sassoon, and regarded himself very much as his social inferior. Nonetheless, after some hesitation, he made Sassoon's acquaintance and, with some diffidence, submitted some of his poems to the already established master. It is much to Sassoon's credit that he recognised his eager pupil's genius and it was he, more than any other who encouraged Owen to become possibly the greatest of the First World War Poets. At Craiglockhart, Owen completed his masterpiece *Anthem to Doomed Youth* and, in this, he received advice, criticism and many suggestions from

Sassoon. In fact, it was Sassoon who substituted the word 'doomed' for 'dead' in the original title. In a letter to his mother, Owen wrote 'met Robert Graves for Sassoon, whom nothing could keep from his morning's golf and took him over to the Course when he arrived'. Thus, Mortonhall had the distinction, in October 1917, of lunching three of the greatest First World War Poets. Sadly, Owen was killed in the last week of the War, having won, like his mentor, the Military Cross. Sassoon's long life ended in 1967 but in 1984, Robert Graves, the author of *Goodbye to All That*, *I Claudius* and many more books and poems, was still living in his 89th year on the island of Majorca. An attempt was made to obtain his autograph on a picture of the Mortonhall Clubhouse as it was when the 'historic' meeting took place in 1917 but unfortunately, as his wife explained, this was not possible:

Canellun Deya Mallorca Spain   September 19th 1984

Dear Mr. Colledge –

Thank you for your interesting letter about the meeting of three poets at your golf club.

Alas, my husband is not able to autograph the card you sent. He has been unwell for some years now, loss of memory among other things, and is unable even to write his own name.

Do you mind if I keep the p.c. of your clubhouse? – I could put it in the book of Wilfred Owen's letters where he mentions the golf course. But if you want it back let me know.

Your sincerely,

Beryl Graves

The year 1918 provided a still dismal prospect on the Western Front and a Special Committee was formed at the Club to consider schemes for raising money for the Red Cross. A concert was considered to be inappropriate, while a golf competition was not thought likely to attract support. Members were accordingly asked for subscriptions – minimum 2/6d – and, by September, £115.8/6d was raised which, allowing for inflation, is equivalent of £2,748 in 1992 terms. A match with beneficial consequences for Mortonhall took place against Officers in the Commander-in-Chief's Office at Rosyth. Shortly afterwards, a letter was received from the Officers of the Grand Fleet stating that it was their wish to present some memento to the Club as a mark of appreciation for the kindness in placing the Course at their disposal during the war. There was a thought that the memento would be a trophy for annual competition, but such was the sense of patriotism within the Club that a signed photograph of Admiral Beattie was preferred. As will, however, be noted from Appendix H, the presentation eventually became a silver cup, known thereafter as the Grand Fleet Cup.

Within the Clubhouse, a whisky crisis developed. In June, a special meeting of the House Committee was convened 'in consequence of a threatened shortage of whisky, the Treasurer having reported that he would only be able to get about 200 gallons to last for the period between June and September'. There was a division of opinion as to whether it would be better to ration the whole Membership of the Club or merely the Temporary Members. This led to the hardly ingenious compromise to instruct the Treasurer 'to endeavour to obtain an additional supply'. Compared with the stalemate existing on the war front, the Treasurer achieved spectacular success within a few weeks in that:

1. the regular supplier, Messrs Cockburn, agreed to supply 20 gallons beyond the normal quota
2. Messrs Crawford would supply 6 gallons and
3. a mysterious Mr Carson, who appeared to have cornered the market, had 30 gallons available.

Immediate authority was given to purchase 'as much whisky as can be got at a price not exceeding £2.7/6d a gallon'. Within a few further weeks, the Treasurer reported that 72 gallons had been safely gathered in. The price of whisky was raised to 1/– a glass except, in the case of Mr Carson's consignment which, having been bottled before the war, was to be sold at 1/8d a glass. The prices of other 'refreshments' available to the diminished Membership were:

Brandy 1/8d a glass	Gin 1/5d a glass	Port 8d a glass
Sherry 8d a glass	All Liqueurs 1/– a glass	Rum 1/– a glass

To the simple question – 'what did Mortonhall do in the War?' the answer was that Members who were fit and of military age went to fight on the battlefields of Europe and the Middle East – strangely only one went to sea – while the aged and decimated remainder struggled to maintain Course and Clubhouse for those of their fellows who were fortunate to return. For the former, the hazards and privations were great; but the contributions of the latter were by no means selfish and insular.

But the war did end on 11th November 1918 and, in Edinburgh, 'there were great rejoicings'. On the news of the armistice, the flag was flown at Mortonhall for a week but events otherwise were quiet as 'few members visited the Clubhouse'. Slowly, Mortonhall's heroes returned from the field — the Roll of Honour showed that 122 had served their King and Country, that 16 had received decorations for distinguished conduct but that for:

Lieut. Colonel E. H. Trotter D.S.O.   Capt. I. Ogilvie Kemp
Major R. B. Trotter   Capt. I. W. Lawson
Lieut. F. Kinloch Anderson   Capt. The Hon Charles H. Lyell MP
Lieut. I. M. Paterson Brown   Capt. J. Martin M.C.
Major G. H. Melville Dunlop   Pte. Ralph Russell (Greens Staff)
Lieut. C. Jamieson   L/Cpl D. P. Watt (Professional)

— there was only 'a drawing down of blinds'. In December 1920, the Captain unveiled a Memorial to them in the Clubhouse.

This chapter ends in 1919 — the war is over and the competitions are to begin again. The Club has at long last recognised that, in 1917, one of its Members, Professor Charles Glover Barkla of Edinburgh University had been awarded the Nobel Prize in Physics. Sixty years later, his portrait was honoured on a Swedish postage stamp.

But Thomson, the Head Greenkeeper, has not returned from France though the Secretary has elicited the information that 'he could not be demobilized at present as he had been 'selected to bring home the guns' — no doubt an acceptable interpretation of what Thomson had probably said — 'Canna come hame — ah hae tae bring back thir bluidy guns!''. The Clubmistress — Miss Campbell — is leaving to get married and Mrs Jessie Taylor is to be appointed in her place. There is another deficit this year — £88 — but the Clubhouse remains wind and water tight, the Course rough but intact and yes — there is still £45 in the Bank. And finally, to whom should be ascribed the title of a 'Mortonhall Man' in this period of sunshine and shadow? Certainly, those 122 who forsook the 'Khyber' for foreign fields — but beyond these, there were few who would merit the title more than certain of the Captains of the period:

George Lorimer   Rev. Professor Malcom Taylor
Professor Sir Richard Lodge   William Greenhill
Henry Brown   Charles F. Scott
Councillor William Inman

for it was they who steered the Club with equal skill
through calm and turbulent waters.

John Ball at Mortonhall (1895)

J. H. TAYLOR
(Ex-Champion)

ALEC HERD

JAMES BRAID
(Champion)

HARRY VARDON
(Ex-Champion)

5

THE CROSSING OF THE RUBICON
1919–1939

> The Die is cast
>
> (Julius Caesar)

On the Near Bank

Slowly the Country and Mortonhall slipped into the post-war era – a quiet and soft prelude, bearing no hint, for the former, of the crazy Charleston period which was to follow or, for the latter, of the momentous decision which was to be taken in regard to the Club's security of tenure.

Strangely, the first act in regard to the Course was the purchase of a new punt for the pond at a cost of £7 and, in 1919, nothing more noteworthy than the return of Thomson who resumed his duties as Head Greenkeeper at £3 per week. In 1923 a row of trees was planted at the 18th green 'for the purpose of sheltering the Course from the view of residents in the houses now built on the opposite side of the road'. As events will show, the rejection in 1923 of the suggestion that a new short 4th hole (in effect, the present 3rd hole) be created, had connotations for the 1979 development. But surely in the Clubhouse, there would be a frenzy of activity – to repair the neglect of the war years and to restore the haven that all had known before. On the contrary, no structural alterations, refurbishments, nor redecorations were undertaken. The shadow, hanging over Clubhouse and Course alike, was that the lease had but 10 years to run.

Mrs Taylor, the Clubmistress appointed at the end of the war, moved serenely along and had her salary increased to £230 per annum in 1920 in order that she could provide four maids. But life was not without its vocational hazards as when, in 1922, she sustained 'a severe cut on her right forearm through the bursting of a ginger beer bottle'. The doctor's bill of two guineas was met by the Club's insurers. Council, nonetheless, showed a proper concern for its servants, in arranging for them all to be vaccinated in 1920 'in view of the prevalence of smallpox' and in sending a maid, who had been seriously ill, on a paid holiday. Beyond matters of health, Council was also committed to labour-saving gadgetry – a vacuum cleaner was purchased in 1921 and an electric cooker in 1924. Against this, Council rejected, in 1921, the introduction of coin boxes for the telephone on learning that this would raise the cost of each call from three farthings to 1d. There was little movement in food prices and the following tariff, fixed in 1919, remained unchanged:

Soup 6d; Cold Meats 1/4d; Hot Meats 1/6d;
Vegetables 2d; Sweets 6d; Bread & Cheese 4d;
Cup of Tea or Coffee – (small) 3d (large) 4d

The same, however, could not be said of the whisky – 1/5d a glass in 1919, 1/6d in 1920, 1/5d again in May 1921 rising to 1/8d in December 1921 when a supply of a greater strength was acquired, and back to 1/7d in 1925.

But if there was little of note occurring either on the Course or in the Clubhouse, there was certainly plenty of activity in the game itself – for this was the era which saw the birth of a uniform handicapping system (1921), the 'standard' 1.62 ball (1921) and the Walker Cup (1922). Mortonhall's response to each of these three major events was mixed. At the end of 1920, a bogey score of 76 was fixed for all handicaps. However, in March 1921, a proposal was received from the Championship Committee of the Royal and Ancient Golf Club in the terms set out as shown opposite.

This matter was seriously considered by Council and Robert Maxwell, a Member of the Royal and Ancient Championship Committee and winner of the Amateur Championship in 1903 and 1909, was invited to assist in determining the scratch score. Mr Maxwell visited the Club in August 1921 and proposed a scratch score of 75 which was subsequently confirmed by the Championship Committee. As far as the 'standard' ball was concerned, the Club adopted a slightly contemptuous attitude – Council expressing the opinion that 'in the meantime, Members should be allowed to play with any ball' – and it is not recorded when the Club eventually assented to the recommendation from the Royal and Ancient. Mortonhall's view on the Walker Cup was something of a volte-face. When subscriptions were sought by the Royal and Ancient in March 1922 'towards the expenses of sending a team of

TELEGRAMS—"ANCIENT."

TELEPHONE—
NOS. 12 AND 13.

CODE—BENTLEY'S.

SECRETARY—
HENRY GULLEN.

THE ROYAL AND ANCIENT GOLF CLUB
OF ST ANDREWS. FIFE.

MARCH, 1921.

To the Hon. Secretary.

Dear Sir,

The Championship Committee of the Royal and Ancient Golf Club has decided that all handicaps in the United Kingdom should be put on a uniform basis, and that in order to arrive at such uniformity—

1. All sympathetic handicapping should be discontinued.

2. A scratch score for all Courses should be fixed by the Championship Committee.

3. The handicaps of all players should be arrived at from this scratch score.

The Committee has further decided to obtain views from the various Clubs and Unions as to whether a National Handicap should also be adopted.

The various Sectional Committees of the Championship Committee were asked to meet delegates from the Clubs and Unions in their district, and lay the above proposals before them. In the case of the Scottish Section the matter is being dealt with through the Scottish Golf Union. It is felt, however, that some Clubs may not be able to be represented at any Meetings which may be held, and I am therefore writing you direct as it is particularly desired that every Club should have an opportunity of expressing its opinion.

The Championship Committee fully realises that no general system of handicapping is possible without the approval and cordial co-operation of individual Clubs. They believe, however, that Golf Clubs generally would welcome an attempt to improve the present confused and unsatisfactory state of matters.

As regards the first proposal. By sympathetic handicapping is meant, the custom of leaving a player at his old handicap although his play has ceased to justify it, rather than hurt his feelings. This, though a natural thing to do, makes any reliable system impossible.

As regards the second and third proposals. The Championship Committee think (1) That the scratch score of a Course is the only sound basis of handicapping, (2) That this scratch score should be founded on the par score of the Course, (3) That in order to obtain uniformity the par and scratch scores should be fixed in each case by a member or representative of the Championship Committee. Any such representative would, of course, rely to a considerable extent on the advice of local players, and I hope that your Club would be willing to co-operate with the Championship Committee in this matter.

As to the question of a National Handicap, it may at first sight seem unnecessary to have two handicaps. The difficulty of a single handicap is that a player who plays much on one course is apt to win competitions, so that his Club handicap must always of necessity be reduced, but his general form away from that Course might not justify from a National point of view his having so low a handicap.

The Scottish Section of the Championship Committee is composed of Mr. W. Norman Boase, C.B.E., Mr. J. L. C. Jenkins, Mr. W. A. Harvey, Mr. Robert Maxwell, Mr. F. M. Richardson, and Mr. J. Gordon Simpson.

I am,

Yours faithfully,

HENRY GULLEN,

83

golfers to the United States of America', the request was refused but, four months later, 'altered circumstances, the selection of one of the Members of the Club, W. Willis Mackenzie' induced Council to change its mind and send a contribution of £21.

There can be little doubt that most of the golfing achievements of the period belonged to Willis Mackenzie. In the Walker Cup, he won his singles match in 1922 against M. Marston by 6 and 5, but fell victim to G. V. Rotan in 1923 when, after being 6 up after 14 holes, he lost 12 of the next 18 holes. As an indication of the general standard, he was playing at number three in the team after the redoubtable Cyril Tolley and Roger Wetherhead. One of Willis's team-mates in the 1922 Walker Cup was W. B. Torrance who became a Member of Mortonhall in 1926 and illustrious as his golfing career was at District and National level, he never succeeded in winning the Championship at Mortonhall. Willis had also been in the victorious Mortonhall teams in the *Evening Times* (1919) and Lothian Team (1921, 1922 and 1923) Tournaments, and had won the individual title in the latter in 1922 and 1923. Along with D. M. More, C. S. Nimmo and W. C. White, he had also won the Edinburgh Inter Club Tournament in 1919 but ultimately crowned these successes by winning the Scottish Amateur Championship in 1924 and by being runner-up in 1925.

Prominent among other players during this time was W. C. White whose record score of 70 in 1912 was equalled in 1922 by J. McCredie, only to be lowered in 1925 to 69 by Willis Mackenzie. While Willie White continued to win many scratch events at Mortonhall, a new name, Archie Carr-Brown, emerged to dent the monopoly enjoyed by Messrs Mackenzie and White. One of the highlights of Carr-Brown's colourful career occurred in the Scottish Amateur Championship when he armed himself with a folding stool, parasol and book to counter the notoriously slow play of Erl Watson of Sandyhills, Glasgow!

Walter Hagen (Open Champion 1922, 1924 and 1928) and Gene Sarazen (Open Champion 1932) were to have played an exhibition match in 1923. Their terms – £15 each – were agreed after some debate but a suitable date could not be found. A pity, as it would have been a pleasure to see the great attacking, overcoming or being defeated by the Course's main features. How might they have fared along the ridge in a stiff south westerly?

The period was not devoid of incident outwith the Course. In 1920, following complaints about cars in the Braid Road, a new gate was formed to allow car parking in the Club's grounds. In the same year, the Lord Provost of Edinburgh asked Council to organise a tournament to raise money for the Royal Infirmary, to which the Club responded by sending a cheque for £21. The Lord Provost, no doubt emboldened by success, then suggested in 1922 a tournament for the Unemployed Relief Fund but on this occasion the Club took 'no action'. Following an unsuccessful effort in 1923 to have the tramway extended beyond the Braids terminus in the 'Penicuik' Road, Council began negotiations to gain access to this road via a field, then lying to the West of the Clubhouse, but it was not until 1928 that the matter was finally concluded. In 1925, a minor furore arose over stones being projected on to the then 2nd hole from blasting operations in the quarry lying to the South of the Course. Despite assurances from the tenants of the quarry that 'great care was being taken' and appeals to the Inspector of Explosives, the bombardment rumbled on till 1927.

Golf, now fast becoming a popular sport, suffered in the eyes of many by its restriction to six days a week and, in early 1926, there was a whisper about Sunday golf. But an important agreement was in the process of being concluded with Colonel Trotter and the murmurs discreetly died away. The 30th Anniversary of the institution of the Club occurred on 29th April 1922 and 30 of the 55 remaining original Members celebrated this event with a competition, followed by a dinner. Two years later, at another dinner, a suggestion that ladies might be 'permitted to be present did not meet with support'. On the financial side, there were, in the Spring of 1920, mutterings that the subscription would have to be increased, and while nothing was done at the AGM of that year, a Special General Meeting in January 1921, increased it from 2 to 3 guineas and raised the Entrance Money from 10 to 15 guineas. At the same time the Membership was increased by 50 to 550 but despite this, there was in a short time a waiting list once more at Mortonhall.

As far as the Club's officials were concerned, Andrew Ker who had been Treasurer since the inception of the Club, retired in 1924 to give way to F. W. Campbell, while in 1919, Alex. Drummond of St. Andrews was appointed clubmaker at the princely wage of £1 per week. Drummond became, like Thomson, part of the folklore in Mortonhall. It was claimed that he rarely ventured from his shop in the Clubhouse and, though regarded as a good teacher, instructed his pupils from the doorway with his hands sunk deep in his pockets. It was averred that he did not know that there was pond at the then 3rd hole!

The period was marked and saddened by the death of the greatest of all the 'Mortonhall Men', Duncan MacLaren, and it is appropriate to leave the following memorial to him on the near bank of the Rubicon:

DUNCAN MacLAREN, S.S.C.
1853 : 1924
'The Father of Mortonhall'

Duncan MacLaren was born in 1853 near Dunkeld of farming stock and   85 on leaving school, he became a law apprentice in Perth. Thereafter, he worked in the Town Clerk's Office before entering into partnership with Duncan Smith, S.S.C. in 1881 under the name of Messrs Duncan Smith and MacLaren at 62 Frederick Street, Edinburgh. He was essentially a family man, living with his wife, two sons and six daughters at Glenquaich Lodge, Cluny Gardens and, in his later years, at Strowan Lodge, Albert Terrace. It is as evident from the recollections of those who knew him, as it is from his portrait, that he was a man of vision and resolution which, allied to a natural energy, enabled him to achieve much in life. Sadly, his two sons died comparatively young men, although one of them, Alasdair, won the Gold Medal at Mortonhall in 1913. His daughters held him in great regard and esteem and inherited something of his strength and determination – two becoming doctors, one a lawyer and another the Head of a Physical Training College. As a sportsman, Duncan MacLaren's great love was golf and he was no mean performer, winning in 1886 the Gold Medal of the Bruntsfield Links Golfing Society at Musselburgh, in 1888, the Chambers Cup of the Tantallon Club at North Berwick with a remarkable score of 78 and, at Mortonhall, the Gold Medal in 1893 and 1901 as well as the Trotter Cup in 1893 and 1894. In 1896, he partnered Lieut. F. G. Tait when the latter achieved his record score of 72 over Mortonhall. But it is for his contribution to golf on the South side of Edinburgh that his name will be remembered. At his instigation the Morningside Golf Club was created in 1891. He was its first Captain and almost entirely due to his initiative the Club acquired the lease 'of the portion of the Braid Hills belonging to Colonel Trotter and now commonly known as Mortonhall for the purpose of playing the game of golf thereon'. Thus did the Morningside Club under its new name of Mortonhall become the first private course-owning club in Edinburgh in 1892. Duncan MacLaren was the first and, at the age of 38, the youngest ever Captain of Mortonhall Golf Club in 1892. He remained in office till 1895 but his contribution did not end there. He remained a Member of Council, acting for a year as its interim Secretary and then as its Law Agent, and, through the Club's formative years, his was the hand on the tiller. He duly became a Trustee before receiving the greatest accolade the Club could bestow – Honorary Membership.

In 1912, Council proposed that 'Duncan MacLaren's services to the Club should be recognised in some suitable manner' and invited subscriptions of 5/– per Member 'to purchase a piece of silver plate or other suitable article for presentation'. When approached, he declined to accept the presentation and informed the Council that 'it would be pleasing' to him if the gift took the form of a gold medal with the inscription 'Mortonhall Golf Club: Championship Medal'. He was approached again and again but apart from suggesting that a trophy take the place of the medal, steadfastly refused all recognition.

> You all did see that on the Lupercal, I thrice
> presented him a kingly crown
> Which he did thrice refuse

On his death at Kilconquhar on 28th November 1924 the Club formally acknowledged Duncan MacLaren as 'the Father of Mortonhall'.

The Crossing and the Far Bank

The Rubicon was crossed in 1926. Scant mention of the negotiations leading up to the great event is, however, to be found in the Minute Books of the Club prior to that date. Fortunately, certain memoranda and notes exist from which it is evident that 'far back through creeks and inlets making' much activity had been taking place since 1921 or earlier. Hence, the reluctance of the Club to embark on any major work on Course or Clubhouse in the immediate post–war period.

Many Members were aware that the lease was due to expire in 1933, but yet it is doubtful if any one individual took the initiative in the purchase of the Course. Nonetheless, there is an indication that, prior to 1921, the Captain for the years 1920/21, James Greig, had raised the issue with Colonel Trotter's Agents. Reference to this approach is contained in a fascinating report to the succeeding Captain, Alexander Mackenzie, by the Secretary, John Anderson, in August 1922. This report is as prophetic as it is important and is reproduced in full in Appendix N. Particular attention is drawn to the following matters:

1. the importance of access to the Course via the Avenue (i.e. the West Drive to Mortonhall House) and by the farm roads (Page 222)
2. the reference to what had become the 'coveted land' South of the 11th hole and the implied criticism of previous Councils (Page 222)
3. the reason for the ground East of the then 4th hole not being leased to the Club and confirmation of the popular belief that the Pheasant or Trotter Wood was planted to hide golfers on the 'Meadowhead Hill Grazing' from the view of the mansionhouse (Page 222)
4. the elimination of the then 12th hole as, at the time, the green was sited on one of the tees for the present 11th hole (Page 224)
5. the importance of the Avenue and the proposal to purchase as omens of events 50 years later (Pages 225 and 225)
6. the possibility that the City of Edinburgh might be a contender for the Course on the expiry of the lease (Page 226)

7. the cost of renting or feuing an acre among Edinburgh Clubs (Page 228) and
8. the Membership statistics of the Edinburgh Clubs and the fact that Mortonhall was the smallest (Page 229)

The first formal step on the part of Council occurred in October 1923 when a Committee consisting of Colonel Stewart and Messrs James Greig, Alexander Mackenzie, George Morris and James Davidson was set up but, apart from a desultory reference to the matter at the AGM in April 1924, the curtain was again drawn till July 1925. However, during the period of 'official' silence, certain documentation is available from which a long series of proposals and counter proposals can be traced and identified.

In September 1924, Colonel Trotter appeared to show his hand for the first time in response to the 'Anderson' plan of 1922 in the following terms:

1. he was willing to grant an extended lease or to feu the present Course for £450 in the first year, for £550 in the next and thereafter at £650 on the basis that one half thereof was redeemed
2. he was not willing either to feu or grant a lease of the Avenue
3. he would consider feuing the whole of Meadowhead Farm (80 acres) at £15 per acre
4. he would insist that any buildings on the ground feued be taken over at a valuation and
5. he would wish to retain his shooting rights over the Course.

General comment on these counter-proposals was contained in a Memorandum by the Secretary in February 1925 and this indicated that Council was willing to feu the Course as it then existed, but was nonetheless concerned at some of the conditions imposed by Colonel Trotter. In particular, these were:

1. the need to maintain the plantations to the satisfaction of Colonel Trotter
2. the requirement for all mutual fences to be maintained at the expense of Mortonhall Golf Club
3. the removal of the rights of access via the Avenue or by the road at Meadowhead
4. the necessity of having to redeem one half of the feu–duty and
5. the retention, by Colonel Trotter, of his shooting rights.

The prospect, however, of having to acquire the buildings on the land, i.e. the cottages at Meadowhead, was not regarded as 'material'. The offer by Colonel Trotter to feu the whole of Meadowhead Farm at £15 per acre was not acceptable as Council could not see its way to pay more than £10 per acre, particularly as the ground was to include the four acres occupied by Pheasant Wood. In addition, the Club was also expected to pay substantial compensation to the tenant of Meadowhead Farm. Between September 1924 and February 1925, the Colonel had apparently a change of heart regarding the access through part of the Avenue but Council considered the feu of £20 per annum per acre plus the value of the timber prohibitive.

In summary, the cost of Colonel Trotter's entire proposals, namely the present Course, the whole of Meadowhead Farm and part of the Avenue, would amount to a feu of £1300 per annum plus a capital outlay for the Meadowhead cottages and compensation to the tenant farmer. Council considered this offer outwith the Club's means and three courses of action were, as a consequence, contemplated:

1. that Colonel Trotter be asked to reconsider his terms
2. that, failing such modification, the Club should consider a smaller scheme and
3. that negotiations for a feu be dropped and an attempt be made to enter into a new lease.

At a Council Meeting in July 1925, it was decided to modify the hopes of the Club on the grounds of finance and to opt for 'a smaller scheme' which essentially comprised a feu of the present Course on the basis that half thereof would be redeemed and certain rights in the Avenue retained. By 31st December 1925, following further unrecorded negotiations, the terms of the arrangement between Colonel Trotter and Council were virtually complete although it is apparent that a hard battle had been fought by the latter to establish its right of access through the Avenue and to protect its interest therein for all time coming. The attention of Council now turned to finance.

The total capital cost of the venture was calculated at £6,687.10/–, which in 1992 terms, was approximately £186,000. Against this, the Club was able to find £1,687.10/– from its reserves, leaving a sum of £5,000 to be raised. Various alternative means of generating this finance were considered and it was ultimately decided to offer debentures to the value of £5,000 to the Members on the basis of interest at 5% and repayable by annual drawings of £200. In addition, the subscription was to be raised from three guineas to £4. A Special General Meeting of the Club was convened on 16th February 1926 and the position admirably set out in the document contained in Appendix O. The proposals by Council were unanimously approved although a lone voice moved that the subscription be raised to £3.13/6d and not £4. Fortune favoured the brave for, at a Meeting of Council in September 1926, the Secretary was able to report that the Debentures had been subscribed in full. While the Club rather grudged the £560 it had to pay for the two cottages at Meadowhead, there was at least some consolation in that the option to feu part of the Avenue was replaced by a servitude in favour of the Club. 89

The final act in the whole saga took place on 27th January 1927 when the formal documents were signed by the Trustees.

Among those entitled to the distinction of being called a 'Mortonhall Man' in this important passage in the history of the Club, the Secretary, John Anderson, comes first but it would be fair to add those who staunchly supported him – James Greig, Alexander Mackenzie and George Morris.

Mortonhall now had a Course to call its own and all the pent-up plans of the post-war years came tumbling out. But these were not to be implemented by whim or fancy. James Braid (five times Open Champion and a previous visitor to the Course with Vardon, Taylor and Herd in 1901) was invited to look over the Course and this he did on 25th October 1926 in a day of 'snow, sleet and rain'. While the original report is not extant, a copy of the great man's opinion is fully recorded in the Minute Book and apart from a number of cosmetic adjustments the following proposals are worth recording:

1. the recommendation that a new 4th hole (the present 3rd) be created is intriguing particularly as a similar proposal was rejected by Council in 1923

2. the siting of the green at the 6th hole (the present 5th) in the plantation behind or alternatively its re-shaping into a two level form was to have reverberations 50 years later

3. the strong recommendation that the 7th green (the present 6th) should be sited on top of the knoll to the north is one which even today has much appeal and

4. the placing of the green at the 12th hole (the present 10th) *in* the plantation beyond seems to confound those who believe in light, air and sunshine for a good putting surface.

The Report concludes with a glowing tribute to the 'great beauty of the Course', 'its many natural features so seldom found in inland greens' and 'the quality and condition of the putting greens which would be hard to beat even on a seaside Course'. In general terms, the response of Council was timid and disappointing and seemed – perhaps understandably – to be dominated by financial restraint. A number of Braid's minor recommendations were carried out but there was to be no change in the green siting at the 6th (the present 5th) and the imaginative position for the green at the 7th (the present 6th) was ruled out on grounds of cost. Council agreed that, for an experimental period, the short 4th (the present 3rd) recommended by Braid, should be tried to the exclusion of the 'Perdition' (the 9th) hole whose tee had been moved to the winter tee of the present 8th hole, thereby making it a 'blind' 9th. By April 1927, Council was, however, reporting to the Club that they were 'of the opinion that the old 9th hole should be retained and while they approved the position of the experimental short hole, they were not meantime prepared to suggest an alteration in the Course to make way for it'. But thirty years later, Braid's proposal came into its own. Braid's report caused the Club to look more closely at the Course and, in 1927, most of the internal walls and fences were removed. The putting green to the North of Clubhouse was also formed during this period although the 12th (the present 10th) green was left *short* of the Plantation.

After this burst of enthusiasm, Thomson and his staff were generally left in peace to mow the grass and maintain the quality of the greens. The early thirties were punctuated by a series of trivial and yet interesting occurrences – in 1933, the Course was formally measured and found to be 5480 yards (by 1976, this had been stretched here and there to 5756 yards); in 1934, the boat was removed from the pond to discourage children who were wont to play there; also in 1934, a novel method of indicating the pin positions at semi-blind holes was introduced in that three tassels were attached to the pin if it was at the back of the green, a central position attracted two tassels while only one was displayed if the pin was at the front; in 1935, an offer and suggestion by Mr John Dougal had an uncanny echo forty years or so later when he proposed to gift the Club £100 to purchase the high ground in the wood near the 3rd tee (the present 2nd) and to construct a tee thereon, but Council did not consider this an improvement; in 1936, the three cottages by the 11th tee (the present 9th) were found to be unfit for human habitation but it was not until 1940 that all became vacant and were demolished.

By 1935, with steel shafts in popular use and the ball being propelled greater distances, it was inevitable that the thoughts of Council should turn to ways of lengthening the Course which was then a mere 5500 yards. A Special Committee appointed for the task produced a number of ideas which were both imaginative and breathtaking but totally impracticable. Swathes would have had to be cut through the Pheasant Wood and more land would require to have been purchased from Colonel Trotter.

Council ultimately resolved to make due enquiry and, somewhat perhaps to their surprise, were informed that Colonel Trotter was prepared to consider feuing the field to the South of the 11th hole (the present 9th) (the 'coveted land') and also that to the East of the 5th hole (the present 4th) at the rate of £20 per acre. Concurrent with this enquiry approaches were made to a number of Golf Architects and the following quotations were received for examining the sites offered:

Mr H. S. Colt – £21 plus expenses
Mr A. Mackenzie Ross – £10.50 plus expenses
Messrs Simpson & Co – £25 inclusive of expenses

After consideration, Mackenzie Ross was asked to undertake the commission. Unfortunately little is known of the plans submitted by Mr Ross except that he submitted two schemes and, of these, Scheme 2 was rejected almost out of hand by the Greens Committee. While Scheme 1 – whatever it was – found certain favour, it was shortly rejected on the grounds that the cost of adding 380 yards to the length of the Course at £1,450, exclusive of the price of the land and the development fee payable to Mr Mackenzie Ross, could not be justified.

After many delays, a compromise plan which, it was thought, would find favour with both Council and Club was submitted by the Greens Committee to Mackenzie Ross in February 1937. This was acceptable to the Architect and was accordingly incorporated in the Report to the AGM in May 1937. The 'scheme' was as follows:

> A new 5th hole of about 215 yards would be made played from the present 5th tee to a green situated near the South-West corner of the ground to the South of the present 5th fairway. This would be followed by a new 6th hole of about 165 yards, played to the present 5th green as reconstructed. The 7th tee would be placed slightly to the East of the present 6th tee and about 15 yards farther back. The second part of the Scheme would consist in the cutting out of the present 9th hole, and the playing of the 10th hole from the present 9th tee. (See Plan on Page 60)

At the Meeting, the adoption of the 'scheme' was moved by Willis Mackenzie but a counter-motion that no action be taken was 'carried by a large majority'. In the twenty years between the wars, when the Course was purchased and the advice of two eminent Golf Architects sought, it is remarkable that so little was done either to improve the Course or lengthen it.

In the matter, however, of Course maintenance, there were some significant changes. The days of the horse-drawn cutters came to an end in the Spring of 1927 when a Fordson tractor and five Shanks Cutters were purchased at a cost of £410. In 1933 there was a brief flirtation with water when consideration was given to the purchase of a water cart for the use of the Greenkeeper, but little seems to have come of this. In 1937, the question of laying on water from the 18th to the 2nd green (the present 1st) was seriously contemplated. While this ambition was restricted to the installation of a hydrant at the Clubhouse for the practice putting green and the 18th green, larger and more expansive ideas emerged concerning the remainder of the greens. Investigations soon revealed that the prospects of a gravity fed system were *nil* and that

92

pumping arrangements were necessary. Undaunted, the Greens Committee proceeded to acquire for £57 a Swinburne petrol pump and engine together with a suction Hose (£2), an extra outlet for the Pump (10/–), a large sprinkler (£5) and 120 ft of hose to enable the 7th green (the present 16th) to be watered from the pond. Fired by this purchase, the Committee then considered it would be more advantageous and economical to erect a 4000 gallon tank near the 7th tee from which pipes would be run to the pond and the distant greens. This would be preferable, the Committee asserted, to watering entirely by hose. But these heroes were before their time and alas! no more was heard of their scheme.

As with the course, schemes and plans to improve the Clubhouse were also not in short supply and it was after careful consideration and much debate that Council submitted proposals to the AGM of 1928 for 'bringing up to date the lavatory accommodation and introducing a foot bath; an extension of the dressing-rooms and boxroom; and building on the plot of ground now occupied as a shrubbery, a room in which Members may receive or entertain lady guests' at a total cost of £1300. To the chagrin of Council, these proposals were defeated by a large majority. After a period of eight years, Council once again took up consideration of alterations to the Clubhouse but, on this occasion, it was on a somewhat different tack – the bedroom and other accommodation of the maids. The remit was entrusted to a Member architect, Forbes Maclennan, and was soon extended to include the rooms of the Clubmistress and the provision of a new shop for the Professional. Mr Maclennan's plans, which represented the most major alteration to the Clubhouse since 1903, were duly submitted to and approved by the AGM of 1937. While the cost was estimated at £1,100, the contract was ultimately concluded in a sum of £1,700 but this included an extension to the Laundry, the construction of a Beer Cellar and certain other improvements.

While the immediate post war era was dominated on the Golf Course by W. Willis Mackenzie, the period to 1939, following the purchase of the Course, saw the continued excellence of his play as well as that of W. B. Torrance and W. C. White. Messrs A. M. Carr-Brown, J. A. Clark, J.M. McCredie and J. Gillespie constituted the next rank of class players though they never attained the eminence of the triumvirate. In terms of individual scores, it was again W. Willis Mackenzie who set the standard in 1926 with a record 68 but this target fell to J. A. Clark who in 1930 lowered it to 66. In recognition of this feat, the Club presented Mr Clark with a silver cigarette box. By 1933, it had become obvious that the bogey of 76 was being beaten so often by so many strokes that the Standard Scratch Score was amended to 71. The year

1933 saw also the introduction of the monthly medal competitions and incidentally a worthy use for the Grand Fleet Cup which had been untouched since its presentation in 1919.

Outside the Club there were a number of notable achievements by Mortonhall Members. In 1927, the individual award in the Lothians Team Tournament was won by W. B. Torrance (albeit that he was not representing the Club on that occasion) with the runner-up, the almost ubiquitous W. Willis Mackenzie. Then, in 1928, Willis once more showed that he was the best amateur in Scotland by winning its National Championship at Muirfield. This achievement was marked by a Club Dinner in the North British Hotel in January 1929 when the toast was given by David Dougal, Captain of the Club. In 1929, Mortonhall represented by W. Willis Mackenzie, W. C. White, J. McCredie and Dr J. L. Cowan defeated Murrayfield in the final of the Inter Club Tournament at Murrayfield. In 1930, the *Evening Times* Tournament was played at Lanark and won by Mortonhall, represented by W. Willis Mackenzie and J. McCredie.

Probably one of the most important decisions made by the Club in regard to golf on the Course related to Sunday play. The possibility had been murmured prior to the acquisition of the Course in 1926 but, for fear of prejudicing the negotiations, the matter was hushed up. The question was inevitably raised again in 1929 and, after considerable procrastination, – or was it reluctance on the part of Council? – the issue was ultimately referred to the AGM in 1932 on the basis that Council was not prepared to express an opinion. While the Meeting resolved that both Course and Clubhouse be opened for play and the use of Members on Sundays, Council was still reluctant to frame the necessary changes to the Bye-Laws. The tentative letter, shown opposite, was issued to the Members in May 1932. Ultimately, the changes to the Rules and Bye-Laws were finally and conclusively approved at the AGM in 1933.

Of wider and more national interest, one of the qualifying rounds for the *News of the World* professional tournament was played over Mortonhall in 1936. In 1938, Miss Gloria D. Minoprio who had caused a minor sensation in 1934 when she appeared at the Ladies Championship *in trousers* and played with one club, offered to play in an exhibition match with the Club Professional, the proceeds of the gate money to be given to charity. Council considered that such a match would not be a success and Miss Minoprio's offer was courteously declined. It is tempting to speculate that the reason for the decision lay with Drummond, the Club's professional, whose activities apparently never took him further than the door of his shop! In March 1939, there was another offer of an exhibition match – this time between A. H. Padgham (Open Champion 1936) and Bobby Locke (later to be Open

53 MELVILLE STREET,
EDINBURGH, 24*th May* 1932.

DEAR SIR,

MORTONHALL GOLF CLUB.

At the Annual General Meeting of the Club on 30th April a Motion (of which due notice was given) was passed to the effect that the Course and Clubhouse should be open for play and use of Members on Sundays.

In accordance with the remit to them, the Council have given careful consideration to the changes in the Rules and Bye-laws necessitated by the Motion. The Council consider it desirable that they should have some experience as to the extent to which Sunday Golf will be taken advantage of before finally deciding upon such changes, and meantime they have temporarily altered the Rules and Bye-laws for Sundays as follows :—

1. The Course and Clubhouse to be open from 9 a.m. till 6 p.m. from 1st November till the end of February, and during the remainder of the year from 9 a.m. till 8 p.m.

2. Subject to the Bye-laws regulating the hours during which the Clubhouse shall be open, the permitted hours for the sale and supply of excisable liquors shall be 12.30 p.m. till 2.30 p.m. from 1st November till the end of February, and during the remainder of the year from 12.30 p.m. till 2.30 p.m. and from 6 p.m. till 8 p.m.

3. The subscription payable by Temporary Members shall be 5s. a day.

4. Members may introduce visitors to play golf, as provided for in the existing Bye-laws, on payment of 2s. 6d. for each visitor. The free tickets issued to Members will not be available on Sundays.

5. Caddies may not be employed on Sundays, nor shall there be any booking of places for starting to play.

Except in so far as above stated, the present Rules and Bye-laws shall apply.

The Council have decided that these arrangements shall come into force on 5th June, being the first Sunday of that month.

Yours faithfully,

J. ANDERSON,
Secretary.

Champion 1949, 1950, 1952 and 1957) – but Council decided to take 'no action in the matter'.

Significant events among the Membership of the Club in the decade prior to the Second World War included the deaths of a number of men who had, in their time, played a prominent part in the affairs of Mortonhall – in 1929, W. B. Taylor, the Irish Open Amateur Champion and Captain in 1925–27; in 1930, W. C. Sturrock, the first Secretary of the Club; in 1936, James Greig, the ex-Captain who had played a prominent part in the acquisition of the Course. In 1932, twenty-five of the Original Members of the Club remained and, on 29th April 1932, fifteen of these celebrated the 40th anniversary with a lunch in the Clubhouse. On the following day the AGM was held and no doubt as a tribute to these stalwarts of 1892, it was agreed that all Members, over 70 years of age and having been Members for over twenty-five years, should have the privilege of remaining Social Members for a subscription of one guinea per annum. In 1935, the Membership was not complete and Council sought to encourage admissions by stating publicly that entry to Membership would be immediate. In 1939, the position had apparently deteriorated to the extent that Council appealed to Members to make 'a special effort to secure new Members'. This did not augur well for the Club as within months, the Membership was further depleted by those who joined HM Forces at the outbreak of hostilities with Germany. The shortage of Members had its inevitable repercussions on the finances of the Club and in the year to 28th February 1939 there was an excess of expenditure over income of £171 and an overdraft of £1303. But then, a 'Mortonhall Man' who was anonymous, presented the Secretary with a £100 Bank Note to be applied against the deficit. In 1932, the Secretary, John Anderson, who had served the Club faithfully and well for 28 years and who had played such a distinguished part in the negotiations leading to the acquisition of the Course, resigned not only as Secretary but also as a Member of the Club. While the appropriate expressions of goodwill and appreciation were made it does seem remarkable that the services of this outstanding servant of the Club were not marked in a more distinctive way. The duties of Secretary and Treasurer were now conjoined and the current Treasurer, F. W. Campbell assumed the post.

Other events were somewhat insignificant in comparison – in 1928, permission was given to the Scots Greys Beagles to follow hares over the Course; on 11th October 1930, the flag was flown at half past as a mark of respect to the funeral that day of the victims of the R101 airship disaster; and in 1933, the trophy case was constructed at a cost of £31.10/–.

W. C. White and W. Willis Mackenzie

The Saddle

The passing scene was not without its moments of colour, curiosity and interest. In 1927, an enlarged stance for motor cars was constructed at a cost of £164.18/9d just in time as it so happened for the visit to Mortonhall by the Prince of Wales. This occasion was recorded in the Minute Book thus:

Visit from H.R.H. The Prince of Wales   14th July 1927

> This day H.R.H. The Prince of Wales visited the Course and played a round with Viscount Hampton. Colonel Trotter and Brigadier Gerald Trotter (the Prince's Equerry) accompanied him.
>
> No intimation of the visit had been given and there was none of the Council or officials present.
>
> The Clubmistress – Mrs Taylor – saw that what was requisite was done and on leaving, the Prince shook hands with her and with Mr John Miller, a Member of the Club.
>
> The Prince expressed himself as greatly pleased with the Course and with his reception.

The privilege of carrying the royal clubs fell to George Burden, then a lad of fourteen summers and the occasion remains in his memory to this day. The Course, he recalls, was deserted but the Prince was not in great form and resorted to irons from the tee. George was equally impressed by the Prince's considerable charm as by his choice of expletives between his not so successful shots.

Within a fortnight, Council enquired whether the Prince would be gracious to accept Honorary Membership of the Club and was almost immediately informed by his equerry, Brigadier General Trotter (the second son of the Club's former Captain, Sir Henry Trotter) of his acceptance.

The period which began with the end of the First World War ended with the beginning of a second and even larger conflagration. Black blinds were purchased for the Clubhouse on 8th September 1939 – 5 days after the declaration of War – and golf – and life – at Mortonhall came to a virtual end for six years.

Who will be remembered as the 'Mortonhall Men' in the 'golf between two wars' beyond those previously mentioned? Who earned the title more than Willis Mackenzie and Willie White?

H

Greenkeeper
for 28 Years,
ALEC
THOMSON.

Professional
for 20 Years,
and a
good Teacher,

ALEX
DRUMMOND

This cartoon is reproduced by kind permission of
The Illustrated London News

6

WAR, SOCIAL CHANGE AND THE NEW MORTONHALL 1940–1969

The old order changeth, yielding place to the new

(Tennyson)

The Forties

It is tempting to compare the effect of two world wars at Mortonhall In the 1914/18 conflict, the Club became moribund, while, in the later Armageddon, it remained alive and reluctant to accept the limitations of war. The reaction to the early air raids on the warships anchored in the River Forth was typical. Members became aware of the hazards of golfing in a raid and suggested that sheets of steel be placed over the shelters to make them splinter proof. This suggestion was not supported by Council. On the other hand, the risk of German planes actually landing on the Course was diminished by the erection of a number of poles.

During 1939–45, no work was carried out on the Course except for the construction in 1940 of a new tee at the 11th hole (the present 9th) which had been made possible by the demolition of the cottages previously sited there. Boundary posts were also erected to prevent players playing the hole by way of the 12th green (the present 10th). In March 1941, in common with all other golf clubs in the country, Mortonhall was approached by the Department of Agriculture for Scotland for 'a contribution to increased tillage in time for the 1941

99

harvest to secure maximum food production'. It was agreed that the field comprising part of the 4th hole and the 5th hole, except the green, be leased to the tenant of Meadowhead Farm for three years. The 4th hole was then played dog-legged to the 5th green and a new tee built for the 6th hole at the edge of Pheasant Wood near the top of the rise. Mortonhall thus became a 17 hole Course and so remained until 1949. As a result of a further visit by the Agriculture Committee in 1942, the Club was obliged to extend the grazing of the Course to dairy cows in the 'North Field' (the present 8th, 9th, 10th, and 11th holes). A lease was entered into with the tenant of Meadowhead Farm on the understanding that he erect a fence from the wood at the 13th (the present 11th) green to the boundary wall at the Braids, the Club being responsible for fencing off the greens. The additional livestock gave rise to the making of a local rule, allowing balls lying in a hoof mark in a bunker to be moved without penalty. It was not until 1949 that the rule could be repealed.

The maintenance of the Course during the war years – indeed as far as 1947 – caused problems. Petrol for the tractor was severely rationed and consideration was given to paraffin-driven vehicles and even the hire of a horse. The Greens staff was reduced to three and, in 1943, in desperation no doubt, it was suggested that Drummond, the Club's Professional, might be willing to cut the practice putting green, the 18th green and the 1st tee. The Minutes are silent as to whether Drummond accepted this proposal. After the war, austerity lasted almost as long as the hostilities. One of the first acts of the Council as far as the Course was concerned was to appoint Mackenzie Ross, Golf Course Architect, from North Berwick, to supervise the restoration of the old 4th and 5th holes (still, in fact the 4th and 5th). Hopes that the area in question would be released by the Department of Agriculture in 1946 were dashed, and it was not until 1949 that Mackenzie Ross could take up his remit. The possibility of engaging the Club's staff to undertake the work was dismissed since they were fully employed on other parts of the Course and ultimately John R. Strutt Ltd. carried out the task for £793.8/– less compensation of £300 awarded by the Department of Agriculture. Grass was sown in the summer of 1949 in the hope – which was realised – that play could commence in the spring of 1951. During the prolonged project, there was understandably agitation to 'find another hole' and so restore the Course to 18 holes. In 1947, a proposal to create a hole, similar in style and design to the present 3rd hole, was rejected and 1948 saw other futile proposals. In 1949, however, the '1947' proposal was resuscitated and a 'temporary' hole created to complete the circuit. The pond which has always been a great feature at Mortonhall, was 'excavated' in the summer of 1947 and a recommendation made by the contractor that it be dragged with chains or the weeds cut by knife. To facilitate this latter task, a small boat was necessary but, as an economy measure, the Council purchased waders for the Greens Staff! So much for the Course in war and peace.

In the Clubhouse meantime, the appropriate air raid precautions had been taken – the black blinds, the shaded lights, the stirrup pumps, the fire parties and the shelter in the cellars – and these, together with shortages of staff, food and drink, dominated the scene. The Clubmistress throughout the war years was Mrs Gray and there is little doubt that the various shortages imposed an ever increasing strain on her administration. There were difficulties in obtaining cooks not solely on account of the wage offered (£1.10/– a week in 1941) but also because of the demands of National Service, of acquiring clothing coupons for material to make maids' uniforms and of coping with the unreasonable demand of a Club Member to be served with a meal during an air raid. It was therefore not surprising that Mrs Gray resigned on health grounds in February 1945 to be replaced by Mrs Selkirk who, though then the manageress of a hotel in Dunbar, had previously served in the Clubhouse. Shortly after her appointment, Council agreed to supply a watch dog provided one could be acquired for 'a cost not exceeding £7'.

In October 1939, the food prices in the Clubhouse Dining room were reviewed and the following increases made:

2 Poached Eggs	8d to 10d	
Bacon & 1 Egg	1/4d to 1/6d	
Welsh Rarebit	6d to 8d	
Potato Chips	3d	where previously no charge
Bread	1d per slice	

Basically, these prices remained unchanged for years and although inflation may never have been a consideration, the consequences of quite severe food rationing certainly caused Council and the Clubmistress problems. Members, but, more particularly, it seemed, Non-Playing Members and their guests, were attracted to the Dining Room to supplement their domestic diet. The playing Members rebelled and Council was obliged to introduce more and more stringent arrangements to restrict the demand for the Club's meagre supplies. At first, meals for 'non regular' Members were delayed until after 8 p.m. on Saturdays and – to rub salt into the wound – were not to be served at the window tables which were now for 'regulars' only. By 1942, Members were restricted to one guest and further the same guest could not be invited more than once per month. The following year, the position deteriorated and meals were reduced to daily lunches of soup and cold meat and to suppers only on Saturdays till 8 p.m. The situation was latterly modified to lunches only on Saturday with no suppers on any day. At the end of the war, shortages and staff difficulties lingered on and it was not until 1950 that the Mortonhall catering slowly returned to something approaching its pre-war levels.

As far as drink was concerned, the first step, shortly after the outbreak of war, was to increase the price of whisky and gin from 1/4d per glass to 1/8d to counter the duty imposed by the Government. While the price rose two years later to 2/– per glass, it was the matter of supply rather than price that exercised many a Council Meeting. Throughout the war, there was apparently no problem in obtaining enough beer or gin – indeed, in 1944, it was reported 'that during the past two months supplies of gin and beer had been obtained from Messrs J. G. Thomson & Co. Ltd., Leith in supplement of the Club's usual quota' but with 'the whisky', it was different. The first rationing arrangements, introduced in January 1942, were as follows:

			Weekly Total
Monday to Friday :	at both bar sessions	– ¾ bottle	7½
Saturday	: 1st bar session	– 2 bottles	
	2nd bar session	– 4 bottles	6
Sunday	: one bar session	– 1½ bottles	1½
			15 bottles

Only small glasses were to be used and 'surpluses' from any session were to be carried forward to the next month. Three months later, the position had slightly improved and a more sophisticated plan was introduced:

			Weekly Total
Monday to Friday :	1st bar session	– ¾ bottle	
	2nd bar session	– 1¼ bottles	10
Saturday	: 1st bar session	– 2 bottles	
	2nd bar session	– 4 bottles	6
Sunday	: 1st bar session	– 1 bottle	
	: 2nd bar session	– 1 bottle	2
			18 bottles

'Surpluses' from all first sessions were to be carried over to the second sessions while all daily surpluses were reserved for Saturday's second session. But, as late as 1947, things were very serious and the weekly issue was reduced to 9 bottles per week. Only Members were to be supplied on the basis of one small whisky per day. Three years later, however, austerity relaxed its grip and Scotland's national drink flowed free once more.

As far as the fabric of the Clubhouse and its environs were concerned, little was done although, during his Captaincy, W. C. White and his brother J. L. White generously had the car park tar-macadamed at their own expense. The ivy which had adorned the Clubhouse walls for so many years was removed in 1942 and, as no licence was required from the Ministry of Works for maintenance costing less than £100, the outside woodwork, rhones and conductors were painted 'with one coat of oil paint' and that part of the wall 'where the ivy had been removed' was coated with one coat of distemper, all for £64.10/–. In December 1941, the Clubhouse was established as a 'Re-inforcement Camp' to accommodate those who might have to be brought into the city as re-inforcements for civil defence personnel. Following his retirement as Captain in 1942, W. C. White requested that he be relieved of his duties as 'Camp Commandant' and the appointment of Past Captain W. West Kerr at the age of 80 as his successor may have provided the latter with the necessary interest and stimuli to reach his century in 1962.

All competitive golf ceased at the outbreak of war although one or two competitions took place on an informal basis with the entry fees going to War Charities – the year 1940/41 yielding £41.1/6d. Competitions re-commenced in the 1946 season but the traditional inter-club matches with Bruntsfield and Murrayfield did not resume until the 1948 season. The players who dominated the scene – truncated though it was – were the evergreen W. C. White and W. Willis Mackenzie, joined by J. A. Clark and I. A. Williamson. The Course was made available – as it had been in the First World War – for Members not only of H.M. Forces but also the American Troops in Britain. In response to pleas from the Lothians Golf Association, the Course was also made available to 'workers' who had been requested by the Government 'to spend their summer holidays at home' on the following terms:

1. 1/6d a round or 2/6d a day
2. all players to have left the 1st tee by 4.30 p.m.
3. facilities only to be available from Monday to Friday and
4. no refreshment of any kind to be served in the Clubhouse.

In financial terms, the Club fared better in the Second World War than it did in the first. The annual subscription was raised in March 1940 from £4 to £4.10/– while, at the same time, those Members of the Club on active service were transferred to a special Supernumerary List for an annual subscription of 10/–. Although income was depressed, expenditure was even more curtailed with the result that the Members' Surplus of approximately £7,700 at 28th February 1939 actually increased to around £11,000 at similar date in 1946. Expenditure deferred invariably means expenditure doubled but to be fair to the wartime Councils of the Club, the opportunity to spend on   103

Clubhouse and Course during the war years did not exist because of shortages of labour and materials and government restrictions. Even with the return of its war heroes and the security of a full Membership, Council was obliged to raise the subscription to £6.6/– on 1st March 1949 and at the same time to increase the Entry Fee from £15.15/– to which it had been raised following the First World War in 1921 – to £21 to meet the following liabilities:

Excess of Expenditure over Income	£780
Repairs to Clubhouse Roof	200
Painting and Decoration of Clubhouse	650
Replacement of Tractor, Mowers & Equipment	800
Extraordinary Expenditure on Course	650
	£3,080

Eighty-three Members of the Club served King and Country and, as in the previous conflict, parcels containing books and cigarettes were sent to the five who had the misfortune to be prisoners of war. Seven Members did not return and the names of:

G. C. Langdon	E. A. Teviotdale
C. MacLennan	G W. Walker
J. W. Robertson	W. K. M. Weir
	J. H. Wilson

were added to the War Memorial at an unveiling by the Captain in January 1948. Other deaths which occurred in the decade to 1950 included those of R. D. Rainie, the Auditor for over 40 years, in 1945, Colonel Trotter in 1946 and Michael Brown, the artist, in 1947.

In 1942 – the year when the celebration of the Club's Jubilee was thwarted by war – the Club elevated the following original Members to Honorary Membership:

Robert Aitken	J. Ogilvie Grey	Robert Millar
W. S. Currie	W. West Kerr	J. M. Rusk
William Gibson	J. M. Brown	A. M. Runciman

An interesting little incident which also occurred in 1942 was the receipt of a letter by Council from a Club Member proposing the name of the next Captain! The Secretary was instructed to reply that the selection of Captains of the Club had always been – and would continue to be – the prerogative of the retiring Captain.

Those who attained the mark of 'Mortonhall Man' in this difficult and austere era were undoubtedly the following Captains:

W. Kinloch Anderson   J. M. Graham
The Hon. Lord Fleming (died in Office)   T. F. MacLennan
Dr J. R. Peddie

and their Secretary and Treasurer, F. W. Campbell.

The Fifties

While the 'Forties' witnessed some of the greatest events and awesome developments in history, they were for Mortonhall a period of stagnation and latterly one of slow recuperation. The 'Fifties', were conversely, for the nation, an era of rehabilitation, enlivened by a Coronation, the last of rationing and the abolition of the stymie (1952) but Mortonhall, on the other hand, underwent some of the most significant changes in its lifetime of 60 years.

Of the 526 Members at the beginning of the Fifties, 357 resigned or died to be replaced by 243 new admissions, leaving the Membership at an all time low of 412 against the full complement of 550 at the end of the decade: the reign of Thomson, the Greenkeeper, and the tenure of Drummond, the Professional, both came to an end, as did the grazing of sheep: there were no fewer than four changes of Secretary and coincidentally of Clubmistress: catering problems engrossed the deliberations of Council and were thought to be due to Members playing much of their golf at the coast: the social change developed and the position of Ladies became more defined and recognised: in 1952, 'sixty glorious years' were celebrated in style at a Diamond Jubilee dinner: the many incidents and innovations of the period were wittily recorded in what became known as the 'Barton Odes' but let the record set all these things in perspective.

As far as the Course was concerned, the decade was dominated by the '4th hole (the present 3rd) controversy' although both the Perdition (the 9th) and the Alps (the 16th) holes were also implicated. (See Plan on Page 60). In 1949, a temporary 4th hole had been created to make a Course of 18 holes but, with the reclamation of the ground at the original 4th and 5th holes, this hole became superfluous. Nonetheless, the Greens Committee had to bow to pressure and re-instate the 'temporary 4th' for a three week trial period in September 1951 at the expense of the original short 9th. The experiment was, however, indecisive and Council, being of several minds, put the matter before the Club at the AGM of 1952. The protagonists of the '4th' claimed it gave a better balance to the Course, separating the two longest holes i.e. the then 3rd and 4th at 442 and 563 yards respectively. This seemed rather spurious as the next short hole was the 12th (139 yards) (the present   105

10th) to be followed in quick succession by the then 14th (260 yards), 15th (211 yards) and 16th (169 yards) holes. By 42 votes to 31, the Club decided to revert to the original Course.

But the problem would not disappear and two years later, the controversy was revived on the basis that the former 16th hole and not the 9th be eliminated. Council again demurred and weakly referred the issue to the AGM of 1955. After considerable discussion, it was agreed that the '4th' be laid out on a permanent basis and, on a vote of 43 to 30, that the 16th be eliminated. While this seemed clear, the Captain, in a mood of perverse democracy, 'undertook' to reconsider the matter. Mackenzie Ross, Golf Course Architect, was consulted and favoured the elimination of the 9th. The Greens Committee were equally divided and once more the problem was referred to the AGM where, in 1956, the diehards proposed that the 4th be eliminated and the 9th and 16th retained. This was, however, defeated and the 'Mackenzie Ross camp' successfully carried by 31 votes to 25 that the 9th and not 16th be eliminated and further that a new tee for the 10th be formed on the old 9th tee (see page 60) – 'Perdition' was thus no more. Apart from a few cosmetic changes to a number of tees, little else was done to the Course in the Fifties. Nonetheless, there were some interesting innovations – markings were put on the trees to facilitate the finding of the sliced tee shot; distance posts were also erected in 1951 at various holes 200 yards from the tee but when the supplier pointed out a pricing error – the posts being 9/– each and not 9/– per dozen – the goods were returned; in 1953, an old fishing net was acquired as a practice net to the South of the 18th fairway to eliminate practising on that fairway.

Few changes there may have been on the Course but new methods of greenkeeping and financial constraints provoked controversy among the Greens staff or, more correctly, with the faithful, forthright and ageing Thomson. Thomson, whose knowledge had been bought by long experience and whose opinions were chiselled on memorials of stone, was hardworking, irascible and defiant. His character did not make him receptive to the suggestions with which he was inundated by a procession of annual Greens Conveners. Formal complaints against him had been lodged as regularly as he had offered his resignation and Captains and Secretaries, in particular, had endeavoured in vain over the years to reason with him over his pin placements and hole cutting technique. Holes were often placed on slopes and cut without the now discredited use of a board ('A tramp it a'roon' claimed Thomson) with the result that 3 and 4 putts were commonplace. Thomson's answer to this challenge never wavered – 'the b.....rs canna putt!' In 1951, there was a major confrontation over a spiking machine. The suggestion was made to Thomson by the Greens Committee that the greens would benefit from spiking and, to this end, it was proposed to purchase a suitable device. Thomson, however, held a contrary view and opined that, if spiking was necessary, it should be done by hand and that furthermore, scarifying would be more beneficial. The Greens Committee persisted and the Secretary was sent to instruct Thomson. Within days, a hurried Meeting of Council was called to be told that Thomson had refused to spike the greens and that, if spiking took place, he would resign. A delegation, consisting of the Captain, Greens Convener and Secretary, was dispatched to meet Thomson once more; fortunately their mission was successful; the spiking machine was bought; the greens spiked and Thomson remained. At the following Captain's Supper, the 'Barton' pen went to work as the following lines reveal:

> 'We're tracking a beast,' said Johnnie
> 'Whose spoor we've lately seen
> It's turning the place into a midden
> Hae ye seen the second green?

> 'You bluidy fools,' said Thomson
> Wi' merriment in his een,
> That's no the spoor o' any beast
> It's the stuff fae wir SPIKING MACHINE'

But Thomson – if out-manoeuvred on this occasion – quickly informed Council that he was having difficulty with 'his' tractor which was now 21 years old. A new Ferguson tractor was purchased for £405.

Around this time, there was controversy concerning Thomson's age – the Club's personnel records being silent on this point. Some four months later, the vital information – extracted no doubt with reluctance – became available – Thomson was 72. Council then made the not unreasonable suggestion that he might retire in 1954 when he would be in his 75th year. This proposal appears to have been ignored by Thomson as, in June 1955, he was informing Council that he was 'required to vacate his lodgings and that his efforts of find alternative accommodation had not been successful'. As a 'temporary measure', Council allowed him the use of the East facing room beneath the Dining Room. It was remarkable that, in October 1955, when Thomson was 75, Council decided, as an economy measure to cope with a falling Membership, to reduce the Greens Staff by one man who, needless to say, was not Thomson. By 1956, however, the depleted and ancient staff were finding it so difficult to keep the Greens cut that the Greens Committee decided to reduce the putting surface of all greens by one third and further, with Thomson's full agreement, to purchase a Ransome Auto Certes with 2 stroke Motor Mower for £83.

The two following verses of a poem, recited by Henry Barton at the Captain's Supper in May 1957, capture the 'Thomson Spirit' and perhaps form an appropriate epitaph for this great servant of Mortonhall:

> 'I'm here' said the Demon 'to fling in your face
> Some of the sins you've committed in this bonny place
> To bring to your mind and make you recall
> Some of your misdeeds at Mortonhall'
>
> 'Ye bluidy auld leer' said Thomson wi' pain,
> 'I've wrocht in this place as if twere my ain.
> I've even got praise, you auld b.....r-lugs
> Frae players and Captains o' visiting clubs.'

On Sunday 4th August 1957, whether by reason of overwork, the new equipment, or simply old age, Thomson was found dead in the Clubhouse – sitting bolt upright in his bedroom chair and facing east over 'his' beloved Course which he had served for a total of 47 years. After Thomson's death, Council proceeded with speed to appoint a new head Greenkeeper and made what proved to be a sound choice in Robert Bulloch, Greenkeeper at Lothianburn. One of the other applicants, Thomas Ainslie, the Professional/Greenkeeper at Inverness, was not considered on account of his age of 57. This was not, however, the last of Tom Ainslie as the record will show.

Off the Course but outside the Clubhouse, there was some concern regarding Drummond, the Club Professional. He had served the Club faithfully since 1919 but had become subject to the criticism that he was no longer capable of playing a round with the Members and that he spent all his time at his shop door or in his workroom under the Clubhouse. The possibility of appointing a younger professional arose at a Council Meeting but the matter was deferred until Drummond's age had been ascertained. As in the case of Thomson, the answer was not readily available and it was three months later before Drummond admitted to 75 summers. Council then proposed that he should retire in 1953 when he would be 76. At a Special General Meeting held in October 1952, this proposal was upheld, despite some strong opposition to defer the retiral for a further three years. Drummond was awarded a pension of £2 per week and a subscription list was opened to yield £275.5/–. Drummond died in 1960 at the age of 83. At the end of 1952, the quest for a successor to Drummond began and after fairly extensive advertising, Andrew Cafferty of the Royston Park Golf Club was appointed in March 1953. This did not prove to be a happy association and Cafferty left in July 1954.

In the light of this experience and the financial constraints of the time, it was decided not to proceed with a further appointment.

The issuing of tickets and the selling of balls was left to the Clubmaster and H. W. Morton of Morningside Road was given the franchise to repair the Members' clubs. In 1958, however, Hugh Morton was granted rent free use of the shop beneath the Clubhouse, on condition that:

1. it would be open from 1 p.m. to 7 p.m. on week days and open all day on Saturdays and Sundays
2. it would be stocked with golfing equipment
3. it would provide caddie cars for hire and
4. its occupant would act as Starter.

A similar arrangement was made for the 1959 season although a rent of £60 was payable. Against this, Hugh Morton was given the right to stamp the clubs he sold with the name of 'MORTONHALL'.

An increasingly popular feature on golf courses all over Britain in the Fifties was the caddie car. In 1950, a shed was provided for them and an annual charge of 5/– per caddie car levied. Several of the cars were purchased for the use of Members and their guests but the control of these became haphazard with the variations of Professional, Starter and Clubmaster. Inevitably the Barton wit had its individualistic contribution to make, anticipating in 1954 the construction of a power driven device. The first model came to a sad although memorable end as will be observed from Appendix I – 'The Barton & Other Odes'.

Before passing on to the Clubhouse, the experience of the Bishop of Edinburgh should not be forgotten – he was 'peppered with shot' from the Edinburgh Gun Club Range adjoining the Course!

In the Clubhouse, events were dominated by the comings and goings of Clubmistresses and Clubmasters, the inadequacy and quality of the catering and the changing nature of social events. In July 1953, Mrs Selkirk, who had been Clubmistress since 1945, intimated her resignation on the grounds of ill-health. She had been a popular and efficient servant of the Club and her resignation was accordingly received with genuine regret. Council decided that the new appointment should be a joint one, with the Clubmaster responsible for Clubhouse and Bar and his wife in charge of the catering. Some of the other conditions were:

1. that meals could be ordered up to one hour before the Clubhouse closing time, which, on a summer Saturday, could be as late as 9.30 p.m.
2. that in the event of the Clubmaster and Clubmistress having a family, a deduction of 15/– per week per member of family was to be made from their wages and
3. that two weeks holiday were to be allowed.

Ultimately, Mr and Mrs Armstrong of the Pitlochry Golf Club were engaged. Unfortunately, the arrangements made did not prove to be satisfactory and after two years, the Armstrongs relinquished their appointment. In January 1956, Council appointed Miss E. Baird, Manageress of the Northern Club, Edinburgh, as Clubmistress and within four months, the catering losses had been turned into a profit. Miss Baird was duly rewarded by a £50 increase in salary within six months of taking up her appointment. Unfortunately, the task proved to be too onerous and Miss Baird intimated her resignation in October 1957. This was received with much regret and marked by a bonus of £100.

Council then reverted to another joint appointment, and in November, offered the posts of Clubmaster and Clubmistress to Mr and Mrs White of Drumrunie Lodge Hotel, Ullapool. Sadly, this encumbancy was not successful and within two years the Club had yet again a vacancy to fill.

Within the Clubhouse, physical changes were relatively few although, in 1952, the old Committee Room (now the Secretary's Office) was converted into a Mixed Lounge and, in 1955, a panel of Captains was erected at a cost of £40. An innovation which became better known by a 'Barton Ode' than by its efficiency, was the installation, in 1950, of two foot baths and a spray. The site of this plumbing disaster was in an old broom cupboard on the East wall of the Locker Room near the present 'dirty' entrance and the opening ceremony was celebrated in verse. (See Appendix I)

As indicated earlier, the decade saw dramatic changes in the Membership of the Club, showing not only that 'the old order changeth' but also a substantial loss of 114 Members. However, in defence of the various Councils of the time, they were far from being idle in the face of the decline, and engaged in many new and imaginative activities to attract and a maintain a full Membership.

Early in 1950, a Junior Membership was proposed by Hay Mackenzie (Captain 1951/53) and, in this, he had enthusiastic support from Henry Barton to whom the task of drawing up the appropriate rules was remitted. The purpose of the proposal was two-fold – it would be a source of new Members and, with this category of Member, Mortonhall would be similar to other Clubs in the Lothians area. At a Special General Meeting in December 1950, the proposal that 'Junior Members be admitted to the Club' was carried unanimously. Council decided to limit the Junior Membership to 50 and, strangely, not to advertise that it was available. Furthermore, no accommodation was to be provided and a list of 'Do's and Dont's' was to be handed to all aspirants. It was not therefore surprising that the response was poor, thus causing Council to approach the Club in October 1952 with an amended set of rules providing for a subscription of £1.11/6d in place of the original proposal of £3.3/– and an increase in the hours of play. These amendments proved partly successful, as the following Membership figures show:

1952 – 10	1956 – 35
1953 - 22	1957 – 30
1954 – 39	1958 – 27
1955 – 32	1959 – 44

Hay Mackenzie was also instrumental in introducing at a Special General Meeting in October 1952 a further new class of Member – the 'Country Member' for those residing outside a radius of 20 miles from the Clubhouse.

In 1952 and 1953, the financial position had so deteriorated that Council was left with no option but to put the following proposals to the AGM of 1953:

1. that the Entry Fee be reduced from £21 to £15.15/–
2. that the Subscription be raised from £6.6/– to £8.18/6d and
3. that a Special Levy of £2.12/6d be paid.

In view of the gravity of the situation, the annual deficit in the year to February 1953 having increased by £944 to £1,254, it was astonishing that the Meeting resolved:

1. to reduce the Entry Fee to £10.10/–
2. to defer a further increase in Subscription and
3. to reduce the Special Levy to £1.11/6d.

Inevitably, Council had to convene a Special General Meeting in January 1954 when, despite suggestions that the Greens staff be reduced, the annual subscription was increased to £8.18/6d. On this occasion, Council took the opportunity to indicate that they 'were unanimous that Lady Members should not be permitted and Morning and Five Day Members were not desired'. Despite an apparent antipathy to Ladies on the Course, financial circumstances dictated otherwise in the Clubhouse. In 1952, 'Ladies Nights' were instituted, to be followed by Cocktail Parties and Bridge Parties in 1956. With even greater daring, Dinner Dances were introduced in 1958 when dancing took place in the Lounge to an almost inaudible record player. From this point, it was almost inevitable that facilities to play golf at Mortonhall would be granted to Ladies and, in December 1958, Council amended the Bye-Laws to enable 'a lady relative or lady relatives over the age of 18 living in family' with an Ordinary Member to play on the Course for an annual subscription of £2.2/– within restricted playing times. This change was intimated to the Members but   111 not considered worthy of a mention in the subsequent Annual Report. It was, however, broadcast by Barton, the 'Poet Laureate', who envisaged gloom in heaven for the original Members over the historic breakthrough:

> This was what caused the depression;
> Their lament was like that of McCrimmon;
> For the rumour got round that the Council
> Was making provision for Women!
>
> They wrung their hands in anguish;
> They saw ruin over all.
> 'Who would have thought we'd see the day
> When there were women at Mortonhall?
>
> Beer and boys are bad enough,
> But women and gin are worse!'

A significant event of the period was the Diamond Jubilee of 1952, which was celebrated in great style in the Freemasons Hall in Edinburgh in April 1952. The Menu and Toast list were as shown opposite:

The principal guest of honour was Francis Ouimet, Captain of the Royal and Ancient, American Open and Amateur Champion, a former Captain of the American Walker Cup Team, on whom Honorary Membership of the Club was bestowed. The occasion was also marked by the presentation by honorary Members of the Club of a Captain's Badge of Office. Shortly after, the Club produced its first tie – price £1.1/–. In December 1954, the Captain proposed and Council accepted that, in future, all Captains of the Club would not be nominated by the retiring Captain but rather by a panel of Past Captains.

On the golfing scene, the Standard Scratch Score of the Course was determined at 69 by the Lothians Association in 1951. At an abandoned Summer Meeting in 1955, D. S. Dougal established, after ratification by the Royal and Ancient, a new Course Record of 68, only for this to be lowered a month or so later by K. B. Munnoch to 66. At this point, W. C. White drew Council's attention to the fact that, in 1930, J. A. Clark had also completed the Course in 66 strokes. While this was indeed true, Council ruled that there had been significant changes to the Course to recognise Keith Munnoch's score as the new record. Four years later, however, in 1959, F. G. Dewar lowered the record to 65 strokes.

In 1952, after a lapse of many years, Mortonhall revived its annual match with the Royal Burgess Golfing Society on the basis that the teams were equally divided between players of first and second class

112

Menu

Melon

§

Consommé Andalouse

§

Filets de Sole Bonne Femme

§

Canard Roti l'Orange   Les Pommes Chateaux
Les Petits Pois aux Beurre

§

Bavarois d'Rhum
Les Fruits aux Liqueurs

§

Tartines de Volaille

§

Cafe

Toast List

THE QUEEN
    The Captain

MORTONHALL GOLF CLUB
    Francis Ouimet, Esq.

Reply
    The Captain

KINDRED CLUBS
    J. R. Peddie, Esq., C.B.E., D.Litt., F.R.S.E.

Reply
    Sir William Wallace, C.B.E.

OUR GUESTS
    D. A. Foulis, Esq., D.S.O., O.B.E., M.A.

Reply
    W. R. Milligan, Esq., Q.C.

THE CHAIRMAN
    R. E. Croall, Esq.

113

I

handicaps. Also in 1952, Mortonhall participated with Kingsknowe and the Merchants of Edinburgh in a Winter League but there is no record of this tournament lasting more than one season. In 1952, Mortonhall was again successful in winning the Lothians Inter Club Tournament by defeating the Royal Burgess Golfing Society in the final at Prestonfield. The team comprised N. McLean, J. H. McLeod, I. McNiven and I. A. Williamson.

On the Queen's Coronation in 1953, Maurice Dewar accepted a wager that, in five minutes, he could not run from the Clubhouse and play out the 18th hole in four shots with one club. While Maurice completed the challenge within the time limit, he lost his bet by taking five strokes! This incident bears a remarkable similarity to one quoted in an official handbook of the Club produced in the 1960's:

> The slope leading down from tee to green seems sufficiently steep as we descend it, but we shall probably think it a good deal steeper if we try to tackle it in reverse. The late A. Drummond, the former professional of the Club, who served his apprenticeship in old Tom Morris's shop, told me that E. F. Storey, the former Cambridge University Captain and British Walker Cup player, once undertook, for a wager, to run from the Clubhouse up to the 18th tee and play out the hole, all within five minutes, and accomplished the feat quite easily. But I understand that another player who attempted to repeat the feat, arrived at the tee so completely out of breath that he was unable to attempt the return journey.

Of the personal golfing triumphs of the decade, Ian McNiven won the Lothians Championship in 1950, while at the end of the decade, G. E. Robertson was selected to play for Scotland in the Youths International. Mention must also be made of the epic final of the Club Championship in 1958 between F. G. Dewar, Scottish Amateur Champion in 1953, and K. D. T. Hall. The Championship was eventually won by Gordon Dewar at the 40th hole (the present 3rd) but only after an amazing stroke of fortune at the 39th hole (the present 2nd but then played from a tee set in the cliffs behind the pond). Gordon's drive, 'shanked' at right angles, struck a tree and thence returned to the teeing ground. Playing his luck, he proceeded to hole out in 3 more shots and secure a life saving half. This situation could not be better described than by the verses of Gordon Dewar himself. (See Appendix I) During the re-construction of the Course in the late 1970's, it was suggested by the Golf Course Architect, F. W. Hawtree, that the tree struck by Dewar's ball be felled but this was stoutly resisted

114

by two of the Trustees. 'Dewar's Tree' is thus still visible from the Clubhouse Lounge.

Early in 1950, F. W. Campbell C.A., who had been Treasurer of the Club since 1924 and Secretary and Treasurer since 1932, tendered his resignation. This was received with great regret as his term of office had been a notable one. He was succeeded by W. M. Berrie CA, who, like his predecessor, also became Secretary of the Scottish Golf Union. Morris Berrie served Mortonhall, and indeed the entire Scottish golfing scene, with great distinction until his untimely death at the age of 57 in 1959. On him had fallen Mortonhall's most troublesome years. Following an interim Secretaryship by Morris's brother, D. S. Berrie, A. J. Cowan was appointed Secretary and Treasurer of the Club in February 1959. Unfortunately, Arthur Cowan resigned for business reasons in August 1959. T. P. J. Nicolson CA was appointed in his stead.

The decade was marked by the deaths of two of Mortonhall's greatest players – W. B. Torrance (1956) and Walter Willis Mackenzie (1959) – and, in reflecting over the period, those who stand out in a fertile field of Mortonhall Men were undoubtedly:

D. S. Anderson	Alex. Dougal
H. Barton	C. Forbes
W. M. Berrie	T. M. Jinkins
J. M. Cooper	A. H. Macdonald
R. E. Croall	W. Hay Mackenzie

The Sixties

After the trauma of the previous ten years, the Sixties were, for Mortonhall, a period of consolidation – changes there were – some significant but none dramatic – and slowly and gradually, the old order disappeared, leaving a younger Mortonhall to emerge and grasp new opportunities.

On the Course, the major activity centred round the provision of water for the greens. In this, Mortonhall, with the financial problems of the Fifties, lagged behind other Edinburgh clubs and there is good reason to believe that a certain loss of Members was occurring due to the fast and fiery greens along the finishing ridge. In all probability, it was the long hot dry summer of 1959 which prompted the request at the AGM in 1960 that Council 'give consideration to the provision of a water supply on the Course'. Council's approach was cautious and it was not until some 18 months later that a Special General Meeting was called to approve a proposal whereby the cost of the installation of water be met   115 by the Club's reserves to the extent of 25% and by the Members for the remaining 75%, the latter contribution being by way of an annual levy of £2.2/- over two years. Ultimately, a scheme was agreed where a tank was sited behind the Greenkeepers' Sheds, then at the car park, and filled each evening from the City's water supply. A pump was installed to carry the water to the various elevations, but its capacity was such that only six greens could be watered each day. In May 1962, an estimate from Charles G. Dobson Ltd. for £2,260.19/d was accepted and, in June 1963, the work was completed. Around 1960, negotiations were entered into with Telecommunications Ltd. for the construction of a shortwave radio mast at the old 16th green. The negotiations proved to be so protracted that it was not until 1969 that a lease was finally signed for this Mortonhall landmark which stood on the skyline of the ridge for over twenty years. There is some doubt as to the precise date of the 80 foot erection but it is popularly attributed to the period of Jock Pyper's Captaincy (1965–1967). A further significant event in 1960 was the almost unobtrusive purchase of ground to the South of the 2nd green (the present 1st). The prudence and foresight of this acquisition was to provide a valuable option some fifteen years later. In 1965, a contract was entered into for the excavation of the pond and, some time later, the Convener of the Greens Committee vaguely reported to Council that the work had been carried out 'as far as the weather had permitted at a restricted cost of £80'. As far as the Greens staff was concerned, a Member of the Club, D. B. Horn was engaged in November 1965 but, after 18 months of acceptable service, left to become Greenkeeper/ Professional at Broomieknowe. But, like General McArthur, he did return.

The main topic of interest in the Clubhouse during the decade concerned the bar facilities. The Bar in 1960 had not changed since the Clubhouse was built – it was small – it was cramped – it was airless – but it had character and was well loved by many. Inevitably, Barton reached for his pen;

> As befits a good Club, it's tucked well out of sight
> Quite near to the Lounge, off the passage to the right.
> Some Members are drawn there, like moths to a light,
> It's the Mecca of Watsonians on a Saturday night.
>
> It's a small box of a room and the comforts just nil;
> There are three hard forms and a broad window sill;
> It's not a place to attract one who seeks comfort particular,
> For the position when drinking is, in the main, perpendicular.

When the place is well filled, there's no room to turn;
For much space is absorbed by a big brass urn;
It's for tobacco and matches and cigarette ends,
And all other junk that the Lord alone kens.

Discussion had taken place in the autumn of 1959, plans had been prepared, estimates had been received and there seemed no doubt that, in the pompous words of Council, the old Bar had to go 'in consideration of a number of factors necessitated by present day staff economies and with an eye to the future requirements of the Club'. In February 1960, a Special General Meeting of the Club was called to approve a scheme which, *inter alia*, converted the old Bar into a room for Junior Members, installed a new Bar in the South West corner of the Lounge – all at an estimated cost of £900, to be met from the reserves of the Club. While Council's proposal was approved, the narrow majority of 41 to 33 caused concern which deepened two weeks later when objections were received from 20 Members. In these circumstances Council rather tamely informed the Club that it was now considering a complete survey of the Clubhouse. While this project lay either dormant or dead, Council set up, in 1963, a 'long term policy committee' consisting of Messrs H. Barton (Chairman) G. Y. Craig, I. Isles (Captain) and E. B. Robertson 'to explore the long term possibilities of disposing of part of the Course for building purposes, the acquisition of other land and the building of a new Clubhouse'. The deliberations of such an eminent committee were deep, serious, and exhaustive, examining restrictions in the Feu Charter, assessing planning difficulties with regard to water, roads, ground levels, and landscape preservation, and weighing up the political consequences. Finally in July 1965, the recommendation was made to Council that it should ascertain from the Mortonhall Estate whether (a) the 'wedge' between the 5th (the present 4th) and 11th (the present 9th) holes, or (b) the 30 acre field lying to the South thereof, was available for purchase. Enquiry was duly made but in October 1965 it was reported that 'there was little likelihood of the ground being available'. While the Special Committee reflected and considered, a new Council returned to the dilemma over the old Bar and, in 1964, entered into a contract for £1,800 to extend the 'small box of a room' southwards into the kitchen servery. This work was completed in 1965.

Concurrent with this activity was the introduction of a fruit machine. During the Sixties, this had been a hotly debated innovation. It had been first considered in 1963 but a decision was deferred until the 'new Bar' was to be opened. Nonetheless, the summer of 1964 saw the arrival of one machine in a month's trial but after 18 days when a surplus of £51 emerged, the equipment was quickly purchased for £450. A year later a further machine was added and, in the first period of four weeks dual operation, a surplus of £282 was obtained. In retrospect, the acquisition of the fruit machines at Mortonhall saw – as it did for so many institutions – the beginning of a marked improvement in its financial fortunes.

The latter part of 1967 found a further new Council unhappy about the amenity of the Clubhouse. Inevitably, an *ad hoc* hoc Committee, under the Chairmanship of A. R. Bade was set up to examine the position and make proposals. This Committee worked quickly and, at a Special General Meeting held in February 1968, a major scheme of reconstruction was approved by a substantial majority. Essentially, this converted the Lounge into its present L-shape, divided the Dining Room with a sliding partition, installed the present Bar in the South West corner of the Lounge, elevated the Kitchen premises from the basement to the Dining Room level, established the present porch on the East elevation and created a 'dirty' entrance to the Locker Room on the North elevation. The cost of the proposals was broadly estimated at £5,000 which the Special General Meeting approved should be met by:

    1. a levy of £5.5/– per Member

    2. the non-returnable monies of the 75th Anniversary Fund (q.v.) and

    3. the capitalised surplus of the Fruit Machines from 1968 and 1969

Throughout 1968, the *ad hoc* Committee planned the operation with great care but had to report in December 1968 that the estimated cost had escalated to £11,500. Council nevertheless authorised the additional expenditure and informed the Members accordingly; the work commenced early in 1969; and after certain delays, the contract was completed in May 1969. When all the accounts were agreed, they totalled £15,941, and, by a display of financial wizardry, were settled thus:

Levy	£2,588
Fruit Machine Surplus (68/70)	5,687
Revenue Account (69/70)	2,441
Deferred Repairs Provision	1,500
Club's Reserves	3,725
	£15,941

The night of 10th/11th August 1969 was a dark one in the history of Mortonhall. The trophies – the cups, the shields and the medals donated over a period of 80 years, displayed with pride and affection, contested for annually, and inscribed with the names of the victors – were stolen from the showcase in the foyer. They were not recovered and, grossly under-insured, their loss to the Club has been inestimable. Behind the theft lay the truly remarkable story which could not be better told than in the words of the person at the heart of the drama – the then Secretary, T. G. Mitchell.

At 11 a.m. on the 1st September 1969, the telephone rang in my office and a voice, unknown to me, enquired if I would be interested in the recovery of the Club's trophies. Naturally, I acquiesced, whereupon I was asked for my home address and telephone number and told that all further commincation would be by 'phone between 2 a.m. and 4 a.m. I was warned that any contact with the police would terminate the negotiations.

I duly contacted the Captain (D. B. Biggs) and the Vice-Captain (E. B. Robertson) and advised them of the position. It was decided to inform the police who recommended the utmost secrecy and the reporting of all further telephone calls. In addition, I was to try and stall for time regardless of the demands.

A few days later in the early hours of the morning, my caller contacted me from a coin box and told me that £3,000 was the price for the return of the trophies. I explained that, as an official of the Club, I could not accept such a demand and that it was a matter for my Finance Committee who were, at the time, mostly on holiday. This explanation was accepted provided there was no undue delay.

A short interval elapsed before I received another nocturnal call – 'Had the Finance Committee reached a decision?' I replied that the Club did not have ready funds of £3,000 and that the Finance Committee was exploring various ways and means of raising the money. The reaction to this further delay was surprising – the Club, said my caller, could recoup the insurance money and have the balance paid by the Members who seemed well-heeled judging by the response to the high-priced Dinner and Presentation to the retiring Secretary, T. P. J. Nicolson, details of which had been observed on the Club Notice Board. Eventually further time was granted for the Club to find the money.

I duly reported the call to the police who formed the opinion that the theft may have been 'an inside job' and proceeded to scrutinise the list of Members. Fortunately this proved negative! It was then proposed that I ask my caller for proof that the trophies were in his possession by suggesting that the Club would play £300 for the return of two cups.

At the next contact, this proposal was turned down flat but proof of possession was promised. A few days later, a postal delivery to the Club contained the lid of the Grand Fleet Cup and this was regarded as conclusive evidence that my caller did have the Club's trophies.

The police advised that I indicate that the Club would now agree to a deal. This was done and I was told to await further instructions. There followed a tense wait before the early morning caller asked 'Was the cash available?' I explained that I required the Captain's signature to cash the cheque and as he was abroad, I'd require a week's grace.

In the time so gained, the police provided me with a package containing the required £3,000 and one week later my telephone rang at the usual hour. I received my first instruction – I was on no account to leave my house during the next four days. A further call would be made in due course.

Two days later at the reasonable hour of 9 a.m. my final instructions were telephoned. I was to pick up the cash from the bank, then walk via Comiston Road, Morningside Road, Church Hill Place, Whitehouse Loan and Warrender Park Road and wait at the telephone kiosk near the Post Office. I contacted the police immediately who assured me that a plain clothes detective would shadow me all along the route. The Captain and Vice-Captain were most emphatic that I should seriously consider opting out of the delivery but my mind was made up.

I duly arrived at the phone box outside the Warrender Park Road Post Office, where, almost immediately, a call came through to say that 'he' could see me from his window and the 'he' had observed 'the package'. I was then asked to synchronise my watch with his and told to look out of the box where I would see a shop on my right and then an open tenement door. At 11 a.m. exactly, I was to enter this door, drop the package into the well area and leave the district immediately via Arden Street.

As I moved into position near the door in question, a very dirty tramp approached where I stood. He picked up a fag-end, lit it and as he shuffled past, head bowed to his knees, I heard him mutter 'You know the drop?' 'Yes' I replied.

At this precise moment, a police car entered Warrender Park Road and stopped 100 yards away. Two policemen in uniform emerged and entered a tenement leaving two other policemen in the car. Almost immediately, the phone rang in the box once more. I picked up the received and was told to 'B.....r off' as I had the place covered with police. I had no option but to pull out.

In retrospect, Tommy Mitchell said it was most unfortunate that the police car – which was on another mission unknown to the detective on the Mortonhall case – should have appeared at the crucial moment. Tommy also recounted that, throughout the whole episode, he was never conscious of any police presence although he was later informed that detectives were posing as counter clerks in Warrender Park Road Post Office. Apart from Colonel Stewart's Medal and the Gordon Thomson Cup which were, at the time, being engraved, the trophies were never retrieved. There was, however, one final flourish when the Coronation Shield was deposited in a smashed condition in the garden of the Vice-Captain, E. B. Robertson.

The social functions, so successfully introduced in the Fifties, continued to thrive during the Sixties. This was largely due to the calibre of the Clubmasters of the period. The new Clubmaster, in succession to the Whites, was Hugh Morton, who, in addition to selling golf equipment in the Professional's Shop, had been a Member of the Club prior to his appointment. Hugh's tenure was marked with distinction and efficiency and lasted till the end of 1962 when he took up duties as Secretary to the Brough Golf Club at Hull. Hugh Morton was succeeded as Clubmaster by another Member of the Club, Jack Dodds who, with his wife, showed much initiative, enthusiasm and enterprise in their stay of some six years. The Dodds left Mortonhall for a similar position at Royal Troon but tragically Jack was killed in a motor accident a few years later. The end of the decade saw the appointment of Mr and Mrs Andrew Thomson who were to render loyal and faithful service to the Club until 1979.

As far as the great game was concerned, the Sixties were remarkable for the inauguration of new tournaments. The year 1960 saw the start on a regular basis of the popular Saturday evening Mixed Foursomes; September 1961 saw the first Invitation Silloth Tournament; the season 1963 saw Mortonhall participating in the Edinburgh Golf League and winning, at its first attempt, promotion from Division II. Next year the Club led the First Division (see photograph facing page 129), a feat which was complemented by the Juniors' victory in the Edinburgh Junior Inter Club Tournament, and then, in 1966, the Mortonhall Open Tournament was born. In the matter of medal scores, the record of 65, achieved by Gordon Dewar in August 1959 withstood the challenges of the decade, the nearest recorded approach being a 67 in 1966. The appointment in June 1963 of Tom Ainslie of Inverness as Club

Professional filled a position which had been vacant since 1954 and proved to be a particularly happy association.

The Sixties saw the Club obsessed with finance. Towards the end of 1960, the subscription of £8.18/6d, unchanged since 1954, was considered inadequate for no better reason than that 'all expenditure, particularly wages, was always increasing'. At a Special General Meeting in January 1961, a resolution to increase the subscription to £10.10/– was approved by 38 to 18 although one Member was sufficiently incensed to have his dissent recorded. Two years later, Council was still unable to match expenditure with revenue and, for no apparent reason, took cold feet in pursuing a proposal to increase the subscription to £12.12/–. But, in 1963, the situation was no better and a Special General Meeting in February 1964 approved an increase to £14.14/–. Whether it was a question of too small an increase too late or whether it was the decline in bar profits, the problem, despite a full Membership, still remained at the end of 1965. Council spoke bravely of maintaining standards and proposed that the subscription be raised to £17.17/–. Somewhat surprisingly, Council's motion was defeated by a substantial majority and it was fortunate that a motion from the floor proposing a levy of £3.3/– for the year 1966 was carried. From this point, annual increases in the subscription became almost routine – although there was, for 1968, a reduction in the Entry Money from £15.15/– to £5.5/–. By 1970, the subscription was up to £21 and the Entry Money established at a similar figure.

In September 1966, a decision was taken to appoint a Sub-Committee for the purpose of raising £5,000 to mark the 75th Anniversary of the Club in 1967. The fund was to be used to improve the Clubhouse facilities and, hopefully, to obviate the need for annual subscription increases. The year 1967 was devoted to a number of fund-raising schemes and the organising committee produced a unique range of activities and appeals. These included:

An Anniversary Fete
An Anniversary Prize Draw
Weekly Raffles
Invitations to 'buy' a square foot of Lounge floor covering
An appeal to the Club's Brewers
A Golfkhana
An appeal to Members for donations
The sale of fallen leaves and grass cuttings as a spring fertiliser
The sale of flowers and plants from a garden cultivated by volunteers
and
The sale of spirits at the festive season at 'cut prices'

In January 1967, Council received the first report on the Members' response – 38 positive replies out of a Membership of almost 500 being hardly encouraging. By May 1967, donations totalling £1,097 had been received and the Fete and Golfkhana were still to come. But, ruefully, in November 1967, Council realised that its bold and imaginative plan was foundering and submitted a resolution to a Special General Meeting in December that the Anniversary Fund be wound up on the basis that monies raised by organised events be credited to reserve and that, if a further £2,500 was not raised from all sources, donations by Members be refunded and a levy imposed for Club improvements. In the event, this target was not attained and donations of £1,176 were returned to Members. A sum of £1,869 was, however, retained and part of this, together with the levy of £2,588, was applied to meet the major reconstruction which had taken place in the Clubhouse.

In Membership matters, the Club's muster in 1960 was 437 but this rapidly increased so that in 1964 Council was able to announce for the first time in many years that there was a waiting list. The decade closed with a Membership of 500, which was now regarded as the maximum. The AGM of 1965 saw the creation of a new class of Member – The Five Day player. The qualifications were basic and straightforward – one had to be over 65 years of age and to have been a Member for over 10 years. The subscription was half that of an Ordinary Member – there was no play at the weekends or after 4 p.m. on weekdays and there was no vote at General Meetings. By 1969, there were only 26 Five Day Players. Motions at the 1968 AGM that consideration be given to the admission of Lady Members and House Members were both defeated by overwhelming majorities.

Other items of general interest included the celebration of the 70th Anniversary in 1962 by a Club Dinner which 43 Members attended at a cost of 15/– per head. Following the death of Willis Mackenzie in 1959, his daughter very generously presented the Club with his Championship Medals and his replica of the Walker Cup. In August 1961, W. West Kerr, a Past Captain and last Original Member of the Club, celebrated his Centenary. He attributed his longevity to 'always keeping busy exercising both body and mind' and, in his younger days, cycled from Edinburgh to Liverpool and back on a penny farthing! On his last visit to the Club in 1957, he said 'I've just come to clear out my locker; I've hurt my back and I won't be able to play any more – I'm 96, you know'. He died in 1962 while October 1964 saw the death of another Mortonhall stalwart, W. C. White.

As far as the Secretaryship was concerned, the decade was presided over with much efficiency, style and panache by T. P. J. Nicolson so much so that when he retired in 1969 an extremely successful and well

123

patronised dinner was held. Tommy Nicolson's successor was T. G. Mitchell whose inauguration at the time of the theft of the club's trophies could hardly have been more spectacular. There were those who worked tirelessly for the Club during the Sixties as well as those who brought great distinction to it. Many of this number happily still survive and it may be for another generation to remember them. But of those who have passed on, the labours of Alec Bade and the skill of Gordon Dewar should not be overlooked – for they were indeed 'Mortonhall Men'.

7

A DECADE OF DEVELOPMENT
1970–1979

There's a divinity that shapes our ends

(Shakespeare)

The Development

In retrospect, Mortonhall could not have chosen a more inopportune time to have engaged in a massive development than in the inflation and economic strife of the 1970's. But the Club was never the master of its own destiny and always had to take 'the current when it served'. Since 1906, successive generations had golfed over the same Course. Minor changes and improvements there had been but the fairways, tees and greens – faithfully maintained by those greenkeeping stalwarts, Thomson and Bulloch – remained kenspeckle. In the 1970's, an opportunity presented itself – or perhaps more accurately half presented itself – and this was enough for the initiative and enterprise of another generation of Mortonhall Men. There then followed a decade of development which dominated life and golf at Mortonhall between 1970 and 1979.

It all started with the following letter, written by the then Captain, E. B. Robertson, to all Council Members on 2nd July 1970:

> Dear Council Member,
>   With a view to obtaining further ground for the extension of our Golf Course I have had meetings with the Solicitors to Mortonhall Estate and also with Mr Alexander Trotter the Estate owner.

At a meeting held on 29th June, Mr Trotter indicated that he was amenable to the proposal of the Club to acquire the area which lies to the north of the 5th hole (the present 4th) and to the south of the 11th hole (the present 9th) (hereinafter referred to as 'the area').

The following points are of importance in considering the acquisition of the area.

1. Mr Trotter is satisfied that he will not obtain planning permission to develop the area in the foreseeable future. While a price was not discussed at our meeting, the inference is that the price level would be based on the existing agricultural use. I estimate that this might be in the range of £500 per acre. The acreage of the area is 28 acres.

2. Mr Trotter is not interested in retaining any part of the area for development.

3. The area is at present part of Meadowhead Farm but Mr Trotter's Solicitors are satisfied that resumption of the area for a sale to our club presents no difficulties because of the terms of the Lease.

4. It will take at least a year from November 1970 at the earliest to give our Golf Club possession of the area.

5. After the ingathering of the harvest Mr Trotter will advise his tenant of our interest in purchasing and Council Members and any Architect employed by us will have permission to walk over the area with a view to considering its merits as an addition to our Golf Course. (I would indeed recommend that the area be regularly inspected during the autumn and winter to ascertain if there are any areas which require drainage, etc.).

Mr Trotter appreciated that the purchase of the area could only be made after the matter had been referred to the whole body of members. It was agreed that I should seek Council authority to employ Golf Course Architects in order to find out how well (or badly) the area would fit in with our present layout, and particularly, whether, as a result of this acquisition, we could cease the use of our last four or five holes. It was further agreed that I should see Mr Trotter again after obtaining the Golf Course Architects' Report.

If the Council agree that the area should be acquired I consider that we should do our best to influence our members to finance the purchase. There should be no difficulty with many of our younger and keener golfers but it is essential to gain the support of our older and less keen members whose financial contribution will be necessary for a project such as this.

I consider that the reference to the Golf Course Architects should contain the following points:

1. Tree planting recommendations for entire Golf Course
2. Bunker placings with advice on better bunker construction
3. Other hazards
4. That a golf course of not less than 6250 yards is desirable containing say 4 par 3 holes, 4 par 5 holes and 10 par 4 holes of which four are over 400 yards
5. A practice area should be available
6. A site adjacent to the West Drive of Mortonhall Estate should be allocated for a future Club House with adequate parking facilities
7. At the site of this proposed new Club House the golf course should be playable in two halves of nine holes each
8. As (in my opinion) we shall be using our present Club House for the remainder of this Century an acceptable (and reasonably safe) mode of using the present 1st and 2nd fairways for our 1st and 18th holes should be devised
9. Consideration should be given to increasing the present car park
10. Additional staff (if any) required
11. Additional green equipment – tractor etc
12. Use of contract labour for laying out the area as golf course
13. Extension of water supply to greens and trees
14. Phasing of operations. What period (if any) will it not be possible to play 18 holes of golf over Mortonhall
15. Estimate of total costs

If the project is found acceptable to the Council we must go to the Membership. A simple acceptance of the idea as being good is not sufficient. The Council should have the money in the Bank before any contract to purchase the area is entered into. Possible methods of raising money are a levy and interest free loans with limitations on repayment. Conditions attaching to new members would require to be drastically revised.

I ask Council members to consider whether the development of the Club should be a matter for Council alone or a specially selected Development Committee. I consider that there are definite advantages in having a special

127

Committee which could include certain Council Members.

At the meeting with Mr Trotter it was put to me by him that he wished to give up the West Drive in his estate – that is the road which runs eastward from Braid Road along the centre of the trees which form our south boundary. A Preservation Order protects the trees from felling and the area from redevelopment. With these conditions applying Mr Trotter confessed that he was interested in discharging his responsibilities as regards the West Drive. I indicated that the West Drive would interest us if we had a Club House erected in the centre of the Golf Course but I felt that this was not possible for many years. I asked for time to think about it. We would have to assess what our responsibilities would be if we took the West Drive over. I think we might get limited permission to fell trees to make new holes but this is bound to be extremely costly. Again I think that the authorities would allow us to make a clearance for a car park in the interests of safety. The matter could come under the reference to the Architects.

So that Council Members' views can be heard it is proposed to hold a meeting of Council at the Club House on Tuesday, 14th July at 7.30 p.m. The next course of action can be decided upon. It is proposed to confine the subject matter of the meeting to the development of the Golf Course.

Yours sincerely

(Sgd.) E. B. ROBERTSON

Captain

It may be valid, at this stage, to note the following matters raised in the letter and then to measure the success of the development by the extent to which each was resolved or fulfilled:

1. Price of £500 per acre
2. Elimination of the last five holes
3. Attitude of the older Members
4. Length and disposition of the Course
5. Availability of a Practice Area
6. Future siting of the Clubhouse
7. Extension of the car park
8. Phasing of operations
9. Raising of finance and
10. Accessability of the West Drive

Council, meeting on 14th July 1970, noted that Mr A. R. Trotter was prepared to dispose to the Club the West Drive of the Mortonhall Estate but recognised that its acquisition would bring responsibilities in

The Pond from the East and from the West

Edinburgh Golf League Team (1964)

D. B. HORN, N. J. ROBERTSON, K. D. T. HALL, D. B. WILSON, E. S. COLLINS, M. G. JAMES, A. F. BROWN

R. G. YOUNG, I. ISLES (CAPTAIN), G. E. ROBERTSON

R. A. DAVIE, I. S. DOUGAL

[ABSENT: L. D. MITCHELL

respect of the upkeep of the woodlands. But this was a matter whose place in the scheme of things was yet to be. Council then resolved:

1. to appoint Mr F. W. Hawtree Golf Course Architect
2. to inform Club Members of Council's intentions and
3. to appoint, in the event of the development proceeding, a committee comprising Club Members having the requisite knowledge and experience.

Mr Hawtree visited the Course in September 1970 and reported his 'definite view that the golf course could be materially improved by the acquisition of the land to the East and the abandonment of the present last five holes'. Attention turned to further factors including, not surprisingly, the maximum sum which the Club could reasonably expect to raise from the Membership. This was estimated at £30,000. A Development Committee was formed to include the following Members:

Planning Sub-Committee	–	W. G. P. Colledge
		H. G. Lindley
		L. D. Mitchell
		D. M. McNish
		T. A. Rankin
Course Sub-Committee	–	J. Brydon
		Professor G. Y. Craig
		A. Steele
		A. N. Sutherland
		C. M. Tasker
Fund Raising Sub-Committee	–	A. M. Aitchison
		D. B. Biggs
		W. G. P. Colledge
		I. Isles
		R. J. A. Michie
		T. P. J. Nicolson
		C. Steven
Publicity Sub-Committee	–	E. B. Robertson
		T. P. J. Nicolson
		J. I. R. Rankine

K. T. R. Clark and I. S. Robertson also joined the Committee in 1975.

The first meeting of the Development Committee took place on 21st October 1970 and appointed the Captain, Eain Robertson, as its Chairman. Prior to the meeting, the Planning Sub-Committee had considered the plan shown overleaf, prepared by Mr Hawtree:

129

K

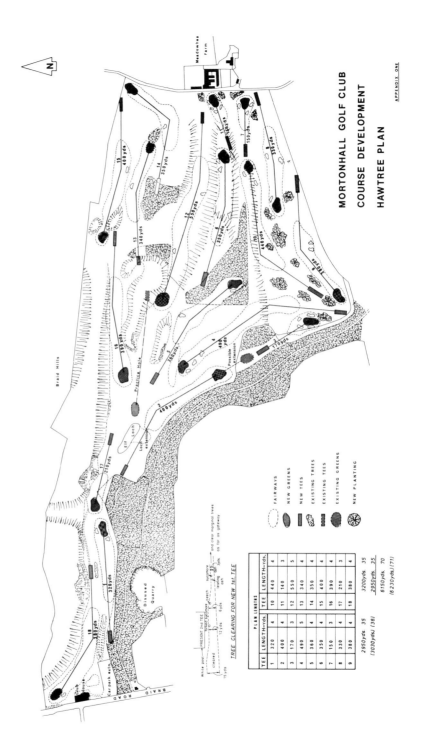

MORTONHALL GOLF CLUB

COURSE DEVELOPMENT

HAWTREE PLAN

APPENDIX ONE

TEE	LENGTH-yds.		TEE	LENGTH-yds.	
1	320	4	10	440	4
2	400	4	11	140	3
3	170	3	12	550	5
4	490	5	13	340	4
5	360	4	14	350	4
6	350	4	15	400	4
7	150	3	16	390	4
8	330	4	17	210	3
9	380	4	18	380	4

PLAN LENGTHS

2950yds. 35   3200yds. 35
(3030yds) (36)   2950yds. 35
          6150yds. 70
          (6230yds) (71)

FAIRWAYS

NEW GREENS

NEW TEES

EXISTING TREES

EXISTING TEES

EXISTING GREENS

NEW PLANTING

130

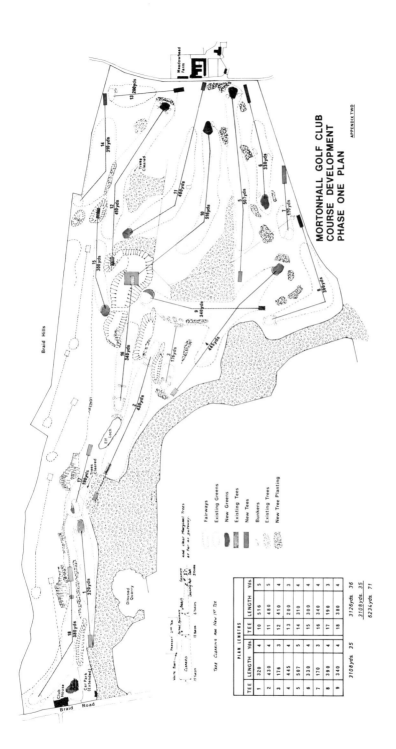

MORTONHALL GOLF CLUB
COURSE DEVELOPMENT
PHASE ONE PLAN

APPENDIX TWO

Fairways
Existing Greens
New Greens
Existing Tees
New Tees
Bunkers
Existing Trees
New Tree Planting

PLAN LENGTHS					
TEE	LENGTH	Yds.	TEE	LENGTH	Yds.
1	320	4	10	516	5
2	430	4	11	480	5
3	176	3	12	410	4
4	445	4	13	200	3
5	507	5	14	310	4
6	330	4	15	300	4
7	170	3	16	340	4
8	390	4	17	190	3
9	340	4	18	380	4

3108 yds. 35

3126 yds. 36
3108 yds. 35
6234 yds. 71

131

Realising, however, that the cost of 12 greens, 14 new tees and a substantial tree clearing operation was well beyond the financial reach of the Club, it also produced a more modest Phase One plan for Mr Hawtree's examination. This was as shown on the previous page.

It was considered – optimistically as events proved – that the implementation of the plan, together with the cost of acquiring the land, could be met within the estimate of £30,000 which, the Finance Sub-Committee proposed, should be raised by a levy of £60 on each Member, and £30 on Five Day Members, payable over a five year period. It soon became clear, however, that this would be impossible and some thought was accordingly given to negotiating a 50 year lease of the ground from Mr Trotter. In early 1971, to all intents and purposes, the project went cold but, in the background, the Chairman, Eain Robertson, was holding long and delicate discussions with Mr Trotter and his agents. It was not until the autumn of 1973 that Eain was able to report to Council that, as a result of plans for the development of a caravan site near Mortonhall House, the way had opened up for the Club to enter into more positive negotiations with Mr Trotter for a long lease of the land between the then 5th (the present 4th) and 11th (the present 9th) holes. A year later, however, it became known that Mr Trotter was prepared to offer the land for sale, provided facilities, similar to those available to the Five Day Membership of the Club, were offered to the temporary occupants of the caravan site. These conditions were acceptable to Council and Eain Robertson was authorised to resume his negotiations on this basis.

At a Meeting on 20th May 1975, Council was informed that a figure of £30,000 had been suggested for the desired 29 acres. An early decision was required. With commendable speed, Council, acting with the Development Committee, concluded the necessary financial arrangements and submitted a comprehensive report to the Membership. The finance required was fixed at £35,000 to take into account not only the purchase of the land but also the cost of de-stoning and sowing the area to grass. To complete the Phase One Plan, it was estimated that a further £30,000 would be necessary. A Special General Meeting was held on 31st July 1975 in Fairmilehead Church Hall and, after leading speeches by the Captain, John Hunter and Eain Robertson, both of whom stressed that the opportunity was unique and that, if declined, the possibility of further development would be gone forever, the following resolution was carried by 188 votes to 3.

> that the Club acquire by purchase an area of ground extending to 29 acres or thereby, lying between the existing 5th and 11th holes and also a small area of ground at present forming

woodland on the South side of the 1st and 2nd holes on the terms narrated in Paragraph 2 of the Development Committee Report (see Appendix P), that the provisions for financing the purchase will be as narrated in Paragraph 5 of the said Report and that the proposals as to detailed planning of the area acquired and the re-development of the Golf Course will be subject to further consideration.

The purchase of the land, together with the necessary Planning Permission for the development, became effective as from 28th November 1975 and arrangements were made for the collection of the levies from 1st December 1975 and the receipt of voluntary loans. Throughout the autumn of that year and the succeeding winter and spring, Council and the Development Committee acted in close liaison and endeavoured to keep the Membership informed of progress by means of regular bulletins. Much work was done on the 'preliminaries' – fences were removed – the new ground ploughed – a new 18th tee on the flat behind the existing first green built – an extension of the car park was considered – and even the re-location of the Clubhouse at the Mansionhouse at Mortonhall examined. Fred Hawtree was instructed to review the Phase One Plan, which had been submitted to the Membership at the Special General Meeting, in the light of the limited finance likely to be available after the purchase of the land. Before the winter was out, Mr Hawtree had produced no less than eight further plans for the consideration of the small planning group on the Development Committee before a compromise was reached on a plan whose essential features were two nines of equal length, sharing the four par 5's and the four par 3's. In addition, the plan would allow 18 holes to remain in play throughout the changeover.

Concurrently, an appeal was launched for interest-free advances of £250 and £500 for which a proportionate reduction in subscription was given. There then followed, 'silently, flooding in the main', a remarkable stream of loans. While it was the case that some of these emanated from younger Members, the vast majority were given by those who, in the twilight of their golfing careers, wished to acknowledge previous pleasure and enjoyment by way of a bequest to Mortonhall. The effect of this financial windfall was two-fold – on the one hand, it restricted the overdraft on the Club's Bank Account, to a mere seven days and, on the other, it encouraged Council and the Development Committee to proceed with the creation of a new Course without delay. This decision, inspired not solely on financial grounds but by the remarkable response of Members could not, in retrospect, have been more brilliantly timed. While inflation had begun   133 its rampage, the economic storm had still some years to run, and the construction industry was in a moribund state. The spring of 1976 saw much activity and discussion on the part of both the Development Committee and Council. The 'compromise' plan was examined in all its many aspects – the ground was walked and shots struck across the stubble – various trees were considered, the formations 'arrowheaded into the wind' – permission for tree felling was obtained for siting the crucial new first tee. Steps were taken to ensure that the funding of the whole operation would be sufficient and timeously available and that the entry monies of new Members were appropriately adjusted. By May 1976, the stage was set and a second Special General Meeting was held in Fairmilehead Church Hall on 26th May 1976 to consider a further report from the Development Commitee (see Appendix Q) and to pass the following Resolutions:

Resolution 1
1. that the plan prepared by Mr F. W. Hawtree, Golf Course Architect, and detailed in the Appendix of the Development Committee Report 1976, be accepted as the new layout for Mortonhall Golf Course
2. that the proposals contained in the aforesaid plan be implemented as soon as possible at a total cost in the region of £35,000
3. that Mr F. W. Hawtree be appointed Architect to the Club for the purpose of implementing the aforesaid plan and
4. that the levy of £12 per annum currently imposed on Ordinary Members and £6 on Five Day Members for a period of five years be extended for a further period of seven years from 1st June, 1981 to implement the aforesaid proposals.

Resolution 2
that, from the 1st June 1976, there will be payable for each year, in addition to the Entry Money due by new Ordinary Members and Five Day Members, the sums of £12 and £6 respectively in connection with the development of the golf course.

While the observations concerning 'THE FUTURE' are of interest, indicating, as they do, the direction in which a generation around the year 2000 might follow, a matter which was to have some influence in the more immediate future was the position of the new 5th green in the woods of the Mortonhall Drive. But of this, more will be written.

The Meeting was addressed by the Chairman of the Development Committee, Eain Robertson, and the Captain, Pat Colledge, and after discussion the two resolutions were unanimously approved. The Captain concluded the Meeting with the following vote of thanks to the Development Committee:

> It is on a full sea that we are now afloat. Many hazards no doubt yet confront us. But we have started our voyage and I am sure Councils of the Club together with the Development Committee will with enthusiasm and determination see us home, safe and dry.
>
> It is for me a very pleasant duty to thank each member of the Development Committee for all that they have done. Collectively they represent a fund of knowledge and a wide variety of skills. Each individual has been called upon to perform those functions most suited to his talents. Each has given willingly of his time and unstintingly of his service. They have done this simply because of their interest, their concern and their affection for Mortonhall.
>
> Personally I am only too conscious of the days they passed in the wind, in the rain and in the mud, of the nights they spent studying Hawtree's plans or wrestling with financial problems and of the steps they took to ensure that no stone was left unturned and no possibility unexplored. I do not mention the Committee by name because they believe that all that they did was done as a team and not as individuals.
>
> There is one – I should and indeed must mention – the 'Team Captain' Eain Robertson. Eain, we have admired and valued greatly your enthusiasm, your persistence, your skill and your foresight in the whole matter. You have never sought any recompense other than the opportunity of doing something for Mortonhall and I trust that you will regard the approval given tonight of the recommendations in your Report as a tangible expression of the Club's deep gratitude.
>
> It is not, as you know, for mortals to command success but we believe you have done more, we think you have deserved it.

After the Special General Meeting, the initiative passed from the Planning to the Course Group of the Development Committee and, in August 1976, Council, realising that to keep an 18 hole Course in play during a major development was too much to expect of any 135 greenkeeper, appointed Douglas Horn, a former Member of the Club and assistant greenkeeper, as Course Supervisor. This appointment, as will be later seen, was a good one. The summer of 1976 was long and hot and looked set so to continue into September. But the new ground had been de-stoned and was ready for grass. It was at the beginning of September that Ian Robertson, an expert on agricultural matters, took the bold decision to sow the seed, and after an anxious wait of eight days, the rains came and a most successful growth flourished. Investigation into the supply of water to the new greens was actively pursued and a quotation for £4,555 accepted from Watermation Ltd. Sixty trees at the new 1st hole were removed under the special licence which had been obtained. Trees were also removed around the new 2nd tee and holes were dug by various Members for young trees on the new ground under the dubious slogan of 'dig a hole for Mortonhall'!

As far as the actual development of the Course was concerned, the work on the new tees was assigned to the Club's Greens Staff under the direction of Douglas Horn while the major work on the new greens and their bunkering was placed out to tender to six contractors. The lowest offer viz. £24, 482 was received from Seafield Landscaping Ltd. and, in view of its established reputation, a contract was duly entered into with a commencement date in the spring of 1977. In January 1977, Council was advised by Douglas Horn that the location of the new 5th Green, surrounded as it was to be by trees, was likely to cause growth and maintenance problems. These difficulties could be overcome if the Club were to acquire from Mr Trotter a small part of adjacent land from which trees could be removed. It was agreed that Eain Robertson should make enquiries. Two months later, he reported that Mr Trotter was not only willing to dispose of the small parcel of land near the new 5th green but also of the entire drive from the Braid Road to the new 5th tee, plus the plantations immediately beyond. This startling proposition with all the attendant attractions of the removal of boundary walls, Course access and extended car parking facilities, was examined with particular reference to price and the maintenance of the substantial woodland, but, in May 1977, Council was faced with an agonising decision. The value of the offer was calculated at £20,000 but it had become known that other interested parties were gathering in the wings. There was no time to convene a Special General Meeting and Council seized on this golden opportunity, arranged overdraft facilities and instructed the purchase of the drive forthwith. While there were those in the Club who criticised Council for its initiative and seeming recklessness, most lived to see the day when the shrewd investment paid out its dividends in a manner beyond all expectations. Oddly, the 5th green was never moved to its planned location. March 1977 brought together the most motley collection of 'Mortonhall Men' when the old, the young, their wives, girl friends and children congregated on the new ground to harvest the stones which the new grass was now thrusting to the surface. These were happy cheerful occasions with the Club literally 'on its knees'!

Many Members of the Club had played their part in various different ways and now the scene was set for the contract to begin. Seafield Landscaping Ltd. moved on to the site and commenced their earth moving operations – gone was that unbroken vista of tree, whin and green and all around great mounds of earth appeared. But within weeks, a cloud cast a dark and ominous shadow over the Course – the parent company of Seafield Landscaping Ltd. was reported to be in receivership. Somehow the contract rumbled on till June 1977 when all operations ceased. The news of the total collapse was shared between Eain Robertson and one of his colleagues on the Development Committee since 1970. After a very substantial but consoling restorative one glorious Sunday morning, they walked sadly over the wreckage of their dreams which a few weeks earlier had held so much promise. What was to be done?

If Mortonhall had a 'finest hour' then it began in July 1977 and ended two years later in 1979 when the new Course was opened. Council and the Development Committee soon established that to have the work completed by another contractor was not possible within the total financial constraint, originally estimated at £35,000 and subsequently amended to £40,000. Acting on advice from Fred Hawtree, Council decided to undertake the task with its own labour, increased as was necessary. Mr Hawtree generously volunteered his services to oversee the work and Douglas Horn was willing to meet the challenge. Council and the two Captains of the period, Adam Aitchison and Leslie Mitchell worked in close co-operation and harmony with the Development Committee; Fred Hawtree fulfilled far more than was ever expected of him; but the hero of the hour was, by common consent, Douglas Horn. His contribution in terms of honest toil was immense and it seemed that the sheer confrontation of the undertaking brought to light an amazing skill and aptitude for shaping bunkers, contouring approaches and building greens. It was therefore no surprise to many when, a few years later, he earned the kind and gracious tribute in Mr Hawtree's authoritative and instructive book – *The Golf Course*. It was a notable achievement that the construction work in the 'new field' and at the new 17th hole was completed in time for the new greens and some of the tees to be sown by the late autumn of 1977. Indeed, this allowed Council to start, in the spring and summer of 1978, a general upgrading of the whole Course under the direction of Mr Hawtree. Virtually, every hole was affected in some way – additional teeing grounds, re-shaping   137 surrounds, re-modelling bunkers etc. One particular problem affecting this secondary development was the construction of the new 7th green in the middle of the old 9th fairway and the subsequent erection of teeing grounds on the old green of that hole. A temporary green was created behind the old 13th (the present 11th) green and play thereto constituted the only variation from the original Course during the development. While, in general terms, Mortonhall had, apart from some minor disturbances around the pond, been free of vandalism, the development was marked by attacks on the water storage tank which had been landscaped into the contours of the ridge at the front of the old 17th tee. Ultimately, £1,000 had to be expended in encasing the tank with a brick wall and barbed wire entanglements. Thereafter the phantom vandal departed leaving the construction to enjoy, unmolested, its nickname – Fort Horn!

The length of the new Course was established at 6548 yards – an increase of 747 yards on the previous circuit – and the holes renamed as follows:

1.	Khyber	10.	Plantation
2.	Moorfoots	11.	Gate
3.	Buckstone	12.	Meadowhead
4.	Poet's Walk	13.	Trotter's Wood
5.	Avenue	14.	Dyke
6.	Pines	15.	Braid Hills
7.	Knowe	16.	Quarry
8.	Cottage	17.	Elfin
9.	Neuk	18.	Warren

Fred Hawtree, on being asked for his reflections on the whole affair, kindly provided the following resumé in his inimitable and distinctive style:

A MORTONHALL MEMORY

It is always stimulating, not to say inspiring for the golf course architect to work in Scotland. The golfing language is precise; the committee, knowledgeable; their co-operation, whole-hearted.

Mortonhall provided all these incentives generously together with a particularly teasing problem – how to get four holes, two out and two back, in a tube one hole wide. This was the logical outcome of surrendering the peaks over which the old 14th to the 17th were played, culminating at the 18th with a vertical descent from a tee in the clouds, down to a fairway already busy with players starting up the first hole.

Fortunately No.1 was not much of a hole anyway so by starting at No.2, not far away, juggling its tees with the new 18th, creating an elevated tee for the new No.2, a 17th short hole and a few contingent modifications, the basic hurdle could be overcome. The new ground presented no difficulties. It had interesting slopes, good length, just enough width and a handsome wood in the middle.

They would not let me make any changes to stop the present 4th being crossed by a returning hole. They thought I had gone far enough already – they were probably right but I am still working on them! However, they allowed the new greens and tees necessary elsewhere to re-number the layout and mix up distances and directions. All the time, they kept a firm eye on the budget and the Membership – both highly desirable when a golf course architect is prowling around!

In all, it was a salutary experience for the designer and not too devastating for the golf course, with Douglas Horn pitching in when Seafield collapsed. Demonstrable benefits have been achieved for the layout without the ugly split right down the middle of the Membership which happens at less well-organised clubs when they see their favourite holes disappearing before their very eyes. I therefore suspect that the PR must have been pretty good, right from Day One, as well, no doubt, as all the other decisions and compromises which had to be made along the way. Perhaps the Committees involved were lucky, But fortune does not favour the faint-hearted – only the brave.

In looking back on the 'development' some 15 years later, Douglas Horn recalls the 'eternity' of the great challenge, the seven day week working necessary to overcome it, the extensive tree planting and the unstinting support which he received from Tom Meolyou (ex Seafield Landscaping), David Winton (now a Head Greenkeeper at Lees Hall, Sheffield) and Donald Menzies (now Head Greenkeeper at Mortonhall). Of the architect, he records that 'I will always treasure my association with Fred Hawtree whose brainchild the whole thing was and from whom I learned so much' and of the final creation, he speaks, with justifiable pride and conviction of Mortonhall having 'one of the finest courses in Edinburgh'.

The grass sown in the autumn of 1977 germinated and thickened to the extent that Council announced its intention to open the new Course for play in the summer of 1979. Soon this event was highlighted when the Royal Bank of Scotland indicated its desire to stage a 36 hole Professional Tournament as well as a Pro-Am Competition at Mortonhall in September 1979 to mark the 100th anniversary of its Golf Club. Mortonhall's own celebrations commenced on 25th July 1979 when a 'farewell medal' took place and continued on the following day when teams selected by the Captain and Vice Captain played the last match on the old Course. No play was allowed on Friday 27th July so as to enable the Greens staff to prepare the new Course – complete with new tee markers and flagpins – for the opening on the 28th. Appropriately, a Champagne Cocktail Party was held on the evening of 27th July. The first shot was struck at 7.30 a.m. on a glorious morning on the 28th by the Captain, Ian Isles, who had, for the first time in the history of the Club, been appointed Captain for a second term. Suitably fortified with champagne at the tee, Ian's opening drive, in the presence of his infant grandson, finished well down the fairway.

The Royal Bank Professional Tournament took place on 13th and 14th September 1979 and resulted in a three way tie on 140 shots involving J. Hay (Waterlooville), S. Torrance (Caledonian Hotel, Ayr) and R. Drummond (Turnberry). In the course of this tournament, Gordon Cunningham established a professional course record of 68. The Pro-Am Tournament took place on 16th September over 18 holes and was won by a quartet which consisted of I. Collins (Kilmacolm), T. M. Moffat, T. D. Collet and L. C. Smith with a score of 58.

The major development complete and the new Course open for play, the question must inevitably be asked – what did it all cost? The position can be summarised thus:

Cost of Land –	Original Estimate	July 1975	£30,000
Cost of Development –	do	May 1976	35,000
do	Increase by Development Committee	Dec 1976	5,000
do	Increase by Council	Sept 1978	14,000
			£84,000

Actual Expenditure to 30th November 1980 when all accounts could be held to have been settled –   £86,943.

As will be recalled, this expenditure was to be settled by a grant from Club Funds of £10,000 and a levy placed on Ordinary and Five Day Members, initially for a period of five years to 1st June 1980 and then extended for a further seven years to 1st June 1987. Clearly in the fullness of time, the cost would be eliminated but that is for another chapter. One minor yet important part of the development programme was resolved in December 1979 when formal permission was received to extend the car park into the West Drive. This enabled a one-way traffic flow through the entire parking area and Council proceeded to have appropriate lighting installed.

The Club had set its hand to a formidable task over a long period of ten years and while its success appeared manifest to all, the most exacting test is to compare all that had been achieved against the objectives set out in Eain Robertson's memorable letter to Council of 2nd July 1970 thus:

1. Price: while the price of £500 an acre doubled to £1000 in 1975 index linking would have produced a figure of £923
2. Elimination of the last 5 holes: this was achieved
3. Attitude of the older Members: the support of the older Membership was magnificent
4. Length and Disposition of Course: a yardage of over 6500 yards (Par 71) had been obtained against a target of 6250 yards and, in addition, four Par 5 and four Par 3 holes have been achieved – only two Par 4 holes over 400 yards had been produced against the target of four, but there were four over 390 yards.
5. Availability of a Practice Area: a suitable area was not possible
6. Future Siting of the Clubhouse: this was not achieved
7. Extension of Car Park: this was achieved
8. Phasing of Operations: a Course of 18 holes was always available during the development
9. Raising of Finance: Members responded nobly to the financial demands placed on them
10. Accessability of West Drive: the Drive was acquired and was to bring vast benefit to the Club in financial terms, as a means of access for Course maintenance, and in perpetual guaranteed amenity.

In the face of such a critical examination it was only just that, in March 1977, the Club acknowledged Eain Robertson's 'innate qualities of industry, enterprise and enthusiasm' and conferred Honorary Membership on him. It was, as the Captain at the time remarked, 'the least and the greatest honour which the Club could bestow'.

Normal Business

There remains little to report as far as the Course is concerned except for a number of matters prompted by the development. There is no doubt that the size of the greenkeeping operations necessitated by the development drew attention to the paucity of the existing facilities. Essentially, these consisted of a series of ramshackle huts leading on to the car park and a broken down shed near the new 2nd tee. In January 1978, the provision of an adequate shed and accommodation for the Greenkeeping staff was raised at the instance of Leslie Mitchell (Captain 1978/79), and a large and impressive building was erected opposite the pond in 1979 for a sum of £13,672. The services to this property were obtained from the Buckstone Estate and, in this, the Club was indebted to Mrs Neeley, a neighbour in Buckstone Crescent, for granting the necessary wayleave through her garden. The last five holes along the ridge of the original Course were used for play in winter of 1979/80 but thereafter the whole area was set aside as a makeshift practice ground. The green of the old 1st hole (the Marsh) was uplifted and used to create an adventurous practice putting green on the old 1st tee. With some landscaping and the planting of trees and shrubs, a very pleasing approach to the Clubhouse was obtained. In retrospect, it was remarkable that a full competition programme was maintained throughout the decade. A new record of 64 on the original Course was set in 1974 by R. A. Davie (Bruntsfield Links G.S., although a former Member of Mortonhall) in the Mortonhall Open.

As the decade drew to a close so also did a period of sound, solid and reliable service to Mortonhall. Andy & May Thomson, who had been Clubmaster and Clubmistress since 1968, decided to retire in November 1979. Their tenure of 11 years was second only to that of Mrs Taylor who reigned for 18 years between 1918 and 1936. Mrs Thomson unfailingly provided a high standard of catering and always enjoyed the whimsical challenge of various Captains for their Annual Supper menu – Jugged Hare, being one of the more memorable eccentricities! Andy, a fine golfing product of the 'Kingdom', presided over the Bar with a quiet efficiency and dignity. A presentation to this kind and gentle pair took place in the Clubhouse in December 1979 and such was the esteem and regard in which they were held that they were granted the courtesy of the Course and Clubhouse for life. Mr and Mrs R. A. Ferguson were appointed in their stead.

Following his appointment as Course Supervisor in 1976, Douglas Horn formed a happy relationship with Bob Bulloch, the Greenkeeper, and Tom Ainslie, the Professional. Sadly, towards the end of 1978, the health of 'Old Tom' began to fail and this popular and faithful servant of the Club died in January 1979 when a severe snowstorm prevented many from attending his funeral at Mortonhall Crematorium. Tom Ainslie was born in 1900 and, after a brilliant amateur record as a member of Leven Thistle in the late 1920's, became professional to the Brora Golf Club in 1931. There he remained till 1946 when he joined the Culcabock Golf Club at Inverness. During his sojourn of over 30 years in the North of Scotland, Tom established a reputation as a coach to young golfers of whom two won the Scottish Boys Championship while a third was a runner-up. On a personal level, Tom was a member of the Scottish Professional Team in 1936 and, in 1957, won his age group (55−60) in the Teachers Senior Championship. Douglas Horn was subsequently appointed as Professional and Course Supervisor.

T. G. Mitchell, who had been appointed Secretary in 1969, served the Club faithfully and well till 1972 when Council granted him non-playing Life Membership of the Club. Then followed a remarkable sequence of events − A. Young succeeded Tommy Mitchell, but after a year had to retire on the grounds of ill health. He was followed by D. Cathcart whose tenure of two months was the shortest on record. His successor, H. Greig, filled the post for a mere five months before taking up a similar appointment at Glenbervie, this leading to the commencement of P. T. Ricketts' Secretaryship in December 1974. As the administration of the Club and the scale of the operations grew and developed, Mrs C. D. Morrison was appointed in 1979 as the Secretary's Assistant. The financial affairs, outwith the provisions made for the Course Development, were, despite the severe inflationary pressures of the period, kept under control by annual increases in the subscriptions and entry monies. In 1970, these both stood at £21 but, by 1980, they had soared four-fold to £88.

At a Special General Meeting in January 1972, it was agreed that the financial year should commence on 1st December and not, as had been the case since the inception of the Club, on 1st March. As a consequence, the AGM which had previously been held in June occurred in March, the first occasion falling in March 1973. Following a revision of the Rules at the AGM in 1978, Council was empowered to increase the annual subscription by 10% without reference to the Club in General Meeting. This arrangement eliminated the practice which had become established of holding a Special General Meeting in the autumn of each year, often for the sole purpose of increasing the subscription.

As far as the Membership and its structure were concerned, several interesting developments can be noted. The total permitted Ordinary Membership stood at 500 in 1970 with a Waiting List of 15, and while it remained at this figure throughout the decade, there was a Waiting List of 162 in 1980. In March 1971, Council gave consideration to a proposal 143 that Five Day Membership be offered to any person over 65 years of age, thus eliminating the previous ten year Membership Rule. A silence ensued in the matter for three years but the AGM in 1974 approved amendments to the Rules whereby such Membership was ópen to all without qualification. At a Special General Meeting in 1975, an attempt to reduce the Ordinary Subscription by 25% to Members who were over 65 and had been Members for ten years was not carried.

As had occurred so often throughout the history of the Club, the question of Lady Members was revived. Council had proposed that proper medal facilities be granted to Lady Visitors and had, in fact, had the Course measured for the LGU in March 1973. In the Annual Report for 1973, it had the further temerity to state that it had 'applied for affiliated membership of the Scottish Ladies Golf Union'. A substantial number of Members raised objections to this action with the result that the offending paragraph was deleted from the Report and the matter referred to Council for further consideration. After much debate, Council reported to the next year's AGM that it had 'decided to take no action' in the matter. The year 1975 marked the death of the then Captain, R J. A. Michie. He had struggled valiantly in his year of office to maintain and uphold the standards and traditions of the Club he so much admired and respected. His was only the third Captaincy to meet with such tragedy – the previous occasions being the deaths of Sir Henry Trotter in 1905 and the Hon. Lord Fleming in 1945. The end of other Captaincies was more happily marked by the annual Captain's Supper. The format remained essentially the same – the Captain – his guest – the Past Captains and Council – the Toast to Mortonhall – the Reply – and the impromptu entertainment. The Suppers were marked in the Seventies by a regular 'State of the Nation' address wittily and hilariously given by Henry Braine and supported by a series of would-be 'Henry Bartons'!

In 1973, Council addressed itself to the method of electing a Captain. Previously the choice was a matter for the Captain of the day and his predecessors in office. On democratic grounds, it was agreed that in future, the choice would be made by a Committee consisting of the Retiring Captain, the Vice Captain, the three immediately preceding Captains and the three retiring Members of Council.

There can be little doubt that the ninth decade of the Club rivalled the first as the most important and traumatic in the history of Mortonhall. Many had played a part; many had given much of their money, time and expertise; some had achieved more prominence than others and yet on that scene when all were on their knees de-stoning the approaches to the greens in the new fields, all were equal.

144   The 'Mortonhall Men'? – it is not, as has been stated before, for this

Douglas Horn

Inter Club Team (1989)

generation to award accolades to the living and so it is perhaps to those who served on the Development Committee and have gone before that special mention should be made – A. Steele, A. N. Sutherland, C. Steven and Past Captains D. B. Biggs and R. J. A. Michie. Nor, too, should be forgotten that grand old man of golf who enjoyed such an Indian Summer – Tom Ainslie!

L

MORTONHALL GOLF CLUB

Champagne Cocktail Party

TO MARK THE OPENING OF THE NEW COURSE
FRIDAY, 27th JULY 1979
19.30 Hours

Price £3.00

MORTONHALL GOLF CLUB

CLUB DINNER

Friday 22nd November 1991
7.30 for 8.00pm

Black Tie

8

THE END OF THE BEGINNING
1980–1992

> Chance and change are busy ever
>
> (Bowring)

It could have been supposed that, in the year following the development of the Course, Mortonhall would have entered a period of consolidation, rest from its labours and enjoyment of its new facilities. But opportunity was once more to beckon and tempt the last generation of Mortonhall Men of the century to embark on a series of ventures which, frustrated though some were, did leave, at the end, the prospect of an exciting form of memorial.

As far as the new Course was concerned, Douglas Horn, the Course Supervisor, kept up high standards with his staff, notably head-greenkeepers, Bob Bulloch (until his retirement in 1982), Hamish Brough, now head-greenkeeper at Broomieknowe, and Donald Menzies. Contours of bunkers were improved, tees extended and particular attention paid to drainage problems. A water pumping system was sited in the new greenkeepers' sheds in 1981, and the old system at the Clubhouse dismantled. In 1985, a complete 'pop-up' sprinkler system was entrenched to serve the greens, tees and approaches at a cost of £29,440 and 1990 saw the surrender of 'Fort Horn' – the previous water supply tank at the old 17th tee. Throughout the 1980's, to meet concern for the ecology of the environment, the pond, woodlands and areas of rough ground were allowed to revert to as natural a state as possible. Many trees were planted and the landscaping of paths and teeing grounds treated with sympathy and respect. The connections   147 between the greens and tees at the 11th/12th, 15th/16th and 17th/18th holes were admittedly imperfect; gradients were improved but the ideal solution still remains a challenge.

The new Course confronted the Members with a formidable golfing challenge. They now faced one of championship length, played most frequently against a stiff Westerly air stream, which, though capable of reducing two of the leeward par 5s to virtual 4s, rendered three of the longer windward par 4s very difficult to obtain. Moreover, the subtleties of slope and distance of the four holes created by Fred Hawtree in the new ground presented intriguing problems of approach and position. Gone was the era of net scores in the low 60s and anything less than 70 was a very good round indeed. An amateur Course record of 67 (one less than the professional record) was set by George McGregor of Glencorse in 1980 and while this was equalled by a Club Member, Keith Clark in 1989, it was reduced the same year to 66 by Walker Cup golfer, Craig Cassells in the South East District Championship.

It was, however, the old West Drive to Mortonhall House, which Council had purchased in 1977, that yielded the opportunity – and the finance – to conclude the century with a substantial development at Braid Road. To appreciate the complex negotiations which took place between 1979 and 1985, it is necessary to identify two areas of woodland at the Eastern extremity of the Driveway purchased. The area to the North adjoined the first part of the 5th fairway and held potential as the site of a new Clubhouse, while that to the South adjoined Buckstone Primary School and the carriageway of Buckstone Loan East (later renamed Buckstone Circle) and carried a financial liability because of the Woodland Dedication Scheme affecting the Drive. In November 1979, Lothian Regional Council sought to acquire, for a modest sum, three acres of the South area for the expressed purpose of providing a playing field for the School. While the disposal of ground of limited use to the Club had its attractions, the then Captain, Ian Isles astutely consulted with Eain Robertson and Colin Tasker, the Club's legal and property advisers respectively, who, on consideration, foresaw the possibility of obtaining an Alternative Planning Certificate from Edinburgh District Council. The Council of the Club agreed to this proposal and appointed a Town Planning Consultant to apply for the certificate. The Planning Committee of Edinburgh District Council rejected the application but, undaunted, the Club opted to appeal against this decision to the Secretary of State for Scotland; a public local enquiry followed in 1981, with the satisfactory outcome that permission was granted for the Residential Development of the ground. Its value, now greatly enhanced, caused Lothian Regional Council to abandon its proposed acquisition, although the Club did considerately grant a rent-free lease of ground abutting Buckstone School as a play area and fire exit.

The Club's intrepid advisers, Messrs Robertson and Tasker, now approached various building firms with a view to the sale of the three acre South area lying at the East end of the Drive. In November 1982, agreement was reached with Cala Homes Ltd. for the sale of the three acres on the basis that it would relieve the Club of the cost of obtaining detailed planning permission for building ten or eleven houses. The Club would receive a percentage of the selling price of each house and would retain a vehicular access and a right to instal services from the roadway to be formed, should the Clubhouse be ever sited in the North area of the Drive near to the 5th hole. Cala Homes Ltd. had to appeal to the Secretary of State for the necessary detailed planning consent and it was not until 1985 that this was achieved, the houses built and sold to benefit the Club to the extent of £140,000. Concurrent with these negotiations, Council created in 1983 a long-term planning committee to review all aspects of the Club's affairs.

These were soon identified as follows:
1. further extension of the Course
2. location of the Clubhouse
3. facilities of the Clubhouse
4. provision of accommodation for senior members of staff and
5. a practice area

By the end of 1983, Council had learned that Mr A. R. Trotter might be willing to dispose of the ground to the South of the 14th hole, which Mr F. W. Hawtree had previously regarded as good golfing country. Some thought was accordingly given to extending the Course, creating a practice area and re-locating the Clubhouse at a central point on the Course. Unfortunately, in 1985, Mr Trotter decided that he did not wish to dispose of the ground; so there the matter ended – if only for the meantime as will be seen later. Thus thwarted, Council turned its mind to the development of the facilities of the existing Clubhouse in the comforting knowledge that the task had been considerably eased by the money from the Cala sale.

A new twist now appeared with the abolition earlier in 1985 of Development Land Tax. Council flirted – indeed for the second time since 1980 – with the prospect of selling the Clubhouse and the 1st and 18th fairways with the renewed possibility of constructing a new building on the Course adjacent to the West Drive. This was examined in depth but the proceeds of the projected sale were not considered sufficient for such a development. Following this diversion, Council presented proposals, in general outline, to the Club at the AGM of 1986 for the restoration of the original entrance to the Clubhouse, the creation   149 of a casual bar, the enlargement of the Lounge and Dining Room and sundry other improvements to meet fire regulations. These plans were reluctantly approved, subject to an assurance that, should the cost exceed £150,000, the matter would be referred back to the Club in General Meeting. A year later in May 1987, a Special General Meeting was – perhaps inevitably – called for Council to report that the costs had escalated to £163,500. After a somewhat acrimonious debate where the general consensus indicated that the expenditure did not justify the benefit to be gained, the proposals were rejected.

Undaunted, a succeeding Council revised the 1986 plans and submitted them once more to the Club in December 1988. On this occasion, the cost was restated at £203,000 but, after a convincing presentation, the proposals were approved. This, however, was not the end of the affair. The lowest tender received in the Summer of 1989 disclosed a figure of £292,000 and, while Council revised this to £270,000, there was no option but to obtain further approval at a General Meeting. This was called in September 1989 but, confronted by a Membership hostile to the increased costs, Council lost the day. Council was in a dilemma. The proceeds of the sale of land to Cala had amounted to approximately £140,000 but this was subject to tax if not 'rolled over' into capital expenditure within three years. With commendable speed, Council entered into a contract to build a house for the Clubmistress on the site of the old Lodge on the West Drive and a new building in the car park to house greenkeeping equipment and the 'buggies' which had been gifted to the Club by Arthur Eddell and the widow of Graeme Menzies. This latter building quickly earned the sobriquet 'The Temple'.

But this was still not the end of the affair – Mortonhall Men are made of sterner stuff. In 1990, a new Council reconsidered the future of the Clubhouse as the top flat was no longer occupied by live-in staff but, more importantly, in the light of the response to a searching questionnaire issued to Members. In November 1990, an imaginative scheme to extend the Clubhouse Southwards – the first proposal ever to be made in this direction – was prepared for submission at a Special General Meeting. The stated purpose was:

1. to improve Lounge facilities for Members dressed in casual attire
2. to improve changing facilities for Visitors
3. to improve changing facilities for Juniors and
4. to construct a new Professional's Shop

The total cost was estimated at £250,000 and, while the initial finance was to be raised by borrowing, Members would be required to meet the ultimate cost by an annual levy of £75 over six years. Some 48 hours, however, before the Meeting took place, Mr A. R. Trotter intimated that he was prepared to enter into negotiations with the Club for the sale of 45 acres or thereby to the South of the 14th hole. This proposal, with so many incalculable benefits to Mortonhall, far outweighed the advantages of extending the Clubhouse. The Captain at once withdrew Council's submission at the Special Meeting and informed the Members of the dramatic news that had so recently reached him.

Some years prior to these major schemes for the Clubhouse, a tasteful refurbishment of the Lounge took place. The project was first mooted in October 1981 and, following the presentation of an outline scheme costing £15,000 to Council in May 1982, a Special Committee, under the Chairmanship of the then Vice-Captain, Jim Saunders, was set up to oversee the operation. A Design Consultant, Mr B. Shields, was appointed; work commenced in November 1982, at a higher cost of £20,000 inclusive of new furniture, and was completed within one month. The final result was greeted with approval – the subtle blend of colour and lighting on the new furniture, carpet and wall fabrics, combined well with the plants and paintings. As far as the latter were concerned, the Club began to amass a collection, which, in their different styles, greatly enhanced the internal appearance of the Clubhouse. To the four excellent paintings of scenes on the Course, purchased out of a legacy by the late Herriot Macdonald, were added six somewhat controversial etchings, colour washed, by Mr Boyd Denver. The original line drawings had been produced for the extension to the Clubhouse in 1968 and had lain untouched since that time. Nonetheless, the pictures were of Mortonhall and were, to the uncritical eye, not displeasing. Two further paintings of depth and sensitivity – one of the Clubhouse and the other of the pond looking West – by the distinguished London artist, Brenda Evans, were donated in 1983 by Eain Robertson. The original Christmas Card, sent to Members of the Club serving in the Armed Forces in the First World War, was framed by an anonymous donor and hung in the Dining Room, while, in 1985, Dr Kenneth Robertson, in a generous gesture, devoted his artistic skill to reproducing, in colour, the Club's copy of Tom Scott's sketch – 'The Golf Stream'. In 1989, attention turned to the Locker Room, and the 'boxes', installed there almost a century ago, were restored in a dark varnish, re-numbered and equipped with uniform padlocks.

In the Clubhouse, Mr & Mrs Ferguson resigned in September 1980 after ten months service, to be succeeded by Mrs Sheila Niven, who had earlier been a popular member of the bar staff and who now brought a cheerful personality to assist in running various functions. Prominent amongst these were the Winter bridge evenings, the Burns Suppers, notable for the contributions of Tom Speirs (the 'Piper') and Neil Hay ('Tam o' Shanter') and the monthly 'international' evenings, where   151 menus from various countries were presented. The Captain's Supper continued as a feature of the Council's year, enlivened by various 'born-again' Bartons. Best remembered of these was Fred Gray (Captain 1982/83) who between 1982 and 1988, the year of his death, presented his annual account of the 'Mortonhall Mafia'. The scene was set in the Clubhouse, where, on a Sunday afternoon, 'an average Member, 5ft 10 inches in height, above average weight, married, one wife and 2.4 children, education average but vocabulary more limited than average, seated at the long window table in the Lounge, overlooking the 18th fairway, surrounded by his friends' holds forth thus:

> This bloody Club's a bloody cuss
> We all should make a bloody fuss
> For no one cares for us
> In Bloody Mortonhall

He proceeds in this way to denigrate the Course and the facilities of the Clubhouse till he realises he is speaking to a visitor. His mood changes at once and the diatribe concludes thus:

> What's that? You're a guest? It's a bloody shame
> Hold on!! *I* would never give the Club a bad name
> For my money, it's the best bloody Club in the game
> Is Bloody Mortonhall

The 'Best of Fred', together with other anonymous efforts, appears in Appendix I.

In 1984, the annual Club Dinner was revived and this proved to be a most popular event. In 1987, the Secretary of State for Scotland, the Right Hon. Malcolm Rifkind Q.C., M.P., did the Club the honour of being its principal guest.

Distinction was brought to the Club by Kenny Gray, a junior internationalist in 1979, who represented Scotland at youth level in 1980 and 1981 and by Keith McCall, who won the British Universities Championship in 1982 and subsequently became Club Champion in 1987 and 1988.

The Mortonhall teams at Senior and Junior level acquitted themselves with much credit through the 1980s. In 1987, the Senior team, Keith Clark, John Evans, Duncan Forbes and Keith McCall, defeated Craigmillar Park at Baberton to win the Lothian Inter-Club Tournament for the fifth time for Mortonhall while the Junior Team, represented by Ian Clark, Fraser Clark, Peter Cockburn, David Fair, Michael Ferguson, Stephen Ferguson, Paul Macari, Gavin Millar and Michael Paterson won the Edinburgh Junior Summer League. Much of the credit for the successes of all Mortonhall teams of the period was due to a series of Team Captains and Selectors – Sandy Anderson, Ross Dawson, Jim Fair, Ian McLaren, Graeme Stark and David Wilson. During the 1980's, the reputation and the quality of the Course was steadily recognised, as evidenced by the District and National Championships which it attracted, including the Scottish Youths Championship (1983), the Lothians Championship (1984), the South East District Championship (1989, 1990, 1991) and the Scottish Police Championship (1989). For 1992, the Centenary Year, the Scottish Golf Union has paid the Club the honour of choosing Mortonhall for the final rounds of the Scottish Amateur Stroke-Play Championship.

Within the period under review, the Membership of the Club was extended to embrace several new categories. In June 1980, the possibility of House Membership was touched on – and dropped as quickly and mysteriously as it was raised – but in 1991 Council did provide this form of Membership for the wives of Members. In 1981, a new category of Membership was created – Special Ordinary Members – to allow those over 65 years of age and with more than 25 years Membership to pay a subscription at half the Ordinary rate. In 1984, a 'Student Membership' category was created for Junior Members who had reached their 20th birthday but were engaged on a course of full time education. This Membership, at one third of the Ordinary rate, would cease on the earlier of the 24th birthday or the completion of education. In 1990 this class was replaced by a 'Youth Membership' which Juniors, having attained their 18th birthdays, could enjoy until the age of 22 at two thirds of the Ordinary Subscription. Concurrently the rate payable by Junior Members was raised from one quarter to one third of the Ordinary Subscription. In 1981, the Club granted Honorary Membership to Ian Isles in recognition of his long and substantial contribution to the Club, culminating in his second Captaincy when, with characteristic poise and efficiency, he had supervised the transition to the new Course. In 1982, the 90th Anniversary of the Club was marked by a Champagne Party on 24th April and by the Trustees raising of the Club Flag on the actual anniversary date, the 29th April 1982. The occasion was further commemorated by the gift of a handsome gavel by the Captain, Fred Gray.

In the mundane field of finance and administration, subscriptions continued to show a relentless increase from £88 in 1980 to approximately £285 in 1992. In the early 'eighties the Club's finances were sound enough to allow repayment in 1982 of the outstanding loans from Members for 'Development' and to abandon the collection of development levies of £12 per Ordinary Member from December 1981 instead of 1986. Regrettably, cash resources, despite the injection of the proceeds of the 'Cala sale', came under heavy pressure towards the end of the century with substantial capital expenditure on Course Equipment (including the 'Pop-up' system) of approximately £70,000 and at the Clubhouse and its environs (including the house for the Clubmistress and the 'Temple') of approximately £200,000. A somewhat controversial innovation occurred in 1980 when a Special General Meeting approved by a majority of 80 to 42 a scheme whereby Members were obliged to buy vouchers to the value of £30 to be redeemed against purchases from the Bar or meals in the Dining Room. The initial value of these vouchers has remained unchanged and a formal motion to continue the system has been carried unanimously at each subsequent AGM.

In 1985, a Centenary Committee was formed under Pat Colledge with an original membership of the then Captain and Vice Captain, Mike James and George Reid. Successive Captains and Vice-Captains automatically joined the Committee and, in 1987, seven Members with specialist knowledge and skills were appointed. The full Committee ultimately comprised:

W .G. P. Colledge	*Chairman*
M. G. James	
G. Reid	
P. G. Duncanson	
P. H. Knowles	
A. C. McNish	
J. Saunders	
G. F. Bolton	– Wines & Catering
R. C. B. Forman	– Social Events
K. D. Isles	– Publicity & Marketing
M. J. R. McCreath	– Finance
L. D. Mitchell	– Technical Services
C. M. Tasker	– Sponsorship
D. W. M. Thomson	– Tournaments

A considerable number of meetings were held and, indeed as this volume goes to press, are still being held. Many other Members serve on Sub-Committees and a programme of competitions as well as social, historic and celebratory events has been designed to enable all Members to participate. The financing of the programme is being met by annual allocations from Club funds since 1985, sponsorships, donations and contributions by Members.

Mortonhall has been well served by its Secretariat. The Secretary is the link between one Council and another, the confidant of Captains and, to a new Captain, 'the guide, counsellor and friend'; he it is who maintains standards of dress and decorum, safeguards the Club's records and possessions and defends its employees; he it is who welcomes guests, placates the intemperate Member and sustains others in time of difficulty and stress; he it is who promotes the Club's interests and remains the guardian of its soul. None who served the Club in this unique and lonely role has failed it, and special mention must be made of those who had a lengthy term of office, or endured particular trials. On this score D. W. Walker, J. Anderson, F. W. Campbell, W. M. Berrie, T. P. J. Nicolson and T. G. Mitchell are not forgotten. To them must be added the name of Peter T. Ricketts, whose term of office of 19 years will extend into the second 'century' and whose portrayal of Santa Claus at the Christmas Party has delighted a generation of Members' children. It was largely at the initiative of Peter and his assistant, Christine Morrison, that the Club's administrative and Membership records, together with the intricacies of the new handicapping scheme introduced in 1983, were incorporated within a computer system, both admired and emulated by other Clubs in the Lothians.

In 1980, the Ordinary Membership stood at 500 with a Waiting List of 162, while at the end of the first 100 years, it still totalled 500 with 120 Members waiting to join in its next century.

The Mortonhall Men of this generation? – such could be an epitaph for Danny Barron, Dr George Brewster, Jim Brydon, Robert Forsyth, Fred Gray, Sheriff Lillie, Willie Mailer, Jack Martin, Willie McFarlane, Willie Murray, Terry O'Riordan, David Reid, David Ross, Pat Scott, George Stark and Jack Wilson. None survived to see the new century but all will be remembered by those who did. And yet beyond these and those to whom the title has already been accorded, there are many others who, privileged to serve on Council, gladly gave of their time from family, friends and golf as a duty to be done.

Four generations of 'Mortonhall Men' have seen in their time the Clubhouse enlarged yet unchanged, the Course extended and yet still where it began. Above all, the Club remains a place for sport, recreation, fresh air and good health. It is still a forum for fellowship, friendship, fun and laughter and yet offers a haven for peace, refreshment, hope and good cheer.

So History has taken its 18-hole course. Or has it?
Surely, Mortonhall golfers can look to the future and rejoice.

'For there is good news yet to hear and fine things to be seen
Before we go to Paradise to putt on the ultimate green.'

(*With apologies to* G. K. Chesterton)

155

EPILOGUE

Now fades the glimmering landscape on the sight
And all the air a solemn stillness holds

(Gray)

The last match has been played – the last shot struck – the last putt holed
– and the flag lowered in an April evening.

Here it has been where the 'Mortonhall Men' have golfed for 100
years not simply for winning or losing but for observing within each
contest of skill and nerve, a convention of customs and courtesies which,
through the centuries, have enriched and ennobled the game of golf.

156

APPENDICES

THE TROTTERS OF MORTONHALL

1. Major General Sir Henry Trotter, G.C.V.O., 11th of Mortonhall
   late Colonel Commanding Grenadier Guards,
   Major General – Home District
   Born 5th January 1844: Died 16th July 1905
   Married 25th May 1866 to the Hon Eva Gifford

Algernon Richard	Gerald Frederic	Edward Henry
(*see 2 below*)	C.B., C.M.G., C.V.O.	D.S.O.
	C.B.E., D.S.O.	Lieutenant Colonel
	Brigadier General, *late*	Grenadier Guards
	Grenadier Guards	Born 1st December 1
	Born 21st July 1871	Killed in Action
	Died 14th June 1945	8th July 1916

2. Colonel Algernon Richard Trotter, D.S.O., M.V.O., 12th of Mortonha
   Colonel 2nd Life Guards
   Born 20th June 1870
   Died 23rd December 1945
   Married 22nd July 1901 to Lady Edith Mary Montgomerie

Henry Redvers	George Richard	Thomas
(*see 3 below*)	Lieutenant Colonel	Lieutenant Colonel
	Royal Scots Greys	60th Rifles
	Born 26th February 1906	Born 11th March 19(
	Died 24th September 1970	Died 1st September 1

3. Henry Redvers Trotter, T.D. 13th of Mortonhall
   Major Notts Sherwood Rangers Yeomanry
   Born 29th June 1902
   Died 6th November 1962
   Married 12th July 1937 to Rona Margaret Murray

Alexander Richard	John Algernon Henry	Fiona Margaret
(*see 4 below*)	Born 12th May 1948	Born 12th April 19

4. Alexander Richard Trotter, 14th of Mortonhall
   Major Royal Scots Greys
   Born 20th February 1939
   Married to Julia Greenwell

Henry	Edward	Rupert
Born 27th March 1972	Born 25th November 1973	Born 7th February

Reginald Baird
Captain
Cameronian Highlanders
Born 25th March 1874
Killed in Action
9th May 1915

Meta m. A. C. Baillie
Born 25th February 1868
Died 23rd April 1944

John
Lieutenant Colonel
Grenadier Guards
Born 31st December 1913
Died 27th October 1983

Joan Catherine m. F. E. S. Beilby
Born 28th June 1903
Died 4th July 1958

List of Members
referred to in,
and signed with reference to,
The foregoing Constitution.

	Name.	Address.
1	Duncan MacLaren, S.S.C.,	Glenquaich Lodge, Cluny Gardens.
2	William Tait, S.S.C.,	7 North St. David Street.
3	A. J. Hodge,	8 Braidburn Terrace.
4	William C. Sturrock,	63 Craiglea Drive.
5	J. Grieve,	110 Craiglea Drive.
6	George More,	29 Morningside Drive.
7	George Cowan, S.S.C.,	41 Morningside Drive.
8	George Whigham,	35 Morningside Drive.
9	Francis S. Cownie, S.S.C.,	Braid Road.
10	Henry Bower, S.S.C.,	40 Gillespie Crescent.
11	George A. Keates,	1 St. Clair Terrace.
12	John T. Watson,	6 Bruntsfield Gardens.
13	Andrew Ker,	23 Craiglea Drive.
14	William Murray,	Morningside Drive.
15	Alex: Black,	272 Morningside Road.
16	George Adam,	47 Morningside Drive.
17	John Wilson, C.A.,	4 Morningside Gardens.
18	A. M. Runciman,	9 St. Fillans Terrace.

160

	Name.	Address.
19	James Rose,	54 Morningside Drive.
20	William Anderson,	77 Comiston Road.
21	Thomas V. Pollock,	71 Comiston Road.
22	David Hunter,	Taymount, Nile Grove.
23	Charles J. Ray,	15 St. Ronan's Terrace.
24	Thomas L. Walker,	9 Crawford Road.
25	John Johnston,	304 Morningside Road.
26	James Walker, S.S.C.,	1 St. Ronan's Terrace.
27	J. A. Fraser Brand,	Hebron Bank, Canaan Lane.
28	Alan C. Sym, M.D.,	144 Morningside Road.
29	J. Kenyon Lees,	32 Woodburn Terrace.
30	D. W. Walker, S.S.C.,	4 Braidburn Terrace.
31	William H. Ross,	Gowanside, Cluny Gardens.
32	William Lindsay,	3 Woodburn Terrace.
33	William Stobie Jr,	28 Grange Road.
34	J. Ogilvy Shepherd,	83 Comiston Road.
35	Graham H. Barclay,	16 Comiston Road.
36	Hew Morrison,	7 Hermitage Terrace.
37	Henry Brown,	54 Craiglea Drive.
38	R. S. Aitchison, C.A.,	15 Morningside Place.
39	J. M. Roberts,	18 Woodburn Terrace.
40	J. Stuart Gowans, C.A.,	33 Charlotte Square.
41	R. Fleming Johnston, W.S.,	Goshen House, Canaan Lane.
42	Thomas Scott,	33 Woodburn Terrace.

M

	Name.	Address.
43	William Paterson,	17 Duke Street.
44	J. A. Nolan,	4 Oxford Street.
45	W. S. Fleming,	Hillside, Braid Road.
46	Thomas Paul,	62 Comiston Road.
47	James Paul,	262 Morrison Street.
48	Andrew Usher,	Blackford Park, So. Oswald Road
49	Harold B. Carlyon,	16 Hartington Gardens.
50	R. J. B. Tait,	7 Ardmillan Terrace.
51	George Fleming,	10 West Castle Road.
52	Walter Dickson,	51 Dick Place.
53	F. Jas. Walden,	Australasian Club.
54	Rev. Wm Stevenson,	6 Montpelier, Viewforth.
55	Arthur Guthrie, S.S.C.,	153 Warrender Park Road.
56	John Macniven,	Cluny Drive.
57	J. Michael Brown,	25 Nile Grove.
58	William M. Manson,	304 Morningside Road.
59	David Anderson, Adv.,	8 Great King Street.
60	D. Kerr,	9 Greenbank Terrace.
61	Professor Don. Mackinnon,	1 Merchiston Place.
62	Robert Aitken,	211 Morningside Road.
63	Robert Cumming, S.S.C.,	15 Lonsdale Terrace.
64	James M. Johnston,	15 Braid Crescent.
65	G. Scott Ranken,	22 Kilmaurs Road.
66	J. H. Forrester,	6 Braidburn Crescent.

162

	Name.	Address.
67	John Rose,	274 Morningside Road.
68	Alexander Croll,	3 Belhaven Terrace.
69	C. W. Donald, M.B.,	Konsgarth, Braid Road
70	John Heggie,	1 Greenbank Terrace.
71	James Clark,	6 Woodburn Terrace.
72	J. Keith Chisholm,	15 Duke Street.
73	C. M. Henderson,	4 Savile Terrace.
74	A. N. Bogle,	University Settlement.
75	Martin McCall Jr.,	5 Lonsdale Terrace.
76	G. H. Elliot,	8 Killbank Terrace.
77	George Elgin,	15 Braidburn Terrace.
78	John White,	79 Craiglea Drive.
79	Archibald Hodge,	8 Braidburn Terrace.
80	Alexander Hay,	33 Cluny Gardens.
81	John Hay,	33 Cluny Gardens.
82	W. P. Sherriff,	6 Morningside Park.
83	James Cowan,	14 Gladstone Terrace.
84	J. Ogilvie Kemp, Adv.,	12 Dublin Street.
85	J. S. Smith,	4 Bath Place, Portobello.
86	Adam Craigie,	165 Ferry Road.
87	W. M. Ritchie,	115 George Street.
88	J. Ogilvie Grey,	37 Gilmore Place.
89	C. J. Munro, C.A.,	46 Hanover Street.
90	Charles Hunter,	Taymount, Nile Grove.

163

	Name.	Address.
91	W. S. Currie,	51 Leamington Terrace.
92	W. M. Welsh,	1 Waterloo Place.
93	A. D. Macpherson,	131 Warrender Park Road.
94	D. Purves,	3 Nile Grove.
95	A. Geoghegan,	26 Cockburn Street.
96	James Barclay,	29 Polwarth Gardens.
97	W. H. Hopkinson,	146 Morningside Road.
98	George F. Scott, S.S.C.,	27 Mayfield Terrace.
99	Charles F. Scott,	27 Mayfield Terrace.
100	L. D. Cotson,	26 Moston Terrace.
101	John Paton,	16 Spottiswoode Street.
102	W. West Kerr,	29 Comiston Road.
103	Andrew Peattie,	16 Craiglea Drive.
104	Alexander Riach,	16 Abercorn Crescent.
105	G. P. Turner,	9 Braidburn Terrace.
106	W. N. Milne,	9 Braidburn Terrace.
107	William Penman, C.E.,	6 Marchhall Crescent.
108	James Coventry,	21 Atholl Crescent.
109	J. Beaton,	55 Craiglea Drive.
110	P. J. Urquhart,	3 Marchmont Street.
111	J. H. Brown,	15 Hope Park Terrace.
112	W. J. Rennie,	64 Princes Street.
113	J. J. Richardson,	10 Napier Road.
114	John F. Richardson,	10 Napier Road.

164

	Name.	Address.
115	H. W. Walker,	6 Blantyre Terrace.
116	A. E. Scougall,	12 Blantyre Terrace.
117	John Anderson,	28 Millhill, Musselburgh.
118	Charles Fell Brown,	19 George Street.
119	W. Birnie Rhind,	St. Helen's, Cambridge Street
120	C. D. Menzies,	6 Braid Avenue.
121	Councillor A. D. MacKenzie,	6 Hartington Gardens.
122	James E. MacLachlan,	Vellore, Craigmillar Park.
123	M. Isaacs,	13 Crawfurd Road.
124	Cossar MacKenzie,	3 Westhall Gardens.
125	W. D. Stewart,	145 Bruntsfield Place.
126	Allan Macdougall,	62 Comiston Road.
127	I. W. H. Smith,	36 Greenhill Gardens.
128	John Sibbald, M.D.,	3 St. Margaret's Road.
129	A. Cromb,	20 Pitt Street.
130	Stephen Mickel,	25 Mentone Terrace.
131	Robert Galloway,	16 Braidburn Crescent.
132	W. J. Moffat,	38 Ann Street.
133	John Byers,	10 Parkside Terrace.
134	T. Bennet Clark, C.A.,	Comiston House.
135	A. B. Campbell,	Milleare, Gillsland Road
136	Hugh S. Smith,	11 Nelson Street.
137	William Lawson,	35 Quality Street, Leith
138	James Martin, S.S.C.,	50 Lauriston Place.

	Name.	Address.
139	J. Stewart Gellatly, S.S.C.,	36 St. Alban's Road.
140	James D. Paterson,	10 Ethel Terrace.
141	John Turner,	23 Dalhousie Terrace.
142	Robert Melrose,	6 Greenhill Gardens.
143	Robert Ellis,	11 Albert Terrace.
144	William Gibson,	7 Alvanley Terrace.
145	George Morris,	339 High Street.
146	David Sime,	27 Dundas Street.
147	James Aylon, S.S.C.,	46 Hanover Street.
148	Alexander Aylon,	4 Mardale Crescent.
149	James Ballantine,	4 Westhall Gardens.
150	John Wallace,	122 George Street.
151	Sydney Mitchell,	34 Drummond Place.
152	John M. Rusk, S.S.C.,	7 Alvanley Terrace.
153	John Battleman,	35 Alva Street.
154	John S. Ferrier,	20 Blantyre Terrace.
155	J. R. Burgess,	Merchiston Castle.
156	R. B. Webber,	Merchiston Castle.
157	Andrew Henderson,	22 Nile Grove.
158	R. G. Wilson,	23 Lauder Road.
159	Dr. Squire W. Allen,	40 Queen Street.
160	William Lees,	12 Morningside Place.
161	St. Clair Cunningham,	March Hall, Marchhall Road.
162	Knight Watson, S.S.C.,	18 Woodburn Terrace.

166

	Name.	Address
163	James Ford,	11 Abbotsford Park.
164	John Macrae,	110 Princes Street.
165	Brigade Surg: John Houston	15 George Square.
166	Patrick Thomson,	16 Craiglea Drive.
167	Rev. George Dodds, B.D.,	F.C. Manse, Liberton.
168	L. M. More,	20 South St David Street.
169	W. J. Haig Scott, S.S.C.,	46 Constitution Street, Leith.
170	D. Menzies, M.B.,	20 Rutland Square.
171	J. B. Young, C.E.,	4 Greenhill Terrace.
172	J. McIntyre,	19 Warrender Park Terrace.
173	George Sinclair,	9 Pilrig Street.
174	J. Andrew, B.A.,	112 Findhorn Place.
175	Rev. W. Whyte Smith, B.D.,	34 Blacket Place.
176	William Ramsay,	2 Hermitage Terrace.
177	Charles Moxon,	21 Comiston Road.
178	T. J. Thyne, M.D.,	2 Dean Terrace.
179	J. G. Girdwood,	65 Queen Street.
180	George Lorimer,	2 Abbotsford Crescent.
181	M. M. Scott,	163 Bruntsfield Place.
182	David Dougal, W.S.,	21 Castle Street.
183	A. M. Douglas,	26 Lauriston Gardens.
184	F. W. N. Haultain, M.D.,	17 Rutland Street.
185	Alexander Gowans,	90 Gordon Street, Glasgow.
186	R. Inglis Watson,	2 Hanover Street.

167

	Name	Address.
187	John Smart,	20 Westhall Gardens.
188	Rev. W. M. Falconer, M.A.,	Garonne House, West Mayfield.
189	William Herse,	21 Greenhill Gardens.
190	David Macfarlane,	8 Chambers Street.
191	John F. Cathcart,	19 Belgrave Crescent.
192	John Taylor,	13 Greenhill Terrace.
193	James Mason,	3 Strathearn Road.
194	Alexander Gordon, S.S.C.	34 Chalmers Street.
195	Rev. George Laing,	17 Buckingham Terrace.
196	Colonel Chas. McInroy,	56 Dick Place.
197	R. Macaulay,	49 Dick Place.
198	I. G. Inglis,	10 Dick Place.
199	Robert Watson, B.L.,	17 Mayfield Road.
200	James I. Fulton,	22 Fountainhall Road.

D Maclaren
? Captain

168

APPENDIX C

THE HONORARY MEMBERS

Date of Election

1892	Colonel Henry Trotter of Mortonhall
	D. F. Mackenzie, Factor to Colonel Henry Trotter
1896	Lieut. Algernon Richard Trotter, 2nd Life Guards
	Lieut. Gerald Frederic Trotter, Grenadier Guards
	Lieut. Edward Henry Trotter, Grenadier Guards
	Lieut. Reginald Baird Trotter, Royal Scots
1897	A. J. T. Allan, Amateur Champion (for 1 year only)
1902	John W. Chesser S.S.C., Captain of Edinburgh Burgess Golf Club
1919	Admiral Sir Charles Madden, C-in-C, Atlantic Fleet
	Vice-Admiral Sir Sydney R. Freemantle
1924	Major Henry Redvers Trotter, Notts Sherwood Rangers
	Duncan MacLaren, First Captain of Mortonhall
1925	G. Lorimer, Past Captain & Original Member
	A. Hay, Original Member
1928	HRH The Duke of Windsor
1930	T. L. Walker, Original Member
1931	Dr T. R. Ronaldson, Past Captain
	Rev. G. Dodds, Original Member
1942	R. Aitken, Original Member (50 Years)
	W. S. Currie, Original Member (50 Years)
	W. Gibson, Original Member (50 Years)
	J. O. Grey, Original Member (50 Years)
	R. Millar
	W. West Kerr, Past Captain & Original Member (50 Years)
	J. M. Rusk, Original Member (50 Years)
	J. M. Brown, Artist & Original Member (50 Years)
	A. M. Runciman, Original Member (50 Years)
1948	W. Kinloch Anderson, Past Captain
	W. H. Hamilton, Past Captain

1949	T. Forbes MacLennan, Past Captain
1951	Dr J. A. H. Duncan
	J. Stevenson
	A. Cowan
	T. P. Manuel
	R. T. G. Paterson
	J. Smail
1952	Francis Ouimet, American Open & Amateur Champion
1954	W. Willis Mackenzie, Past Captain & Scottish Amateur Champion
1957	W. C. White, Past Captain
1962	J. M. Graham, Past Captain
1964	★ Lieut. A. R. Trotter, Royal Scots Greys
	F. W. Campbell, Former Secretary
	A. Dougal, Trustee
	H. W. McIntosh
	J. L. White
1966	Sir Alexander Brebner
	A. D. Mackenzie
1969	A. H. MacDonald, Trustee
	T. M. Jinkins, Trustee
1970	Dr J. R. Peddie, Past Captain
1971	R. E. Croall, Past Captain & Trustee
1977	★ E. B. Robertson, Past Captain & Trustee
1981	★ I. Isles, Past Captain

★ Surviving Honorary Members

171

THE CAPTAINS

1892–95	Duncan MacLaren	1942–44	T. F. MacLennan
1895–97	Hon. Lord Stormonth Darling	1944–45	Hon. Lord Fleming
1897–98	F. W. N. Haultain		*(Died in Office)*
1898–1900	Sir Mitchell Thomson Bt.	1945–47	J. R. Peddie
1900–01	J. Ainslie	1947–49	J. M. Graham
1901–02	Rev. W. Whyte Smith	1949–51	W. Willis Mackenzie
1902–05	G. L. Crole	1951–53	W. H. Mackenzie
1905–06	Sir Henry Trotter	1953–55	D. S. Anderson
	(Died in Office)	1955–57	R. E. Croall
1906–07	D. A. Tod	1957–59	H. Barton
1907–08	T. R. Ronaldson	1959–61	R. H. Hood
1908–09	G. Lorimer	1961–63	H. M. Braine
1909–10	Sir Richard Lodge	1963–65	I. Isles
1910–11	H. Brown	1965–67	J. E. H. Pyper
1911–12	W. Inman	1967–68	J. M. B. Wilson
1912–13	Sir Thomas S. Clouston	1968–69	T. G. O'Riordan
1913–14	J. S. Gowans	1969–70	D. B. Biggs
1914–16	Rev. M. C. Taylor	1970–71	E. B. Robertson
1916–18	W. Greenhill	1971–72	A. R. Bade
1918–20	C. F. Scott	1972–73	G. Y. Craig
1920–21	J. Greig	1973–74	T. P. J. Nicolson
1921–22	D. S. Stewart	1974–75	R. J. A. Michie
1922–23	A. Mackenzie		*(Died in Office)*
1923–25	G. Morris	1975–76	J. J. Hunter
1925–27	W. B. Taylor	1976–77	W. G. P. Colledge
1927–28	J. A. S. Millar	1977–78	A. M. Aitchison
1928–30	D. Dougal	1978–79	L. D. Mitchell
1930–31	G. W. Simla Paterson	1979–80	I. Isles
1931–33	A. MacKelvie	1980–81	J. Thomson
1933–34	W. H. Hamilton	1981–82	A. C. McNish
1934–35	Hon. Lord Pitman	1982–83	F. M. M. Gray
1935–36	R. D. Rainie	1983–84	J. Saunders
1936–38	W. West Kerr	1984–86	M. G. James
1938–39	Sir John Jeffrey	1986–88	G. Reid
1939–40	W. Kinloch Anderson	1988–90	P. G. Duncanson
1940–42	W. C. White	1990–92	P. H. Knowles

THE CHAMPIONS

1913	W. C. White	1957	F. G. Dewar
1914	W. C. White	1958	F. G. Dewar
1915/19	*No competition due to war*	1959	F. G. Dewar
1920	W. C. White	1960	K. D. T. Hall
1921	Dr C. S. Nimmo	1961	R. P. White
1922	A. M. C. Brown	1962	G. E. Robertson
1923	W. C. White	1963	D. B. Wilson
1924	W. H. Hamilton	1964	G. E. Robertson
1925	W. D. McNiven	1965	R. A. Davie
1926	W. C. White	1966	A. F. Brown
1927	J. A. Clark	1967	I. F. Johnston
1928	J. McCredie	1968	D. M. Forbes
1929	W. Willis MacKenzie	1969	J. A. Mather
1930	J. McCredie	1970	L. D. Mitchell
1931	W.H. Taylor	1971	A. Hardie
1932	J. McCredie	1972	A. C. McNish
1933	J. A. Clark	1973	L. D. Mitchell
1934	W. H. Taylor	1974	K. T. R. Clark
1935	J. McCredie	1975	J. C. Leckie
1936	J. McCredie	1976	M. R. Scott
1937	I. A. Williamson	1977	M. R. Scott
1938	I. A. Williamson	1978	A. C. McNish
1939	J. McCredie	1979	D. W. M. Thomson
1940/45	*No competition due to war*	1980	K. T. R. Clark
1946	A. W. Jamieson	1981	D. W. M. Thomson
1947	I. A. Williamson	1982	A. C. McNish
1948	I. A. Williamson	1983	I. D. Currie
1949	H. P. Crosbie	1984	J. K. Evans
1950	I. A. Williamson	1985	M. R. Scott
1951	J. H. McLeod	1986	J. K. Evans
1952	J. H. McLeod	1987	K. G. McCall
1953	J. H. McLeod	1988	K. G. McCall
1954	I. S. Dougal	1989	D. M. Forbes
1955	N. McLean	1990	K. T. R. Clark
1956	H. P. Crosbie	1991	A. C. McNish

THE OFFICIALS

THE SECRETARIES

Date of Appointment

1892	W. C. Sturrock
1892	D. W. Walker
1903	D. MacLaren (Interim)
1904	J. Anderson (Retired 1932)

(*Note*: The post of Secretary was combined with that of Treasurer in 1932)

THE TREASURERS

Date of Appointment

1892	A. Ker
1924	R. D. Rainie (Interim)
1924	F. W. Campbell

(*Note*: The post of Treasurer was combined with that of Secretary in 1932)

THE SECRETARIES & TREASURERS

Date of Appointment

1932	F. W. Campbell
1950	W. M. Berrie (Died 1959)
1959	D. S. Berrie (Interim)
1959	A. J. Cowan
1959	T. P. J. Nicolson
1968	T. A. Rankin (Asst. Secretary – resigned 1971)
1969	T. G. Mitchell
1973	A. Young
1974	D. Cathcart
1974	H. Greig
1974	P. T. Ricketts
1979	Mrs C. D. Morrison (Secretary's Assistant)

THE AUDITORS

Date of Appointment

1892	J. S. Gowans
1904	R. D. Rainie
1934	Messrs Brewis, Rainie & Boyd
1946	W. M. Berrie
1950	D. S. Anderson
1953	J. Whitton
1956	D. S. Anderson
1964	J. Whitton
1970	R. J. R. Richardson
1989	Messrs Coopers & Lybrand Deloitte

THE PROFESSIONALS

Date of Appointment

1894	J. Simpson (Died 1895)
1900	W. Cunningham
1904	T. Drummond
1909	R. B. Martin
1910	D. P. Watt (Died of wounds in First World War 1917)
1919	A. Drummond
1953	A. Cafferty (Resigned 1954)
1963	T. Ainslie
1979	D. B. Horn

THE GREENKEEPERS

Date of Appointment

1892	P. Lees
1894	J. Durie
1900	W. Cunningham
1908	W. H. White
1911	A. Webster
1913	A. Thomson
1957	R. Bulloch (Retired 1981)
1979	D. B. Horn (Course Manager)
1984	H. Brough
1987	D. Menzies

THE CLUBMASTERS AND CLUBMISTRESSES

Date of Appointment

1892	Mrs P. Lees
1893	Mr & Mrs J. Sales
1896	W. Cockburn (Died in 1897)
1897	Mrs W. Cockburn
1906	Mrs A. Miller
1912	Miss B. Campbell
1918	Mrs J. Taylor
1936	Mrs Gray
1945	Mrs Selkirk
1953	Mr & Mrs J. Armstrong
1956	Miss Baird
1957	Mr & Mrs White
1959	Mr H. Morton
1963	Mr & Mrs J. Dodds
1968	Mr & Mrs A. Thomson
1979	Mr & Mrs R. Ferguson
1980	Mrs S. Niven

THE TROPHIES

The origin of a number of trophies at Mortonhall Golf Club extends back to the last century and it is a matter of considerable regret that all those in existence in 1969 were, with the exception of Colonel Stewart's Medal and the Gordon Thomson Cup, stolen from the Clubhouse on the night of August 10th/11th 1969.

None was recovered and the insurance monies received were applied in the purchase of replacements which, attractive though they are, lack, inevitably, the antiquity and craftsmanship of their more valuable predecessors.

The history of each trophy is recorded in order of its seniority.

The names of the winners of the trophies are recorded in a separate book in the Clubhouse.

THE HANDICAP CUP (WATSON) CUP – For the lowest handicap score at the Spring Meeting

This is the oldest trophy, being originally a silver cup presented by an anonymous donor for annual competition 'on such terms as the Council might think fit to fix' on 3rd February 1893. After its loss in 1969, it was replaced by a cup, presented by the late A. Steele, in memory of his first wife, a former Miss Watson, hence the present title – THE WATSON CUP.

THE TROTTER CUP   – For the lowest scratch score at the Spring Meeting

This trophy was originally a silver bowl, presented by Colonel Henry Trotter, on the occasion of the formal opening of the Clubhouse in February 1893.

THE GOLD MEDAL   – For the lowest scratch score at the Autumn Meeting

The original Gold Medal was purchased by the Club from Messrs Hamilton & Inches at a cost of £15 and was first played for in the Autumn Meeting of 1893.

THE GORDON GILMOUR CUP   – For the lowest handicap score
at the Summer Meeting

In October 1894, Captain (subsequently General) Gordon Gilmour of Liberton and Craigmillar presented a silver cup for annual competition, stipulating that it was 'to become the property of the Member, first winning it three times in succession'. Fortunately for the Club, this has never occurred, although A. A. Mitchell won the trophy in two successive years.

COLONEL STEWART'S MEDAL   – For handicap foursomes hole
and hole Competition

In June 1896, Colonel Stewart intimated to the Council his intention to present a prize for foursomes hole and hole competition but, for some reason, to would appear that his medal was not presented until 1903, when it was first competed for.

This medal was not stolen in 1969 and consequently it is now the oldest original trophy in the Club.

THE WALKER SILVER CLUB   – For the lowest scratch score at
at the Summer Meeting

At the AGM in 1900, the Secretary, D. W Walker, presented the Club with a silver driver, similar to the one presented by the Corporation of Edinburgh to the Honourable Company of Edinburgh Golfers.

THE MORTONHALL STAR OF INDIA – For the player most holes
up on bogey in annual
Competition

In May 1902, the Anglo-Indian Members of the Club presented a small gold medal to be known as 'Star of India' for annual competition under bogey conditions. Colonel McInroy of the Burn 'complained that the name – Star of India – chosen by the Anglo-Indian Members was a very inappropriate one in respect that it was the title of an order of the Crown'. Council thereafter resolved to alter the name of the trophy to 'The Mortonhall Star of India'. The trophy was first competed for in 1906.

178

THE CORONATION SHIELD   – For the annual singles hole and hole Competition

To mark the Coronation of Edward VII in June 1902, arrangements were made to hold a display of fireworks 'on one of the hills, the first rocket to be set off at 10 pm.' Members of the Club were accordingly asked for subscriptions, not exceeding 5/– per Member, to defray the cost thereof and, in due course, fireworks to the value of £30 were purchased.

Due, however, to the King's illness and the consequent postponement of the Coronation, the display was cancelled and, after some hard bargaining, the fireworks were ultimately re-sold for £7.10/–. An appeal was once more made to the Members and a further sum of £42.16/7d was raised. After meeting the loss of the 'firework transaction', the balance was used to purchase a shield to be known as the 'Coronation Shield'.

THE DUNCAN MacLAREN CUP   – The award for the Club Championship

No man has made a greater contribution to Mortonhall Golf Club than Duncan MacLaren, its first Captain. It was almost entirely through his initiative and enterprise that the Club was formed and in due course he became known as 'The Father of Mortonhall'.

In April 1912, Council proposed that 'Duncan MacLaren's services to the Club should be recognised in some suitable manner' and invited subscriptions of 5/– per Member 'to purchase a piece of silver plate or other suitable article for presentation'. When approached, Mr MacLaren declined to accept the presentation and informed the Council that 'it would be pleasing to me if the gift took the form of a gold medal with the inscription – Mortonhall Golf Club 1913 – Championship Medal'. When Mr MacLaren was again approached in March 1913, he once more refused any presentation but agreed that a trophy be purchased instead of a medal.

The trophy was duly purchased in 1913 and inscribed thus: 'The Duncan MacLaren Cup – presented to Mortonhall Golf Club by Duncan MacLaren, S.S.C., first Captain of the Club 1892–95'.

While for many years the trophy was regarded as the award for the Club Championship, it was not until 1953 that it was officially so recognised.

THE GRAND FLEET CUP — For the winner of a
competition between the
season's medal winners

In December 1919, The Commander in Chief of the Atlantic Fleet, Admiral Sir Charles E. Madden, presented to the Club a silver cup 'in grateful recognition of the hospitality shown to the officers of the Grand Fleet during the Great War'. The actual presentation was made by Vice-Admiral Sir Sydney R. Freemantle who, along with Admiral Madden, were thereafter made Honorary Members of the Club.

After receipt of the cup, Council recommended that 'it be not competed for, but simply displayed', but in 1932 it was decided to introduce it as a competitive trophy.

THE SHANGHAI CHALLENGE SHIELD — For the winner of a hole
and hole Competition among
the sixteen players returning
the lowest handicap scores
at the Spring Meeting

In April 1921, A. Dorward Smart of Singapore presented a silver shield to the Club for annual competition 'As a memento of the many happy days he spent as a visiting member of Mortonhall in 1919'.

THE STOBIE BOWL — For annual handicap
Competition by Members of
50 years of age or over and
who have been Members of
the Club for not less than ten
years

In 1922, Dr William Stobie, son of William Stobie, an Original Member of the Club, presented a cup (later renamed a bowl) in memory of his father and suggested that it be played for by older Members of the Club.

This trophy, along with that of the Adam Tait, was competed for during the 1939/45 War but the names of the winners were not recorded.

THE ADAM TAIT COMPETITION – For annual handicap
(ROBIN HOOD TROPHY)   Competition by Members of
                                     60 years of age or over

In 1934, Adam Tait, a Member of the Club, an uncle of Sheriff Lillie
and a former General Manager of the Royal Bank of Scotland,
presented the Club with £500 worth of 4% debenture stocks,
London Midland and Scottish Railway Company Limited, on the
understanding that one half of the income would be used to provide
a prize for competition by Members over 60 years of age, and the
other half a prize for competition by Members of the Royal Bank of
Scotland, resident in Edinburgh, and retired members of staff – both
competitions to be played over Mortonhall. In 1970, the widow of
Robin Hood, a former Captain of the Club, presented a silver salver
to be competed for in conjunction with the Adam Tait competition.

THE HASTIE BRYDON CUP   – For handicap foursomes hole
                                 and hole Competition, played
                                 over the winter months

In April 1951, the trustees of the late J. Hastie Brydon intimated that
it had been the wish of Mr Brydon that one of his racing cups should
be presented to the Club. Council thereafter decided that it be used
as the award for the winners of the Winter Foursomes.

THE PATERSON PUTTING PRIZE – For the winner of an annual
(THE O'RIORDAN PUTTER)   putting Competition

In March 1955, it was intimated that the late R. T. G. Paterson had
bequeathed the sum of £50 to endow an annual prize for a singles
putting competition 'in memory of his old Membership of the Club'.
    T. G. O'Riordan, famed for his putting, died in 1987 and his
family presented his putter, a 'Mortonhall Special' to the Club in his
memory – the club to be used as the trophy for the Paterson Putting
Competition.

THE ADAM QUAICH — For the lowest handicap score at the Summer Meeting by a Member under 35 years of age

In May 1955, it was intimated that the late D. Bruce Adam had bequeathed the sum of £250 'to provide, in the first instance, a cup for competition among the younger Members of the Club'. Council thereafter decided that the competition for the trophy should be restricted to Members under 35 years of age.

THE J. GORDON THOMSON TROPHY — For the winner of the the Junior Championship

In April 1956, Mrs Munro, daughter of the late J. Gordon Thomson, intimated that her father derived great pleasure from his Membership of the Club and in view of this, she presented a cup to be known as the 'J. Gordon Thomson Cup' for competition by Junior Members. The Council thereafter agreed that the trophy would be for the Junior Championship. This cup was fortunately not stolen in 1969 and as a consequence remains an original trophy.

THE WALTER LOWNIE PRIZE — For the winner of an annual handicap foursomes medal Competition, each couple to consist of one Senior and one Junior Member

In January 1957, K. C. Lownie, son of the late W. F. Lownie, presented a sum of £30 to purchase a prize to be known as the 'Walter Lownie Prize' for annual competition. In July 1959, Council ultimately decided that this would take the form of a foursome medal competition, each couple to consist of a Senior and Junior Member.

THE BALFOUR CUP — For the winner of an annual putting competition between Members of 50 years and over, who have been Members of the Club for at least ten years.

In October 1958, it was intimated that the late C.G.C. Balfour had bequeathed to the Club a silver cup to be called the 'Balfour Cup' and 'to be competed for on the putting green each year by Members of 50 years and over and who have been Members for ten years'.

THE JUBILEE CUP — For the lowest scratch score in the high handicap section of Autumn Meeting

In July 1967, J. Brydon donated a cup for annual competition by Junior Members of the Club. As it appeared not possible to organize a suitable competition, Council decided in July 1969 to use the trophy as an award for the scratch prize for the high handicap section of the Autumn Meeting.

THE AINSLIE LINDSAY QUAICH — For the lowest handicap score at the Golf Foundation Competition

In March 1970, T. Ainslie, at that time the Club Professional, and J. Lindsay, whose shop at 41 Comiston Road was the first meeting place of the Morningside Golf Club in 1891, presented a trophy for the Golf Foundation Competition.

THE DUNCAN MacLAREN TROPHY — For the winner of the 'B' Championship i.e. the supreme scratch award for the second class handicaps

In April 1970, H. H. Considine (the son-in-law of Duncan MacLaren) presented a trophy which he desired to be known as 'The Duncan MacLaren Trophy'. Council thereafter decided that it should be awarded to the winner of the 'B' Championship.

183

THE NICOLSON CUP   — Awarded to winners of annual match between the Councils of Mortonhall and Murrayfield Golf Clubs

In June 1970, T. P. J. Nicolson, who had retired from the position of Secretary of Mortonhall in 1969, presented a cup to be used as a challenge trophy in an annual match between the Councils of Mortonhall and Murrayfield — this in recognition of the close connections of the Clubs and of his friendship with Donald Sutherland, Secretary of Murrayfield.

THE McIVOR TROPHY   — For the lowest handicap score in an annual Competition over 36 holes

In November 1971, a number of the friends of the late Joe McIvor, a popular and enthusiastic Member of the Club presented a trophy for annual competition over 36 holes.

THE BURMA CUP   — For the winner of the Junior singles hole and hole Competition

In 1974, Dr I. S. Robertson presented a trophy to be known as 'The Burma Cup' for competition by Junior Members.

THE JUNIOR AUTUMN CUP   — For the scratch winner of a Junior 36 hole competition

No history has been recorded.

THE BOB KING TROPHY   — For the handicap winner of the 36 hole Bob King Trophy Competition

In July 1978, Robert King presented a cup for competition by Junior Members.

| THE VETERANS CUP | – For the lowest handicap score in a Veterans Competition |

In December 1980, Mrs Steele, the widow of the late A. Steele, a former City Architect, presented a trophy to the Club to be competed for by the 'veterans' of the Club.

| THE ROYAL BANK QUAICH | – For the scratch winner of an annual 36 hole open Competition |

In April 1982, the Royal Bank of Scotland presented to the Club a Quaich to be awarded to the winner of an annual open low handicap competition. This recognized the long and close association between the Club and the Bank.

| The McLAREN CUP | – For the winner of an annual putting Competition for Junior Members |

In 1982, I. S. McLaren presented a cup in appreciation of the happy times enjoyed by his sons, Keith and Craig, as Junior Members of Mortonhall.

THE GORDON DEWAR MEMORIAL QUAICH – For the winner of an annual Junior open Competition

In 1983, the Bank of Scotland presented a quaich to be competed for in annual Junior open competition. Gordon Dewar, who was with the Bank of Scotland, was Club Champion at Mortonhall in 1957, 1958 and 1959. In addition, he gained many golfing honours, including being Scottish Amateur Champion, a Scottish Internationalist, and non-playing Captain of the Scottish Team during the 1960s.

THE WILLIAM MAILER TROPHY – For the winning Tri-Am team competing on a better ball basis

In 1986, a group of Bill Mailer's friends, saddened by his death earlier in the year, donated to the Club, in his memory, a cup to be awarded to the winners of the Tri-Am Competition – in which Bill had taken a great interest.

THE SENIORS V JUNIORS FOURSOMES TROPHY – For the winning team in the annual match

In 1991, Ron Goodwin presented an imaginatively designed trophy, (three small silver clubs, a putter, iron and wood, resting on a drum-shaped base showing the Mortonhall crest) to be awarded to the winners of the annual Seniors versus Juniors Foursome match.

THE CENTENARY SALVER – For the winners of an annual Senior/Junior Stableford Competition

In 1991, Ian Isles presented a silver salver to commemorate a 50 year association with Mortonhall for the Boyd (his father-in-law) and Isles families. The trophy is to be first competed for in 1992 by a Senior/Junior partnership on a Stableford basis.

THE BARTON & OTHER ODES

'KEEP YOUR 'EE ON THE BA''
(Lord Stormonth Darling)
A Ballad of the Beginner

When on Musselbro's famous old green
There was gorse by the slumbering sea,
When the golfer was lord of the scene,
And the lark piped his carol of glee,
When the turf was as prim as could be,
And the air bore the scents of the spring –
It was then I first sought for the key
To the game that is fit for a king.

The caddie that fell to my lot
Was old, hard of hearing, and wise;
His face had a hue that was not
Entirely the work of the skies:
He knew how the young player tries
To remember each tip all at once,
And, forgetting the vital one, sighs,
And despairs of himself as a dunce.

So, deep in his mind he had set
A rule that pervades all the rest;
'Tis the maxim you ne'er can forget,
If you wish in your game to be blest:
'Tis the greatest, the first, and the best,
The beginning and end of golf-law;
And 'twas thus by my caddie expressed –
'Now, mind, keep you e'e on the ba'.'

If I asked – 'Am I standing too near?'
'Am I holding my hands right, or not?'
'Is the ground to the left rather queer?'
'Is the bunker in front very hot?'
To each query the answer I got
Was that rigid, inflexible saw
(Of deafness and wisdom begot),
'Now, mind, keep you e'e on the ba'.'

I was wroth at the time, I confess,
That my longing for help should be vain:
I sighed for a 'no' or a 'yes',
And I cursed that eternal refrain:
I saw not – what now is so plain –
That there's nought, when a golfer is raw,
Like Burning well into his brain
The rule 'Keep your e'e on the Ba'.'
            Envoy
Whate'er be the mark to be hit,
This truth from that caddie I draw –
In life, as in golf, you'll be fit
If you aye keep your e'e on the ba'.

'ECK AND THE DEIL'
(Henry Barton)

Here is a tale I now recall,
Of further doings at Mortonhall.
'Twas the time the Captain was Bobby Croall,
A jovial and a genial soul.

At the Captain's Supper one night in June,
The Council were in merry tune,
They had dined full well with healthy zest,
They were full of wit and sparkling jest.
For those who don't know the locus well,
There are some details I must tell.

The dining room it will be found,
Is above a bedroom, half underground,
Used by Thomson, the Head Greenkeeper,
At times a deep and sonorous sleeper.

Now on this night of the Captain's feast,
There was Thomson asleep, with his feet to the East,
Pointing to the window and privet hedge,
And the bushes that waved above the ledge.

The din upstairs it rose and fell,
Sometimes guffaws and whiles a yell,
As someone's story or ribald jest,
Was related with spirit and gusto and zest.

What Thomson was thinking when he went to sleep,
Is locked in the bosom of mystery deep,
Maybe he'd eaten some cheese from Leyden,
Unsurpassed as the stuff that dreams are made on.

Or 'twas maybe a salad with sliced cucumber,
Which disturbed his normal peaceful slumber.
But he half awoke with a stifled yell,
And thought from the din he was down in Hell.

I'm not sure if I've got this right,
But through the window came a shaft of light,
From the moon new risen behind the trees,
Which made bits of the room seem in a bleeze.

Whether the light and the bushes had played a trick,
But he saw quite plain, the shape of Auld Nick.
Two muckle horns and a forkit tail,
Which lashed about like a harvest flail.

'What the Hell dae ye want, ye black devil wi' me?'
Said Thomson quite loud, wi' wrath in his e'e.

'I'm here' said the Demon, 'tae fling in y'r face,
'Some o' the sins ye committed in yon bonny place,
'Tae bring tae y'r mind and mak' ye recall,
'Some o' y'r misdeeds aboot Mortonhall'.

'Ye bloody auld leer' said Thomson wi' pain,
'I've wrocht in the place as if 'twere my ain,
'I've even got praise, ye auld b.....r-lugs,
'Frae players and Captains o' visiting Clubs.

'If you've cam' here wi' fauts and blame,
'By God I'll send ye hirplin hame.
'Just wait till I get on my buits;
'An' we'll damn soon see wha first cries – Quits'.

'Man Thomson, said Beelzebub,
     'Ye're a man o' my ain he'rt,
'I admire your spunk, you've spirit and guts,
     'And that's definite cert.
'I'm glad that I have met ye,
     'And found oot for mysel'
'That there's nae room for the twa o' us.
     'In yon place they ca' Hell.   189

'There would be nae leevin' thegither,
    'That's as plain as can be,
'So I'll just prescribe some penances,
    'And then let ye go free'.

'Free be damned' said Thomson,
    'Let's hear from y'r blasphemous lips,
'The things they say against me,
    'And then we'll get to grips'.

'Well, first of all' said Nicky Ben,
    'The things folk canna thole,
'Is the way ye look for hidden slopes,
    'Before ye cut the hole,
'An' then ye use the cuttin' tool,
    'The best the Club can afford,
'An' ye leave the edges a turned up,
    'Why dinna ye use a board?'

'Awa back hame tae y'r depths o' Hell'
    Said Thomson wi' a froon,
'Efter I've cut the blastit hole,
    I tramp it a' aroon.
'Naebody can say that when I've done,
    'The holes are no weel cut
'I'll tell ye what the trouble is –
      'THE B.....S CANNA PUTT!'

'BATH TIME'
(Henry Barton)

I had a dream last night that I must recall,
Of a gathering of Members at Mortonhall.

They were there in the Lounge and Dining Room,
In the Bar there were serried ranks
There were more – still more – in the Locker Room,
Plus the place that's equipped by Shanks.

There had been weighty deliberations; the Council all felt sure,
That something really must be done, to keep the Members pure.
There were signs their morals were slipping, Virtue was half alive,
So if Godliness weren't possible, then for cleanliness they must strive.

The purpose of the gathering – this crowd in bright array
Was the opening of the shower bath – or if you like – the spray.
The Council was assembled at the door of the little cell
There was Willis Mackenzie, the Captain and his namesake, Hay,
as well.

The Captain was dressed like the ancient Greeks,
A toga round him and no thought of breeks,
And hovering near, just cheek by jowl,
Was Morris, the Secretary, bearing a towel.,

With some well chosen words he declared the place open,
And held out his chest for Morris to put soap on.
When the anointing was over, he got under the shower,
And turned at the handle with vigour and power.

With a heart rending yell – though his spirit was bold,
'Twas not what he reckoned – the water was cold.
The handle got stuck – he danced in his frenzy –
The oaths were the pet ones of Willis Mackenzie.

His antics continued – he'd given up hope,
When without warning he trod on the soap.
He was upside down when he came to rest,
And hard on the window his bottom was pressed.

Outside there was gathered an interested crowd,
Expectant, excited and talking aloud.
There was Thomson, the Greenkeeper, supported by Drummond,
Mrs Selkirk and others whom her daughters had summoned.

Meanwhile inside there was a Helluva din,
They gape round the door at the Captain within.
'Get him out' shouted someone. The Council concur.
Hay Mackenzie leads the rescuers with his slogan 'Moncur'

They rescue him dripping, his skin like a puddock's,
And Morris wraps the towel round his quivering buttocks.
He's led in procession to seek some place warm,
To keep the ex-champion from coming to harm.

They carry the hero. Its not very far.
The first place they make for is naturally the Bar.
He's borne there in triumph by two Merchistonians
But they can't get near it for 'Bloody Watsonians'!

'THE NEW TROLLEY'
(Henry Barton)

There was once a brother Member
Was as keen as he was jolly,
And to help transport his golf clubs,
He acquired a brand new trolley.

He loved his new contraption,
His tubular brand new trolley,
He loaded on it all his kit,
And on wet days took his brolly.

Besides being a useful golfer,
He had an inventive mind,
He thought 'Why pull the barrow?
It needs an engine of some kind.'

He cast around for ideas,
And then he felt impelled,
To discard a piston engine,
He'd have one Jet-propelled.

He screwed on a combustion chamber,
Complete with louvres and vanes,
He adjusted exhaust and intake
And took no end of pains.

He brought it round to the Clubhouse,
That the Members might admire,
But they viewed it from a distance,
Lest the damned thing went on fire.

Then out came the Green Committee,
To see if they'd allow,
Such a queer and droll contraption,
That looked like a mechanised plough.

The inventor started the engine;
It got going with grunts and snorts;
It then backfired and set alight
The seat of *Haddow's shorts.

It flew through the air like a rocket;
Blue flames streaked out at the back;
It hit the rocks on the hillside
With a resounding crack.

And then came a dreadful explosion,
Dense smoke rose up from the ground,
The machine was in bits with its maker,
Their spare parts were scattered around.

The Members raced up and stood awestruck
Till the voice of the Captain was heard;
'We must quietly gather the remnants
And get them immediately interred'.

He added 'Let this be a warning,
To all with inventions oppressed.
We'll bury our friend on the fairway
At the top of the very hill crest#'

* Later to become Sir Douglas Haddow
# The mound on the left of the 18th fairway, 250 yards from the tee.

'THE ROAD TO THE ISLES'
(Henry Barton)

Sure by Marsh and then the Khyber Pass,
Around the Course I go,
With knolls and woody places far beyond.
If it's thinking in our inner heart,
The air is always pure,
You've never smelt the guff from off the pond.

'THE LITTLER GOLFER'
(Henry Barton)

I'm a little golfer, fat and small
Frisking like a rabbit over Mortonhall,
Sometimes on the fairway, sometimes in the rough.
I'm a happy little golfer and I never get tough.

See me on the next tee, waggle my bum,
Hey little golf ball, here I come.
I swing my little driver as a golfer should,
Then away flies the ball to the blasted wood.

o

'THE LAST TEE'
(Anonymous)

The Captain stood on the eighteenth tee
Whence all but he had driven.
Before him lay his golden chance
For seventeen holes he'd striven.

Two under fours – the marvellous score
From this rebuilt machine
A birdie here – a birdie there
Pure art from tee to green.

One hole to play – a simple four
He'd do it on his head
The silver cup was surely his
As down his driver sped.

'THE SALVATION OF JAMES THOMSON'
(Anonymous)

James Thomson was a golfer bold
Of class beyond recall
A Heriot born Captain, eke was he
Of famous Mortonhall.

He first to golf was introduced
Upon his mother's knee
With baffy, cleek and cut-down spoon,
The tools of the TSB.

It was on Edinburgh's Goldenacre
The golden wonder grew.
They told him it was Paradise,
And he believed them too.

194

'THE CAPTAIN'S CLUBS'
(Anonymous)

There's a little yellow idol,
To the East of Mortonhall.
It bears no fond inscription
Except a club and ball.
No human bones are there interred
Amid the flowering shrubs.
The silent tomb alone contains
The present Captain's clubs.

'CAPTAIN FRED'
(Anonymous)

At Mortonhall where golf is played,
We call our Captain, Fred.
A friendly fellow by whose hand,
The Council still are led.

His chat is smooth and bright his smile,
As drinks he pours around.
With silver tongue and honeyed words,
His charm is quite renowned.

'MORTONHALL MAFIA'
(Fred Gray)

This bloody Club's a bloody cuss,
We all should make a bloody fuss,
For no-one cares for bloody us! –
                    In bloody Mortonhall.

The bloody greens are bloody small,
The whins are just too bloody tall,
And only O'Riordan finds his ball! –
                    In bloody Mortonhall.

When bloody clouds bring bloody rains,
The fairways are swamps – no bloody drains.
The greens staff's got no bloody brains! –
                    In bloody Mortonhall.   195

All the drinks are bloody dear.
Over a quid for bloody beer.
Are the brands the best? – no bloody fear

In bloody Mortonhall.

Victors we praise, our great Inter Club Team
How did we win? Things are not what they seem.
'Twas the absence of Watsonians did it, I deem

In bloody Mortonhall.

When Fred Gray was Captain, he must have gone off his rocker.
The showers were re-furbished, but the result was a shocker.
So it's only fair justice, dry rot's in his locker

At bloody Mortonhall.

Greens Convener Stark needs a bloody rocket
He must be in Dougie's bloody pocket
All he does to advice is bloody block it

At bloody Mortonhall.

On the bandit, press 'P for Peter' if you're really on the ball
And our Captain presses 'P' when he wants to walk tall
How else would he keep repeating
      'I know what's best for Mortonhall'

In bloody Mortonhall.

The present Captain's bloody stance
Is more like an Indian Totem Dance
He should have lived in bloody France

Not bloody Mortonhall.

All the Councils I've known have been bloody showers
I could speak of their faults for hours and hours,
You'd think it was bloody Fawlty Towers

Not bloody Mortonhall.

What's that? You're a guest? It's a bloody shame!
Hold on! *I* would never give the Club a bad name.
For my money, it's the best bloody Club in the game,

Is bloody Mortonhall!

'THE CLUB CHAMPIONSHIP (1958)'
(Gordon Dewar)

Two holes passed without mishap, as Ken teed up at the Third
He hit a good one down the right, that flew past the pond like a bird.
I staggered on to the Khyber Tee, intent on the final knock
And swung my club like one possessed, more a blacksmith than a
                                                    Bobby Locke,
The club descended – my knees collapsed – the teeing ground shuddered
                                                    with shock.
The ball flew up – a rocket in flight – the stricken trees rattled and
                                                    rocked.
The crowd was still – the end was near – 'He's had it' said one of the
                                                    crowd,
Then Dame Fortune smiled – as welcome a sight as beer to Johnny
                                                    McLeod
The ball landed back on the teeing ground, like a roysterer home from
                                                    a revel,
And one or two glanced fearfully around for signs of Auld Nick or the
                                                    devil.
Jock Pyper's long chin dropped another twelve inches, his teeth they
                                                    chattered disjointed
And Terry's pipe went out for good, some blokes are sure anointed!

THE DIARY

Year	Event
1892	Constitution of Mortonhall Golf Club approved.
1892	Nine Hole Course opened.
1892	First competition (Bogey).
1892	Willie Park, Junior, visited Mortonhall to advise on Course.
1893	Clubhouse formally opened by Colonel Trotter.
1893	'North Field' leased from Colonel Trotter.
1893	First Caddies authorised.
1893	Record Score of 82 by Duncan MacLaren over two rounds of original Course.
1894	Jack Simpson former Open Champion, engaged as Club's first professional.
1894	First 18 hole Course opened.
1894	First Extension to Clubhouse completed.
1895	First Club Match against Borders Golf Association.
1895	John Ball of Hoylake played over Course.
1896	'Triangular' Field leased from Colonel Trotter.
1896	Record Score of 75 by W. B. Taylor over first 18 hole Course.
1896	Record Score of 72 by Lieut. F. G. Tait over first 18 hole Course.
1897	Second 18 hole Course opened.
1898	Plantation sown at East end of Elf Loch.
1899	18th green levelled by blasting rock.
1900	Footbridge over Elf Loch removed.
1900	Harold Hilton of Hoylake played over Course.
1901	Harry Vardon, J. H. Taylor, James Braid and Sandy Herd played Exhibition Match over Course.
1901	100-a-side Match against Edinburgh Burgess Golfing Society.
1902	Second 100-a-side Match against Edinburgh Burgess Golfing Society.
1903	Land North of the Drive leased from Sir Henry Trotter.
1903	First Trustees appointed.
1904	Second Extension to Clubhouse opened by Sir Henry Trotter.
1904	Record Score of 69 by D.G. MacKenzie over second 18 hole Course.

1905	First Lothians Inter Club Tournament.
1905	Sir Henry Trotter appointed Captain.
1905	Death of Sir Henry Trotter.
1906	J. H. Taylor visited Mortonhall to advise on Course.
1907	Third 18 hole Course opened.
1909	Record Score of 71 by W. C. White over third 18 hole Course.
1910	Visitors Fees introduced.
1911	Electricity installed in the Clubhouse.
1912	Record Score of 70 achieved by W. C. White.
1912	Reunion of Original Members on 20th Anniversary.
1913	First Council Match against Murrayfield.
1914	Lothians Inter Club Tournament won by Mortonhall.
1914	D. P. Watt, the Club Professional, won the Scottish Professional Championship.
1917	Professor C. G. Barkla, a Member of the Club, awarded the Nobel Prize in Physics.
1917	Siegfried Sassoon, Wilfred Owen and Robert Graves lunched at Mortonhall.
1919	*Evening Times* Tournament won by Mortonhall.
1919	Lothians Inter Club Tournament won by Mortonhall.
1921	Lothians Team Tournament won by Mortonhall.
1922	Lothians Team Tournament won by Mortonhall.
1922	Reunion of Original Members on 30th Anniversary.
1922	W. Willis Mackenzie played for Great Britain in Walker Cup.
1923	Lothians Team Tournament won by Mortonhall.
1923	W. Willis Mackenzie again selected for Walker Cup.
1924	W. Willis Mackenzie won Scottish Amateur Championship.
1924	Death of Duncan MacLaren – 'the Father of Mortonhall'
1925	Record score of 69 by W. Willis Mackenzie.
1926	Record score of 68 by W. Willis Mackenzie.
1926	James Braid visited Mortonhall to advise on Course.
1927	Negotiations for purchase of Course completed.
1927	First Tractor purchased.
1927	H.R.H. Prince of Wales played over Course.
1928	W. Willis Mackenzie won Scottish Amateur Championship.
1929	Lothians Inter Club Tournament won by Mortonhall.
1930	Record score of 66 by J. A. Clark.
1930	*Evening Times* Tournament won by Mortonhall.
1932	Reunion of Original Members on 40th Anniversary.
1934	Boat removed from Elf Loch.
1937	P. Mackenzie Ross, Golf Architect, visited Mortonhall to advise on Course.

1937	Professional's Shop, Bedroom accommodation and Beer Cellar added to Clubhouse.
1941	Present 4th and 5th holes cultivated for food production.
1947	Elf Loch cleaned.
1950	Junior Membership created.
1950	Ian McNiven won Lothians Championship.
1951	Present 4th and 5th holes re-opened for play.
1952	Lothians Inter Club Tournament won by Mortonhall.
1952	Annual match with Royal Burgess Golf Club resuscitated.
1952	Club's Diamond Jubilee celebrated in Freemasons Hall.
1952	Captain's Badge of Office presented by Honorary Members.
1954	Mid-week medal introduced.
1955	New record score of 66 by K. B. Munnoch.
1955	Captains' Panel erected.
1958	Wives and Daughters of Members granted playing rights.
1959	Record score of 65 by F. G. Dewar.
1959	Death of W. Willis Mackenzie.
1959	G. E. Robertson selected as a Youth Internationalist.
1961	Silloth Tournament inaugurated.
1961	W. West Kerr, an Original Member, celebrated his centenary.
1963	Water installed at all greens.
1964	Junior Inter Club Tournament won by Mortonhall.
1964	First Fruit Machine installed.
1964	Edinburgh Golf League won by Mortonhall.
1964	Death of W. C. White.
1965	Five Day Membership created.
1966	Mortonhall Open inaugurated.
1969	Bar installed in Lounge.
1969	Champions' Panel erected.
1969	Club Trophies stolen.
1969	Junior Inter Club Tournament won by Mortonhall.
1970	Major Course Development Project initiated.
1972	Financial Year changed to 30th November.
1974	Record score of 64 by R. A. Davie.
1975	29 acres of land at Meadowhead purchased.
1976	Juniors' Honours Board erected.
1976	Plan of new Course agreed.
1977	West Drive to Mortonhall House purchased.
1979	New Course opened for play.
1979	Royal Bank 36 hole Professional Tournament.
1979	Record score (Professional) of 68 by Gordon Cunningham (Troon) over new Course.

1979	New Greenkeepers' Sheds erected at 2nd hole.
1979	K. W. S. Gray selected as Junior Internationalist.
1980	K. W. S. Gray selected as Youth Internationalist.
1980	Record score (Amateur) of 67 by George McGregor (Glencorse) over new Course.
1981	K. W. S. Gray again selected as Youth Internationalist.
1981	New Water Pumping System installed.
1982	Major refurbishment of Lounge.
1982	British Universities Golf Championship won by K. G. McCall.
1985	Pop-up Sprinkler system installed.
1987	Lothians Inter-Club Tournament won by Mortonhall.
1987	Edinburgh Junior Summer League won by Mortonhall.
1987	Secretary of State for Scotland attended Club Dinner.
1989	Lodge House for Clubmistress and 'Temple' constructed.
1989	Record score of 66 by Craig Cassells (Murcar).
1991	D. Patrick won Scottish Under-16 Strokeplay Championship.

Constitution
or
Rules for the Government
of the
Mortonhall Golf Club,
as adopted at a
Special General Meeting of the Club
on
29th April 1892.

1. The persons whose names and addresses are specified in a List signed with reference hereto by the Captain of the Club hereby constitute and form themselves into a Golf Club to be named and designed "The Mortonhall Golf Club", and they hereby enact and declare that the following Rules shall be the Rules for the government of the said Club, videlicet :—

2. The Club shall be governed by Office-Bearers consisting of the Captain, Secretary, Treasurer, Auditor, and ten Members, all to be elected by the Club, which Office-Bearers shall form the Council of the Club. The Council shall have the management of the whole affairs of the

the Club, subject to such directions, as may be given at an Annual General or Special Meeting of the Club.

3. The financial year of the Club shall commence as from 1st April. The Annual General Meeting of the Club shall be held in the last week of March each year, when the Office-Bearers shall be elected by a majority of votes of the Members present. The Captain, Secretary, Treasurer, and Auditor shall hold office for one year. One half of the remaining Members of Council shall retire each year, and all retiring, both Office-Bearers and Members of Council, shall be eligible for re-election; and in the event of any vacancy occurring amongst the Council, they shall have power to fill up the same till the first Annual Meeting.

4. A Special General Meeting of the Club may be called at any time upon the request of the Council, or upon the requisition of not fewer than twenty five Members of the Club, addressed to the Captain or Secretary.

5. The Captain shall be the preses of all Meetings, and

and in his absence the Secretary, Treasurer,
or a Member of Council present, whom all
failing such preses as the Members present
may appoint. The preses for the time shall
have in all cases of equality a casting, in
addition to a deliberative vote.

6. The Secretary shall keep a correct record of
all the proceedings of the Club at their General
and Special Meetings, and at the Meetings of
the Council, and shall call the Meetings of the
Club and Council, and take charge of the papers,
books, and records of the Club.

7. The Treasurer shall receive and disburse all
monies due to and by the Club, and in particular shall collect the Entry Money and
Subscriptions, and any other fees that may be
due by the Members. He shall keep Audit
Accounts of his intromissions, and present a
full and complete Account thereof at the Annual
General Meeting of the Club, which shall previously be examined and certified by the
Auditor. The Council may at any time require him to present to them an Account
of his Intromissions and of the State of the
Funds

Funds of the Club. All monies to be collected by the Treasurer to be paid by him into Bank.

The Annual and Special Meetings of the Club shall be called by written notice addressed to each Member, on at least two days' notice. — The Members present at such Meetings shall have power to transact all competent business. Meetings of Council may be called at any time by the Captain or Secretary by written or verbal notice to each Member resident in Edinburgh at the time, and four Members shall be a quorum.

The persons whose names form Numbers One to ninety-seven inclusive of said List signed as aforesaid, shall for the current year, but without prejudice to Rule 13 hereof, pay the sum of £1..1/- each, and the remaining persons whose names appear on said List shall, for the current year, pay to the Treasurer of the Club the sum of £3..3/- each, and the said payments shall form and be held to be the contributions of said persons respectively for the year current to 31st March 1893. The said

said Contributions shall be payable on or before 15th May 1892.

10. Members to be admitted hereafter shall pay as Entry Money the sum of £3.,3/- in addition to the Subscription for the year then current. The Subscription payable by Members annually is fixed at the sum of £1.,1/-, and shall be payable on or before the 1st day of May in each year, except in cases where Members are admitted after the said last-mentioned date, when the same, along with the Entry Money, shall be payable within one month from the date of entry to the Club.

11. Any person failing to pay his Contribution, Entry Money, or Subscription, on a request for payment from the Treasurer within ten days after the lapse of the periods specified in the two preceding Rules, shall thereupon cease to be a Member of the Club, and shall from said date forfeit all right and interest he may have had as a Member thereof, but any Member who through inadvertence may not have timeously paid his said Contribution, Entry Money, or Subscription may be reinstated on payment

206

payment of the sum due by him, if the Council think fit to do so, on application by him.

2. Any Member wishing to resign the Membership of the Club must give written notice to the Secretary at least one month previous to the 31st day of March in each year.

3. The Council shall have power within the current year to call upon those Members of the Club whose names form Nos 1 to 97 inclusive of said List, to pay an additional sum not exceeding £1..1/- towards defraying the cost of erecting a Club House and other expenses of the Club, and any such Member who may refuse or delay to pay such call shall cease to be a Member of the Club after the lapse of thirty days from the date of demand. The Club, by a majority of votes, shall have power at any Annual or Special Meeting to assess the whole Members for payment of such sum equally as may be considered necessary for liquidating the obligations of the Club, and any person failing to make payment of his share within thirty days thereafter, upon written notice from the Treasurer, shall cease to be a Member of the Club

Club, and have his name struck off the Roll of Members, but he shall, notwithstanding, remain liable for his share of said assessment.

14. The Membership of the Club shall be restricted to 200. This number shall not be exceeded, except with the approval of the Club by a majority of votes at an Annual or Special Meeting duly called. New Members to fill up vacancies may be admitted by the Council, until this power is recalled at any Meeting of the Club. No person can be so admitted, unless the Council are unanimous, but any person rejected by the Council may be admitted by the Club at any Meeting, provided there be a vacancy, and provided also that not fewer than three-fourths of the Members present vote for him.

15. The whole Office Bearers and Members of Council shall be the Trustees for the Club in the Lease between Colonel Trotter of Mortonhall and the Club — (a majority being) at all times a quorum) — and the said Trustees shall continue as Trustees until death or resignation, or until any new Trustee or Trustees shall be appointed

208

appointed in their place at any General, or Special Meeting. The said Trustees shall have full power to contract debt for the construction and furnishing, and completion or alteration of the Club-house, and to borrow money on the security thereof, either by granting a Bond and Assignation in Security, or Personal Bond or Bills, or other habile security, which Deeds shall bind the whole Members of the Club, present and future, as if they had individually subscribed the same.

6. The Club shall have full power and authority, in all questions between it and any of its Members, to sue and be sued in name of the Captain, Secretary, and Treasurer thereof for the time being; and no Member of the Club shall, in any action or suit raised against him by the Club, be entitled to object to or impugn such instance; and any person or persons by becoming Members of the Club hereafter shall be held to have agreed to this rule, and to waive any objection competent to him or them thereanent, or to the sufficiency of such instance.

17. The Council shall have power, by a two-thirds' majority of votes of the whole Members of Council, upon their being satisfied that any Member has infringed any one of these Rules, or any of the Bye-Laws framed or to be framed, or otherwise has made himself offensive, to suspend such Member from exercising his privileges as a Member of the Club, and in the event of three-fourths of the Members present at the first General or Special Meeting confirming the Council's decision, the said Member shall therefor be expelled the Club, and in that case the Club or the Council shall not be liable for repayment of any part of the subscription of such Member, or for any claim at his instance in respect of such expulsion; and any Member so expelled shall thereupon forfeit all right and interest he may have had as a Member of the Club.

18. The Council shall have power to alter and amend the Bye-Laws of the Club, and to make new Bye-Laws, which shall be binding on the Members until the first Annual or Special Meeting of the Club, when the same shall be confirmed or otherwise determined by the Club.

19.

9. The foregoing Rules shall not be altered or added to except at an Annual Meeting of the Club. Notice of any alteration or addition must be lodged with the Secretary two weeks before the date of such Meeting, which notice shall embody a statement of the alterations proposed.

0. The game of Golf shall be played according to the Rules of the St. Andrews Royal and Ancient Golf Club, subject to such Bye Laws as may be necessary having regard to the nature of the Course, and as may be made from time to time by the Council.

D Mackaren
Captain, Chairman

211

Bye-Laws of the Club
referred to in,
and signed with reference to,
Minute of Council dated 9th June 1892.

II. Special Bye-Laws
Framed in view of the terms of the Lease.

1. No person shall be admitted to the Private Course and Club-house, except Members of the Club and such persons as may be admitted in terms of the Bye-Laws, and no Member shall on any pretext whatever enter upon the Course on a Sunday.

2. Every Member of the Club shall wear the Club Uniform or Cap.

3. No Caddies shall be brought upon the ground by Members unless this Rule is altered by the Council with the sanction of the Proprietor.

4. No dogs are to be admitted, and no Member of the Club shall enter the plantations of Morton-hall estate upon any pretext whatever, with the exception

212

exception of such portion of the plantations as the Proprietor may fence off.

5. Only one access from the Penicuik Road shall be used, and no Member shall be entitled to climb the walls, or to obtain access, otherwise than by the gate provided.

6. No Member shall touch or interfere with the game, hares, or rabbits upon the Course or upon Mortonhall Estate.

7. The Servants of the Proprietor and the Greenkeeper shall have right to enforce these Special Rules, and to prevent or report any infringement thereof. Members also are expected to do the same, and to do all in their power to prevent unauthorised persons from entering upon the Course, and to report any infringement of these Rules on the part of another Memb. or other person to the Council or any Member thereof.

_II._

II. Ordinary Bye-Laws.

8. The question of handicapping shall be arranged exclusively by the Council, who shall have full power to alter and adjust the handicapping of Members as often as may be considered desirable; but it is agreed that the maximum allowance to be given in any stroke competition of 18 holes shall not exceed 18, and in any hole match, 9 holes.

9. All competitions shall be arranged by the Council alone, and full power is conferred on them to make such alterations as may seem expedient or desirable, either as regards dates and places of Competitions, regulations for play on the green, nature and value of prizes, or otherwise. All disputes arising at any competition or match must be referred to the Captain in the first instance, whom failing to any Member of Council present whose decision shall be final and binding. Any Member playing in a Competition with one who is not also a Member

&c.

214

of the Club will be disqualified in that particular Competition, unless with sanction obtained.

5. Each Member shall be entitled to introduce only one Stranger at a time, and the Member and Stranger introduced by him shall be bound to play together or in the same party. Strangers shall not be allowed to play on Saturdays after One o'clock, or on Public Holidays; but Strangers who have commenced to play before One o'clock on Saturdays shall be entitled to complete the round they may be engaged in on the arrival of that hour.

6. Players are expressly prohibited from playing in the reverse order of any of the holes.

7. A party desirous of entering on a second round immediately after completing a first round, shall be entitled to take precedence of all players then waiting to commence play, except those next in order to strike off; but where there shall be more

more than one such party desirous of entering on a second round, such parties in their order shall only be entitled to strike off alternately with the parties in their order then waiting to commence play. This Rule shall not extend to players proposing to start for a third round, nor to players who, having completed one round, combine with a party waiting to commence play.

13. In the event of any players causing undue delay, either in playing the game or otherwise, so that the hole next that to which they are playing is entirely unoccupied, the players immediately behind shall be entitled to pass such players, who shall be bound to permit this on being so required.

14. A ball driven outside the limits of the Course shall be treated as a lost ball.

15. If the ball lie or be lost in the marsh, the player may drop a ball and play from behind the hazard, losing a stroke, or

or he may play it where it lies without a penalty. If the ball lie or be lost in the pond, or in the fenced-off part of the plantation near the second teeing-ground, the player may drop a ball and play from that part of the Course next to where the ball lies or is supposed to lie, losing a stroke, or he may play the ball where it lies without a penalty.

16. No balls may be driven or played from off any putting-green. When a ball lies on a putting green on the way to another hole, it must be lifted and dropped beyond the green and not nearer the hole being played to, without a penalty.

17. If a ball lodge in a rabbit-hole or scrape, the player may take it out and tee it a club's length behind the hazard, losing a stroke. If, however, the hole or scrape be in a hazard, the ball may be lifted and dropped behind, but not out of the hazard, under

under the same penalty. If a ball lodge in a rabbit-scrape within ten yards of the hole it may be taken out and placed behind without any penalty.

18. Any turf cut or displaced by a stroke in playing must be at once carefully replaced by the player, and pressed down with the foot.

DMacLaren
Captain

REPORT BY J. H. TAYLOR – 1906

Richmond
Surrey, 9th October 1906.

Gentlemen,

In terms of your instructions I visited Mortonhall Golf Course on Monday 24th September and spent the day in a thorough examination thereof; in the forenoon accompanied by the Secretary and in the afternoon with the Captain and several Members of the Green Committee.

In the first place I have considered how the field recently sown down to the south of the present fourth hole and taken with the object, I am informed, or lengthening the course can best be utilised.

In my opinion the best method of working this field into the course is to play from a tee on the hill at the present third hole right out to the south east corner of said new field to the putting green now there, thence teeing at the boundary wall to a hole on a green to be formed near the bend of the wall at the north west of said field, and thence teeing at said bend to the present fifth hole, which would then become the sixth. If necessary 50 or 60 yards of the wall short of the present 5th hole could be taken down to improve the approach, but I hardly think this would be found necessary. This would give one long hole of about 500 yards and would also add about 100 yards to the present fifth hole; the new hole would be about 230 yards. In answer to objections raised by the gentlemen I met, I may say I consider there is ample room to play through the gap between the two plantations. There would be a crossing in the gap, but I do not see how it can well be be avoided if a long hole is to be got, and I do not consider it is at all dangerous or objectionable as the players would be in sight of each other. Bunkers should be placed at the sides of each other. Bunkers should be placed at the sides to catch sliced or pulled shots and a large bunker made in the face of the rising ground to the south of the road in said new field. None of the bunkers should be nearer the hole than 40 yards. I indicated the precise positions to the Secretary on the ground. By the above plan one hole has been gained, and I would further suggest that the present 10th and 11th holes should be thrown into one playing from a tee south of the cottage to the 11th green. All the rest of the course could remain as at present. This I consider is the best that can be made of the ground now at the Clubs disposal. It is not possible to work in the new field and get more long holes owing to the shape and size of the field, but I consider that this plan will certainly improve and lengthen the existing course.

I was asked in the second place if I considered a better course would be made by taking in more ground. I think that the field to the south of the present 11th hole lies naturally into the course and that it would have been better if this field had been taken. Had that field been available a good course would have been made by playing the first seven holes as at present, throwing the present 8th and 9th into one; playing a hole (new 9th) along the eastern boundary right over the hedge into the new field; a long hole (10th) right up west in the new field; thence back east (11th) thence a short hole to near the Roundel Plantation (12th) and thereafter home as at present. This I consider would give a very good course indeed.

So far as the advantage of the two fields are concerned I have no hesitation in saying that the field at the 11th hole would enable much the better course to be made, but the question to my mind is chiefly a financial one, as of course if this field were now to be taken in the Club would lose the money spent on the other field and would have to face additional expenditure. If they are prepared to do this then I recommend giving up the field at the fourth hole and taking and laying out that at the 11th hole.

As regards the rest of the course I have the following suggestion to make.

All the bunkers should be enlarged and made at least five or six yards wider filled with sand and the cops removed. New bunkers should be made at the places indicated to the Secretary. The first green should be extended eight or ten yards.

I am, Gentlemen,

Your obedient Servant.

J. H. Taylor

REPORT BY JOHN ANDERSON, SECRETARY
(1922)

Mortonhall Golf Club.
Private and Confidential.

Report to The Captain by the
Secretary, in regard to extension
of course.

August 1922.

Dear Sir,

I beg to report that in my opinion the time has arrived when it is desirable that additional ground should be taken in to the golf course. I make this report not because I consider the present course too short, or is in any way inferior to others in the district but for the following reasons:—

1. Certain holes (e.g. the 4th and 12th) are lacking in character and could with advantage be eliminated,

2. The scheme which I suggest would obviate to some extent the present congestion through the green, and

3. I may further say there is a want of space in the vicinity of the Club House.

In order to place you in possession of the circumstances affecting the matter and to enable you to consider it fully, I think it necessary to refer to the following.

History of the course.

The annexed shows the extent and rent paid at different periods:—

1892	55 ac	rent £60	rate p. ac. £1
1893	73 "	" £125	" £1, 14 –
1896	82 "	" £155	" £1, 18 –
1903	96 "	" £338	" £3, 10 –

It is to be noted that these are all maximum rents, and that with the exception of the first mentioned all these rents include the grazing rights. With reference to the last mentioned, it may further be noted that the rent of the course then stipulated for was based upon a rate of £4 per acre for the additional ground then acquired.

In 1903 an endeavour was made to secure a feu or a 99 years lease, but was unsuccessful. The Club however obtained a feu of half an acre for the site of the Club House at a feuduty of £20, no feuduty being payable during the Club's tenancy of the golf course.

The present lease expires at Whitsunday 1933.

All the ground added to the course since 1892 has been sown down to grass by the Club. The average time which has elapsed between sowing down and opening for play has been 3 years. In every case with the exception of a single putting green the putting greens and tees were turfed.

Present Conditions.

Under the lease there are numerous restrictions in the Club's possession, viz:—

Prohibition to entrance to the course on Sundays.

Reservation of game &c.

Restriction on admission to the course except by main entrance.

Prohibition against crossing fences.

Restriction as to employment of caddies.

Some of these conditions have not been rigidly enforced for some years, but they exist, and can be enforced at any time.

The Club have the important privilege of a cart access through the proprietor's avenue, and by the farm roads.

Comparison with other Clubs.

Appendix I is a comparative statement showing the extent of, and rents paid for other courses in the district.

Extension proposed in 1903.

When the course was last extended in 1903 the proposal originally made to the Club was to take in the field lying to the south of the 11th hole; but this was not approved owing chiefly to an erroneous impression that this field was rocky and poor and so unsuitable. The ground wherein the 4th hole is situated was then leased, it was of much smaller extent, but the proprietor would not at that time let a larger part of it, owing it is believed to the remaining part being within view of the Mansionhouse windows. There is little doubt that the Council's original proposal in 1903 would have provided for any extension that in future might have been deemed necessary. What was actually done has however as I along with many more Members of the Club believed would be the case, turned out to be only a temporary measure.

To take in the field above referred to now would no doubt answer the present suggestion, but is open to the objection that if this were done the ground last leased would not be required, and that ground, which is now in fairly good condition, would be lost to the Club and all the money expended on it would be thrown away.

Suggested Extension.

The suggestion I have to submit is that the remainder of the field east from the 4th hole and extending to about 13 acres should be leased, if possible. If this were approved I would suggest the following:

Re-arrangement of the course:

Hole 1. The Khyber Pass – the present 2nd – a tee being made at the western or Club House end of the range of hillocks on the southern side of the course there, which hillocks should be lowered to allow of the tee being placed near the boundary wall so as to be out of the way of tee shots played to the 18th hole. As the second shot to this hole would be a long one the whins on the left hand side of the approach to the hole would require to be removed.

Hole 2. The Warren – the present 3rd.

Hole 3. A new hole to be made in the dip short of the service road crossing the line to the present 4th hole (Note. This hole used to be played before the last addition to the course was made).

Hole 4. A new long hole right down to Meadowhead (in the new ground) the tee for which would be across (or on the southern side of) said service road.

Hole 5. A new short hole in a southerly direction across the new ground.

Hole 6. A long hole back to the present 5th green.

Hole 7. The present 6th played from a tee on the top of the rising ground east of the new 3rd hole (Note. This hole used to be played before the last addition to the course was made).

The remaining holes would be the same as now, with the exception of the 12th hole which would be entirely eliminated, and that green would be utilised as the tee for the 13th hole, a somewhat long walk from the 12th (present 11th) green to that tee would be necessitated, but this seems unavoidable.

Proposed additional ground.

This forms part of Meadowhead Farm and is let to Mr Spence on lease of which several years have yet to run, with a break at Whitsunday 1925 on giving one year's notice. The rent of the Farm is £242; The extent is not accurately known, but is believed to be between 80 and 100 acres.

Suggestion for a new Lease

I think Col. Trotter's Agents should at once be approached and negotiations entered into not only for a lease – for an extended period – of the 13 acres referred to, but of the whole course including the suggested extension. There is no doubt that an increase in rent will require to be faced, but the Club is well able to afford it, and as will be seen from Appendix I the present rent is comparatively moderate. It has to be kept in mind that the taking of 13 acres from a very small Farm may have the effect of making the latter more expensive to work, and might depreciate its value from the proprietor's point of view. It is believed the Estate is entailed and the Club would probably have to bear the expense of an application to Court for authority to enter into the new lease. Moreover there would be compensation to pay to the tenant not only for unexhausted manures in the soil, but also for the termination of his tenancy in terms of the Agriculture Act 1920. If it were desired to enter upon the scheme at once probably an arrangement could be made, but this would probably mean more compensation to the farmer for loss of profits during the period of his lease yet to run.

I have not made any estimate of the cost of laying out the ground, but will do so if desired.

Purchase.

As I have pointed out the conditions of the lease have frequently been the source of much irritation, and may become so again. The ground game are a source of constant damage to the course, and consequent annoyance; and projects for improving the course have occasionally had to be abandoned for lack of the proprietor's consent. All these would disappear if the Club owned the course.

Extent of ground to be acquired.

I am of opinion that to acquire the ground occupied by the golf course and that only would not be sufficient. One of the greatest charms of Mortonhall lies in its amenity, and unless the Club were in a position to preserve this great asset the attractiveness of the course would be much diminished. A great feature is the wood which partly forms the southern boundary. It is true there is no prospect of this being destroyed meantime and so long as it forms, as it now does, an approach to Mortonhall House. But changes come very rapidly; ground at one time considered unsuitable for buildings is now covered with houses; if it were possible to build upon the ground now used as Avenue the mere fact of its adjoining the course would make it the more desirable for that purpose. If this did happen the course up to the Khyber Pass would become unplayable. Apart from the destruction of amenity by the removal of trees, there would arise continual friction with the householders on account of balls driven out of bounds, and what is of great importance – as there is no cart road through the course – the access through the Avenue to the eastern part of the course would in all probability be done away with. That a golf course cannot exist surrounded by houses is such a well known experience that cases in support do not need to be cited. I therefore suggest that if a purchase can be arranged the Avenue *ex adverso* of the course up to the present 4th hole should be included. To make a compact holding the field adjoining the present 11th hole should also be acquired. With the exception of the field just mentioned the additional ground (i.e. the Avenue) does not seem to be valuable; probably the chief value there lies in the timber. If desired by the proprietor a servitude of access to Mortonhall House could be given over the Avenue. No doubt this scheme would leave the Club with a larger extent of ground than is at present required. But this is no disadvantage, as it would place the Club in a secure position against the future. Land in the vicinity of a City always becomes more and more valuable with the lapse of time. Any ground not presently required could be sown down to permanent grass and grazed, or let to the adjoining farmer. Moreover the Club would be enabled to provide a house for the greenkeeper at Meadowhead which is very much required. In any arrangements to be made care would require to be taken to provide outlets for the drains from the course, several of which have outlets beyond the boundaries of the course, including the overflow from the pond.

Price.

I cannot give anything but the most vague indication of the price likely to be asked; and in the circumstances I think it prudent not to specify any figure.

Possible Competition.

There seems to be a prevalent idea that the City, when the Club's Lease expires, is likely to become a competitor for the course, but for reasons which need not be entered into here, I consider this improbable.

Finance.

The proposal to lease the additional 13 acres does not require that any financial scheme should be formulated. The Club have sufficient money on hand to meet the expense of laying out the ground, and the additional rent would form a charge on the income of the Club.

But a scheme for purchase is different and provision would require to be made for raising the capital sum. I have heard it suggested that a private Company should be floated to buy and lease to the Club. I do not approve of this at all, and I am sure the Club would not, as they would desire to have complete control in their own hands.

A considerable part of the purchase price could be raised by Mortgage over the property, provision being made out of the Club's revenue for payment of interest and sinking fund for redemption of capital spread over a period of years. The balance could be provided in one of several ways or by some or all of them combined.

1. Issue of Debentures.

(a). To Members of the Club for a sum the interest on which at a certain rate would be equivalent to the annual subscription. These would be non transferrable, or transferrable only to members of the Club, and terminable at a fixed period.

(b). To any individual approved of by the Council, bearing no interest but for such a sum as might be determined. These would be perpetual, and would entitle the holder to membership without further payment, and would be transferrable only to an individual approved of by the Council. The objection to this class of security is that provision requires to be made for a certain number of members from whom the Club derive no income at all, and further that in the event of competition for admission to the Club such debentures would probably rise in value without any benefit to the Club.

(c). Debentures for a fixed sum bearing a fixed rate of interest and redeemable at a fixed period.

2. Election of a fixed number of Life Members.

The advantages of this are that on the death of a Member a portion of the debt is extinguished; and also that should he remove from the district the Club get the benefit of the money he has paid without obligation to him. In order to make Life Membership attractive a preference would be given to them over other candidates desirous of joining the Club.

3. Contributions from Members by –

(a) a levy;

(b) Increase of Entrance Fee; and,

(c) Increase of annual subscription.

4. Enlargement of the Club's Membership.

With an extended course the Club's Membership could probably be increased, without inconvenience to the present Members. Several Clubs have a larger Membership, as is shown in Appendix II. How far any increase in membership would entail an extension of the Club House is matter for consideration.

226

Present position in regard to purchase.

Negotiations for purchase of the course have already been opened with Col. Trotter's Agents, through the good offices of Mr James Greig. The position so far as Col. Trotter is concerned is explained in a letter from his Agents to me dated 1st April 1921, in the following terms:-
'We have had the matter on which you write in view since Mr Greig mentioned it to us, and we have discussed it with Col. Trotter. He is not yet in a position however, to open negotiations from his side, as there are other matters pending in connection with the Mortonhall Estate which, if they became active, might present a suitable opportunity for dealing with the permanent position of the Golf Course. On the other hand if from your side, you care to put forward a definite proposal we should of course submit it to our client, but perhaps the best thing might be if you were to leave it in abeyance for some months yet, unless we find ourselves able to raise the matter with you.' Col. Trotter (it is understood) is reluctant to part with any portion of the Estate, but Mr Greig had received an assurance that in the event of its coming into the market the Club will have the first offer of the course. It has not been considered expedient to press the matter further. It seems to me that, as I have already suggested, if Col. Trotter were approached in regard to a lease of the proposed additional ground and an extension of the present lease an opportunity might be afforded for discussing the question of purchase.

I am,
Yours faithfully
J. Anderson
Secretary.

Showing extent of golf courses in
district and rent paid therefor.

Course.	Extent.			Rate per Acre
Bruntsfield	108 ac	Feu - - - - - - £ 847		£7, 17, –
		Grazing rent	140	
			£ 707	£6, 10, –
Burgess	102 "	Feu - - - - - - £ 773		£7, 11, –
		Grazing - - - - -	135	
			£ 638	£6, 5, –
Liberton	65 "	Rent - - - - - £ 550 ★		£8, 9, –
		Grazing &c - - -	250	
			£ 300	£4, 12, –
Prestonfield	83 "	Rent - - - - - £ 585		£7, - -
		Grazing - - - - -	250	
			£ 335	£4, - -
Duddingston	100 "	Rent - - - - - £ 600		£6, - -
		Grazing - - - - -	200	
			£ 400	£4, - -
Murrayfield	100 "	Rent - - - - - £ 462		
		Feu - - - - - -	49	
			511	£5, 2, –
		Grazing - - - - -	150	
			£ 361	£3, 12, –
Mortonhall	96 "	Rent - - - - - £ 338		£3, 10, –
		Grazing - - - - -	88	
			£ 250	£2, 10, –
Baberton	94 "	Rent - - - - - £ 301		£3, 4, –
		Grazing - - - - -	150	
			£ 151	£1, 12, –

★ Includes Mansion House, Gardens &c rated at £250.

Showing membership of Clubs in district.

Burgess	Gentlemen	860	★			Total	860
Kingsknowe	"	–		Ladies	–	"	700
Murrayfield	"	400		"	300	"	700
Baberton	"	500		"	150	"	650
Prestonfield	"	500		"	150	"	650
Bruntsfield	"	600				"	600
Duddingston	"	600				"	600
Liberton	"	–		"	–	"	560
Mortonhall	"	550				"	550

★ Ordinary 750, Country 60, Playing Candidates 50,
Total 860.

APPENDIX O
Heads of Agreement for Feu between Colonel Trotter of Mortonhall and the Captain and Council of the Mortonhall Golf Club.

1. Colonel Trotter will feu to Trustees for the Club (*a*) the ground embraced under the existing Lease as indicated by an irregular stipple on the enclosed Plan, and (*b*) the Plantations indicated by cross lines and marked A B, D, E, F, and the western portion of

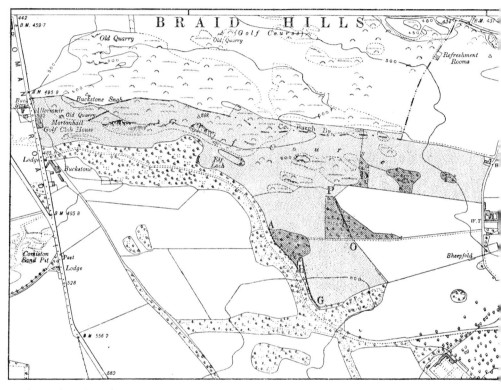

C on the Plan, the eastern boundary of the said portion of Plantation C being a straight line marked P O on the Plan from the north-west corner of the field which lies to the south of the cart track leading from Meadowhead to the West Drive or Avenue leading from the old Braids Road to Mortonhall House, to the most westerly point of the field lying

230

to the north of said cart track; (c) the two cottages and gardens at the north-eastmost corner of the Golf Course as at present leased by the Club. Entry to be as at Whitsunday 1925 notwithstanding the date hereof.

2. The feu-duty to be at the rate of £450 per annum from Whitsunday 1925 to Whitsunday 1932, £550 from Whitsunday 1932 to Whitsunday 1939 and £650 thereafter, these sums to include the feu-duty of £20 payable in respect of the ground feued in 1904 for the erection of a Club House. The Club shall redeem the feu-duty to the extent of £325 per annum, being one half of the ultimate feu-duty by payment of the sum of £5687, 10s. or seventeen and a half years purchase of that portion of the feu-duty at or prior to the term of Whitsunday 1928.

3. The Club will pay to Colonel Trotter the value of the cottages and gardens referred to at No. 1 (c) above, as such value may be fixed, failing agreement, by arbitration. The Club will also grant to Colonel Trotter a lease of one of the cottages to endure so long as Meadowhead Farm is let by him or his successors as an agricultural subject—the rent being at the rate of 6 per cent. on the price paid by the Club for such cottage.

4. The Plantation A B shall be retained as a Plantation and no trees or shrubs shall be cut down without the written consent of the Superior for the time being, and the dyke round the said Plantation shall not be interfered with unless with such consent. The other Plantations included in the feu shall generally be retained as Plantations but the same or any of them may nevertheless be used by the Club for any purpose (such as the making of tees, putting greens, the widening of the fairway of the course, etc.) in connection with the Golf Course, and for such purpose they may cut down and remove any trees, and also remove at any time any fences, fallen or decayed trees, bushes, rocks, stones or the like. The Club shall when called upon to do so erect boundary fences along the lines A B and P O in so far as these are not already fenced. The Club shall not be bound to maintain any fences round the Plantations except in so far as the same or any of them may form boundaries of the feu, nor will the Club be bound to replant any portion of the ground presently occupied by the Plantations; the remaining boundary fences of the feu, except so far as adjoining the Braid Hills and the public road, shall be maintained at the mutual expense of Colonel Trotter and the Club. The march fence or boundary wall with the Braid Hills shall be maintained at the mutual expense of the Club and the Corporation of Edinburgh as proprietors of the Braid Hills.

5. The Club will be given the same rights of access to the feu as they at present have under the Lease, and also, in so far as Colonel Trotter has right thereto, access by the road which runs northwards from Meadowhead Farm to join the public road, the Club always paying a just proportion of the cost for which Colonel Trotter may be liable of maintaining the said road, and Colonel Trotter will on the other hand be entitled to reserve a right to use for estate purposes but not as an access to feus, the cart track leading from Meadowhead to the West Drive or Avenue.

6. Colonel Trotter will be entitled to take from such places as may be pointed out by the Club, gravel from the hillside between the first hole and the Elf Pond for the maintenance of the avenues leading to Mortonhall House, together with a right of access for removing such gravel, but such right only to be exercised during such time as Colonel Trotter or his sons retain a predominant interest in the said House and so as not to interfere with the Club's free enjoyment of the feu.

7. The ground feued to the Club in 1904 for the erection of the present Club House shall be held under the same conditions and with the same rights as stated in the Feu Charter then granted and the whole ground now feued shall be used only as and for the purposes of a Golf Course and (but that only with the consent of Colonel Trotter and his successors in Mortonhall which shall not be unreasonably withheld) for the erection of such buildings as may be necessary for the purposes of the Club, including any extension or extensions of the existing Club House, the erection of garages, shelters, toolhouses or houses for employees, all which the Club shall with said consent have full power to carry out, erect, renew, or enlarge at any time.

8. The Club will grant a lease of the shootings over the whole feu to Colonel Trotter and any son or sons succeeding to him in his rights in Mortonhall Estate for their lives and the life of the survivor, at a nominal rent; under reservation of the right to the Club to keep down the rabbits if at any time the proprietor of Mortonhall does not in the opinion of the Council of the Club keep them down sufficiently for the proper enjoyment of the Golf Course. The right of shooting conferred by the said lease shall always be exercised by the grantees and others holding under them so as not to interfere with the full enjoyment of the subjects feued.

9. The whole assets of the Club, including the Club-house cottages and other buildings on the ground feued, will form security for the feu-duty, but the feu rights will be so expressed that the members of the Club and the trustees therefor and the members of the Council or of any committee thereof will not incur any liability as individuals in connection with any of the obligations of the feu charter or contract of feu.

10. If at any time prior to Whitsunday 1945 the superior shall propose to feu in accordance with a feuing plan the ground forming the west avenue or approach to Mortonhall House or the ground lying to the south thereof so far as *ex adverso* of the feu, and shall have definitely feued or entered into a contract or contracts to feu not less than two acres of the ground included in the said feuing plan (other than the strip of ground immediately hereinafter referred to) as the same may be certified by the superior's factors for the time being he shall first require the Club to declare whether it will agree to feu the strip of ground north and east of the avenue from the West Lodge to the point marked G on the Plan or any part thereof mutually agreed upon at the rate of £20 per acre and to take over the trees thereon at a valuation. If the Club agrees to feu any such additional ground, they shall have six months from the date of a requisition made to them to the above effect by the superior, to declare

whether they agree to feu the whole or any part, and if so what part, of the said strip of ground on the above terms, and in the event of the Club agreeing to do so they shall be bound to take a charter of such area as is agreed to be feued containing stipulations that the ground feued shall be deemed to form part of the Golf Course whether the same shall actually be used as part of the Golf Course or retained by the Club in whole or in part for the protection of the amenity of the latter, provided always that any additional ground so taken by the Club shall be fenced in by them at their own expense with a fence of a character and design to be approved of by the superior and that such ground shall not be used for any purposes otherwise than in connection with the uses of the Club as before specified, and in particular shall not subject as aforesaid be subfeued for the erection of dwelling-houses nor used for any purpose which might be injurious to the amenity of neighbouring feus. The Club shall also take over at valuation the trees on any additional area forming the whole or part of the said strip which they so agree to feu. If the Club do not timeously as above provided for agree to feu the whole or any part of the said strip their right to do so shall forthwith cease ; Provided always that in the event of the superior making no requisition as aforesaid prior to Whitsunday 1945 then the option which the Club have of feuing the said strip of ground shall be continued thereafter from year to year, but the superior shall have right to withdraw the option at any time thereafter on one year's previous notice in writing ; In the event however of such notice of withdrawal being given the Club shall nevertheless have the right at any time before the expiry of the term of the said notice to feu the whole or any part of the said strip on the terms hereinbefore mentioned. During the subsistence of the Club's option over the said last mentioned strip of ground, the superior will not cut any trees without consultation with the Club and consideration of their interests.

11. A renunciation of the Club's existing lease will be accepted by Colonel Trotter to take effect as from Whitsunday 1925, and (subject always to the provisions of Article 7 hereof) the Club will also reconvey to Colonel Trotter the feu on which the Club House has been erected. The new Feu Charter will then include the whole ground held by the Club.

12. As regards the Captain and Council of the Mortonhall Golf Club this Agreement shall have no force or effect unless and until approved of by the Club in General Meeting, and in the event of such approval of this Agreement by the Club not having been intimated to Colonel Trotter before the fifteenth day of May 1926 Colonel Trotter shall be entitled to declare this Agreement to be at an end.

REPORT OF DEVELOPMENT COMMITTEE –
JUNE 1975

1. Background

The Golf Courses on the South side of Edinburgh are mainly hilly and short in length. It is considered that only Mortonhall has the capability of acquiring suitable ground for expansion and to thus become the outstanding Golf Course on the South side of the City.

Over the years successive Councils have looked at the problem of obtaining additional land adjoining our Course with a view to extension and the elimination from play of the last five holes of our present lay-out. These last five holes are unpopular with many members and are undoubtedly the main reason why the Club has lost a substantial number of its most promising young golfers.

It is clear that only at the East end of the Golf Course can any expansion take place. The only land currently available to the Club is that lying between the existing fifth and eleventh holes. These fields extend to about twenty nine acres and are owned by Mr A. R. Trotter, the proprietor of Mortonhall Estate and are farmed by the tenant of Meadowhead Farm. Mr Trotter has indicated that he is prepared to sell to the Club the land between the fifth and eleventh holes (hereinafter called the 'new field') and to settle any claims by the farming tenant. Mr Trotter is also prepared to include in the sale parts of the wooded area on the North side of the West Drive of Mortonhall Estate.

It was agreed with Mr Trotter that the Club should first consult with Golf Course Architects to establish whether the acquisition of the new field would materially improve the Golf Course. The advice was sought of Mr F. W. Hawtree, Hawtree and Son, Featherbed Lane, Addington, Croydon, Surrey, who is an internationally well known Golf Course Architect.

Terms of reference to Mr Hawtree were prepared and he carried out an inspection of the Course and the new field in September 1970. Mr Hawtree gave as his definite view that a materially better Golf Course could be laid out involving the new field. Indeed he was genuinely enthusiastic about the possibilities of a first class Golf Course being created at Mortonhall. It was clear however that the development of the Course to the extent envisaged by Mr Hawtree would be very costly and for that reason could not be undertaken as a single operation.

With the assurance of Mr Hawtree as to the excellent prospects of a first class Golf Course which would not contain 'blind' holes and which would be considerably longer and flatter than at present, the Committee undertook the investigation and further work necessary preparatory to submitting this report.

2. Terms of Purchase

The main terms of purchase are:–

(a) The price will be THIRTY THOUSAND POUNDS (£30,000).
(b) The purchase will be subject to the Club obtaining Planning Permission to use the new field for the purposes of golf.
(c) The date of entry is Martinmas (28th November) 1975.
(d) Mr Trotter is to settle the claims of the farming tenant.
(e) Mr Trotter will obtain the value of any timber cleared from that that part of the woods to be involved in the Golf Course extension.
(f) Mr Trotter will retain shooting rights over the new field.

The Committee have been professionally advised that the purchase consideration is fair and reasonable.

3. General

There is enclosed a copy of Mr Hawtree's plan (see page 130). This plan was considered by five leading golfers in our Club who are members of the Development Committee. It was agreed that the plan could not be adopted in whole because of cost and a modified plan was produced known as the Phase One Plan (see page 131). The Committee recommend that the Phase One Plan be accepted in principle as the layout for golf to be played over Mortonhall for at least the next twenty five years and that the adoption of further parts of the Hawtree plan be left over meantime.

The Committee recognise that the Phase One Plan does not provide a Practice Area near to the Club House and also there is no convenient second Starting Place and Finishing Hole near to the Club House. So long as the Club House remains at Braid Road such facilities are considered impossible.

STARTING AND COMPLETION DATES

With sufficient finance, works could commence in 1976 and all works involved in the Phase One plan could be completed by the end of 1979. If sufficient finance is not available it is recommended that the field be 'de-stoned' and sown to grass. For a period the field could be let for grazing and the income therefrom used to reduce costs. The Committee would however like the position to be achieved as soon as possible whereby two holes in the new field could be brought into play and thus the new first hole could be introduced.

PERIOD OF TRANSITION

Care has been taken to ensure that play can continue over the entire 18 holes of our existing course until the new layout comes into use. At the following holes however there will be relatively minor interference with play:–

Existing hole 2 – Green for new No. 1 hole to be formed. Existing green to be extended to bunker forty yards from hole. Tee for No. 18 hole to be formed.

Existing hole 5 – Green for new No. 4 hole to be formed to south of fairway. Tee for No. 5 hole to be formed to north of fairway.

Existing hole 9 – Green for new No. 15 hole to be formed.

Existing hole 10 – Green and tee for new No. 14 hole to be formed.

Existing hole 11 – Green for new No. 12 hole to be formed.

At various parts of the Course tree planting will commence.

DRAINAGE

It has been found that drainage is generally satisfactory throughout the new field except for relatively small areas. It is proposed to drain where necessary in the new field and also to put drains in our existing 13th fairway which is generally regarded as being the wettest part of our present course.

SOIL REPORT

Soil tests throughout the new field have been carried out by officials of the East of Scotland College of Agriculture and their report is very satisfactory. In order to ensure a satisfactory surface for the playing of golf a large part of the new field is to be 'de-stoned' by a special machine.

TREE PLANTING

It is proposed to plant trees to a considerable extent at many holes. In this connection the Development Committee have been advised by one of

236

our members, Mr John Cousens of the Department of Forestry and Natural Resources. It is proposed to follow Mr Cousens' advice both as to the types of trees to be planted and their care after planting.

SHELTERS AND STARTER'S BOX
At least two shelters will be required in the new field and a Starter's Box near to the new first tee is desirable.

EXTENSION OF WATER SUPPLY TO NEW FIELD
Provision has been made for extending the existing water supply system to all new greens and certain tees.

EXTENSION OF CAR PARKING
The present car parking facilities are considered entirely inadequate. The adoption of a revised layout will enable the existing car park to be enlarged in an easterly direction. It is proposed to increase the parking area by 2,200 square yards giving accommodation for fifty additional cars. The total car capacity of our car park will then become ninety cars.

PLANNING PERMISSION
An application will require to be made to the Secretary of State to rezone the new field as a 'private recreation area.' It is not anticipated that this will present any difficulties but if any objections are lodged there could be the necessity of a Public Enquiry. It is proposed to fell and remove trees to form tees at the new first and second holes and to widen the access to the new seventeenth green. Because of the Tree Preservation Order affecting these trees an advertisment of the intention to fell must be made in the local press to enable any objections to be heard.

It is not necessary to advertise the intention to fell trees at the new twelfth hole.

4. Estimate of Costs

A. WORK NECESSARY TO EXISTING COURSE
  1. Clear tree roots at 1st, 2nd, 12th and 17th holes.
  2. Form 6 new tees (including reshaping existing).
  3. Form 5 new greens to reduced specification.
  4. New tree planting.
  5. New bunkers.
  6. Extend car park.

B. CONSTRUCT NEW HOLES IN EXTENSION
1. Prepare ground including de-stoning.
2. Form and seed new fairways.
3. Seed rough and tree planting.
4. Provide and lay polythene water pipes 1000 L.Y.
5. Provide new water hydrants.
6. Form 6 new tees.
7. Form 4 new greens to full specification.
8. Construct new bunkers.
9. Necessary drainage.

It is anticipated that expenditure in the range of £30,000 will be incurred in the above works in terms of current costs.

A substantial part of the work to be done is planned to be carried out by our own staff.

5. **Proposals as to Finance**

It is the view of the Development Committee that the costs of the development should be borne by all members in the categories of membership equally. It is recommended that:–

(a)   levy of £12 per annum be imposed on Ordinary Members and £6 per annum on Five Day Members for five years commencing at 1st June 1976. The charge to levy will not apply to Junior Members and Lady Visitors.

(b)   Voluntary Loans of £250 or £500 should be sought from members. These loans will be repaid in full at or before 1st June 1991 or on death or resignation. During the period of the loan in the case of a loan of £250, an Ordinary Member will be required to pay only two thirds of his subscription and a Five Day Member one half of his subscription. In the case of a loan of £500, an Ordinary Member will be required to pay only one third of his subscription and the Five Day Member will not be called upon to pay any part of the subscription.

(c)   Entry Fees for members joining the Club after 1st December 1975 should be adjusted having regard to the levy liability.

The Council of the Club have agreed to contribute the sum of £10,000 from the reserves of the Club for the proposed Development, and the

Club's Bankers have agreed to advance the sum of £25,000 repayable over 5 years. Interest at 2½ per cent over Base Rate (currently 9½ per cent) will be charged but by reason of substantial sums being at credit of the Club for a large part of the financial year the interest charge will be calculated on a much lesser figure than £25,000.

★   ★   ★

6. The Committee's Recommendations

The Committee submit this Report and recommend its adoption in the firm belief that if it is accepted by the members, Mortonhall will become one of the premier Golf Courses in this City.

REPORT BY DEVELOPMENT COMMITTEE – MAY 1976

1. BACKGROUND

Reference is made to the Report of the Development Committee in June 1975 and the decisions made at the Special Meeting held on 31st July, 1975. Reference is also made to the Development Committee Bulletins which have been posted in the Club House.

In broad terms, the above meeting agreed that the Club should proceed to purchase the new field. The proposals as to finance which were approved at the meeting were designed to cover the purchase of land, de-stoning, ploughing and sowing to grass.

The levy imposed for a five year period commencing in June, 1976 was intended to reduce year by year and finally eliminate the Bank facilities of £25,000 which had been arranged. In making its calculation, the provision for Members Voluntary Loans contained in the 1975 report was totally discounted by the Committee, although it was hoped that several loans would be made in order to reduce the amount of the Club's Bank borrowing. Support by way of Voluntary Loans, however, surpassed all expectations. Within a very short time £20,000 was produced and there is evidence of more loans to come. Further, many members made advance contributions of the levy for the year 1976, and some paid the whole five years levy in advance. As a result of this high level of financial provision from members, the Club's Bank Account was overdrawn for only seven days following the payment of the purchase price of the new field.

Encouraged by this financial support, the Committee has been strengthened in its desire to make immediate progress in reconstructing the Course so that the new field can be brought into play in this decade.

Being satisfied as to the financial viability of undertaking the development immediately, the Development Committee submit this Report.

2. GENERAL

(a) The Plan
In view of the proposal to accelerate development, Mr Hawtree was recalled to Mortonhall to consider a Plan. He made it clear that because of problems of connection it would not be reasonable to retain, even for

a temporary period, any of the present holes 14–17 in an acceptable revised layout. He was thus asked to prepare a plan omitting these holes.

There were two constraints placed on him. Firstly, the total cost was not to exceed £35,000 and, secondly, his plan should ensure that play could continue over the existing 18 holes until the reconstructed course was ready. Mr Hawtree was also informed that it was extremely unlikely that the site of the Clubhouse would be altered in the foreseeable future and he should prepare his plan accordingly.

After two visits and consideration of several alternative schemes it was decided to adopt a plan which Mr Hawtree had prepared based on acceptance by the Committee that the present crossing holes (5th/7th) and the present 11th hole would be retained.

It is the Committee's intention to use available funds in ensuring that all new holes be constructed to the highest standards. For that reason only six new holes (4 in the new field and a new 7th and 17th) are being introduced. Of these six new holes, only the new 7th hole is considered as not being a permanent hole in the ultimate development of the Golf Course. With the area of the present 9th green being the pivot in the Plan, it is, however, necessary to introduce the new 7th as a 'link' hole. It is intended that the existing 5th, 6th and 7th loop and the existing 10th, 11th, 12th and 13th loop be redesigned some years hence when funds are available. The Plan which Mr Hawtree has produced is shown in the Appendix.

(b) Implementation of the Plan

It is proposed to employ Sports Works Contractors for the construction of the holes in the new field, the new 17th hole and the green only on the new 7th hole. Contractors will also be employed for the extension of the water supply and on the large tree planting programme. Contract work could commence in the Summer of 1976 and, given reasonable weather conditions, the new holes will be ready for play in July, 1979. It is proposed that the Greens staff (probably increased in number) carry out the following works in the years quoted:–

1976/77	New Hole 1	Prepare tees and carry out improvement works near green
1976/77	New Hole 2	prepare tees and new green
1979/80	New Hole 5	prepare new green
1979/80	New Hole 6	prepare new tees
1978/79	New Hole 7	prepare temporary tee
1979/80	New Hole 7	prepare permanent tees
1980/81	New Hole 8	prepare new tees
1977/78	New Hole 10	prepare new tees
1975/76	New Hole 18	prepare new tees

The Greens Staff will also lay tracks linking greens and tees where required. The works allocated to the Greens Staff will be carried out partly as Winter work and partly on an overtime basis throughout the Spring, Summer and Autumn.

The Development Committee take the unanimous view that Mr Hawtree should be appointed Architect to the Development with overall responsibility for detailed planning and supervision of contractors and the Club staff for work carried out by them. Mr Hawtree's fee will be in the region of £5,000. It is strongly urged that members will take an early opportunity to walk over the proposed holes in the new field. Until the date of the Special General Meeting members of the Development Committee will be available in the Clubhouse each Sunday at 2.30 p.m. to accompany members over the new field and to discuss any points.

(c) Shelters and Starters Box
The existing Shelter at the present 14th tee will require to be moved. As soon as funds permit two additional Shelters will be provided and a Starter's Box will also be erected near the first tee.

(d) Extension of Car Parking
The permanent extension of the present Car Park cannot be brought into use until 1979 when it is hoped that play on the present 1st and 18th holes will be discontinued. The Council have agreed that they will take over responsibility of providing the Car Park extension from the Development Committee.

Mr Trotter has kindly permitted the Club to use, for a temporary period only, part of the woodland to the South of the existing Car Park for overflow parking. Because of tree removal via the West Drive it is uncertain when the use can commence. The use will be discontinued in the 1979 Season.

(e) Planning Permission
Prior to the completion of the purchase of the new field, Planning Permission in principle was granted by the City of Edinburgh District Council to the use of the new field for the purposes of golf. The Club are required to submit a Plan of the proposed new layout. Subject to the approval of Mr Hawtree's Plan at the Special General Meeting that Plan will be submitted to the Planning Committee. The Plan will also show the proposed area of tree felling and permanent and temporary Car Parking areas. Site meetings have already taken place with staff from the Planning Department regarding the only aspects which have caused slight problems namely the tree removal at the new first hole and the temporary Car Parking area.

3. ESTIMATE OF COSTS

Mr Hawtree's estimate of the cost of works is in the region of £27,500 excluding extension of the water supply scheme, tree planting, and his professional fee. As it is not realistic to allow for less than £5,000 for each completely new hole, the Development Committee consider that the total cost of development will be in the region of £35,000.

The Development Committee did not feel that Mr Hawtree should be instructed to provide a schedule specifying works in detail for the purpose of obtaining estimates until the Club members authorise his appointment on the basis sought by the Committee.

4. THE FUTURE

The elimination of the crossing holes and the present 11th hole must be faced by another generation of our members. Discussions are currently taking place with Mr Trotter regarding a possible future interest of the Club in the 30 acre field lying to the South of the new field as well as further areas of woodland on the North side of the West Drive to Mortonhall Estate with, possibly, the drive itself.

5. THE RECOMMENDATIONS

It is recommended:
1. That the plan prepared by Mr Hawtree which accompanies this Report be accepted as the new layout for Mortonhall Golf Course.
2. That the proposals contained in the Plan be implemented as soon as possible at a total cost in the region of £35,000.
3. That Mr Hawtree be appointed Architect to the Club for the purpose of implementing the Plan.
4. That that the levy of £12 per annum currently imposed on Ordinary Members and £6 per annum on Five Day Members for a period of five years be extended for a further period of seven years from 1st June, 1981 to implement the current development proposals.
5. That as from 1st June, 1976 the Entry Monies payable by new members shall be increased by £12 in each year in connection with the development apart from any increase which the Council of the Club may recommend for reasons unconnected with the development.

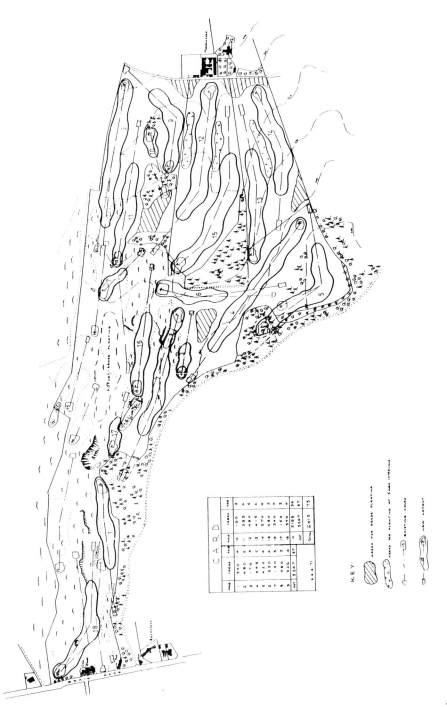

245

TABLE OF CHANGING MONEY VALUES

The following table is based, as far as the years 1892–1914 are concerned, on an Index of Wholesale Commodity Values and thereafter on an Index of Consumer Goods and Services. It is considered that it reflects a reasonable trend in the value of the £ over the century 1892–1992.

It is accordingly hoped that it will be of assistance in relating the monetary values of any year to the present time thus:

Value of £7,000 in 1926 = in 1992 terms: $\dfrac{£7,000}{.36} \times 10 = £194,444$

Currency has been referred to in terms of Pounds, Shillings and Pence until 1971 when decimalisation was introduced. A simple means of relating the former to the latter is to divide the Shillings and Pence by two – hence 18 Shillings and 4 pence equals:

$$\frac{184}{2} = 92p$$

Reference is made in the text to the Guinea. This is an obsolete currency expression representing £1 and one Shilling – hence two Guineas = £2.2/– and three & half Guineas = £3.13/6d.

Based on Value of £10 in 1992		_Based on Value of £10 in 1992_		_Based on Value of £10 in 1992_	
Year		_Year_		_Year_	
1892	.17	1923	.36	1960	.93
1893	.17	1924	.37	1961	.96
1894	.16	1925	.37	1962	1.00
1895	.16	1926	.36	1963	1.01
1896	.15	1927	.35	1964	1.05
1897	.15	1928	.35	1965	1.10
1898	.15	1929	.34	1966	1.14
1899	.16	1930	.33	1967	1.17
1900	.17	1931	.31	1968	1.23
1901	.17	1932	.30	1969	1.29
1902	.17	1933	.29	1970	1.37
1903	.17	1934	.30	1971	1.50
1904	.17	1935	.30	1972	1.61
1905	.17	1936	.31	1973	1.76
1906	.18	1937	.32	1974	2.04
1907	.19	1938	.33	1975	2.53
1908	.19	1939–45	N/A	1976	2.95
1909	.19	1946	.55	1977	3.42
1910	.19	1947	.59	1978	3.70
1911	.19	1948	.64	1979	4.20
1912	.20	1949	.65	1980	4.96
1913	.20	1950	.67	1981	5.54
1914	.21	1951	.73	1982	6.02
1915	.26	1952	.77	1983	6.30
1916	.30	1953	.79	1984	6.61
1917	.37	1954	.80	1985	7.01
1918	.42	1955	.83	1986	7.25
1919	.45	1956	.86	1987	7.55
1920	.52	1957	.89	1988	7.92
1921	.47	1958	.92	1989	8.54
1922	.38	1959	.92	1990	9.34
				1991/92	10.00

INDEX

This index records the names of those appearing in the text of Chapters 1–8 but does not include those appearing in the Appendices.

In many cases the christian names are not known and the following code has been adopted:

if single name, name in full, if known otherwise initial only

if more than one, initials only

if name not known, 'Mr' only

if known by two names, both shown e.g. Kerr, E. West